D1707321

The Ministers' Minders

The Ministers' Minders

PERSONAL ADVISERS
IN NATIONAL GOVERNMENT

James Walter

Melbourne
Oxford University Press
Oxford   New York   Auckland

OXFORD UNIVERSITY PRESS

Oxford New York Toronto
Delhi Bombay Calcutta Madras Karachi
Singapore Hong Kong Tokyo
Nairobi Dar es Salaam Cape Town
Melbourne Auckland
and associates in
Beirut Berlin Ibadan Nicosia

National Library of Australia
Cataloguing-in-Publication data:

Walter, James, 1949–   .
    The ministers' minders.

    Bibliography.
    Includes index.
    ISBN 0 19 554590 7.
    ISBN 0 19 554589 3 (pbk.).

    1. Political consultants – Australia. 2. Politicians –
    Australia. I. Title.

354.9407'22

Edited by Lee White
Cover designed by Guy Mirabella
Typeset by Syarikat Seng Teik Sdn. Bhd., Kuala Lumpur, Malaysia
Printed by Kyodo Shing-Loong Printing, Singapore
Published by Oxford University Press, 7 Bowen Crescent, Melbourne
OXFORD is a trademark of Oxford University Press

CONTENTS

For Robyn —
and for Alice, Tom and Jenny

ACKNOWLEDGEMENTS

My thanks are due, first, to those members of ministerial staff who allowed themselves to be interviewed or who completed questionnaires during the course of my research. Most of these remain anonymous at their own request.

The institutions which made this work possible must be acknowledged. The project was supported initially by a Griffith University Research Grant, and thereafter by the resources of the School of Humanities Research Sub-Committee at Griffith University. The secretarial, typing and word-processing services of the School of Humanities were an essential support. A period of attachment as a Visiting Fellow to the Politics Department, Research School of the Social Sciences, Australian National University, in August 1983 allowed for concentrated work in Canberra, and I am grateful to Professor Don Aitkin and Dr John Warhurst for facilitating that visit. During the same period, I was permitted to use an office in the Legislative Research Service in Parliament House which considerably assisted my interviewing programme. I am grateful to Dr Frank Frost for this arrangement, and to the Head of the Legislative Research Service, Dr George Webb, for his permission. I was also aided by being granted access by the Parliamentary Librarian, Mr H. deS. C. MacLean, during August 1983, to the unparalleled newspaper files of the Legislative Research Service's Current Information Section. A sojourn as Visiting Fellow at the Center of International Studies, Princeton University, in September and October 1983 allowed me to do valuable comparative work on American and Canadian systems of political advice, and to gain a broader perspective on the theoretical issues involved in this project: thanks are due particularly to Professor Fred Greenstein of the Woodrow Wilson School at Princeton University for arranging my visit.

Some of the survey materials reported in chapters 5 and 6 were first published in my article 'Ministerial staff under Hawke', *Australian Journal of Public Administration*, vol. XLIII, no. 3,

September 1984, pp 203–19. They are reprinted here with permission. The lines from Waterman/Kenny, 'I could be so good for you' (the *Minder* lyric) are reprinted here by the kind permission of Chappell & Intersong Music Group (Australia) Ltd.

There are many individuals whose advice and discussion helped in this work. I would like to thank Graham Little, Roy Forward, Fred Greenstein, Alan Davies and John Langmore for fruitful suggestions and stimulation during early stages of this research. Robyn Sloper and Paul Lewis provided research assistance. Robyn Walter was closely involved in analysing the results of the surveys reported in chapters 5 and 6. Alan Davies, Graham Little, Andrew Graham, and Allan Patience read and commented helpfully on sections of the manuscript. Clem Lloyd provided a constructive critique of the entire manuscript which was a great help in revision. Many of the typing and word-processing staff of the School of Humanities laboured over successive drafts, but my thanks go in particular to Robyn Pratten who has always carried the bulk of my work. I am grateful for the sympathetic professionalism of Louise Sweetland at Oxford University Press, and for the deft editing of Lee White. Finally, I want to thank my own 'minders' — my wife Robyn and my children Alice, Tom, and Jenny — who kept me alert to the pretensions of the solitary scholar, reminded me of other pleasures, and demanded an appropriate perspective on work. This book is for them.

James Walter
August 1985

1

Introduction

Ministers, Minders and Mandarins

The British television programme, *Minder*, has a cult following among Wran's staff and associates; they replay lines, quips and scenes to raucous laughter and exaggerated Cockney accents. . . It has a natural appeal for the political mind. . .   (*Sydney Morning Herald*, 19 June 1982, p. 34.)

— Do you know that in this State we are quite widely known as 'minders'?
— Is the term borrowed from that television series?
— No, No. . . I don't think so. It's more like a corruption of the two words, *min*isterial advis*er* . . . so 'minder' . . . Do you see?
                    (Conversation with an aide to the Victorian Premier, 1983.)

Hawke can waffle. He has a capacity for circumlocution. But his minders prepare him very well. They give him short, sharp phrases to answer questions.
           (David O'Reilly, ABC-TV *Nationwide*, 29 November 1984.)

If you want to I'll change the situation,
Right people, right time just wrong location.
I've got a good idea,
Just you keep me near,
I'll be so good for you,
(I'm gonna help ya!)
. . . I'll do anything for you. . .
                    (Denis Waterman, *Minder* lyric, Thames Television.)

This book is about the role played by ministerial staff in Australian federal government. It is particularly concerned with the potential influence on policy making that this group may have through their capacity to advise ministers. It is, then, about the nature of the relations between personal advisers and their principals — a general issue that can be explored through history, and in countries other than Australia (see chapter 2). From the outset, however, it is important to differentiate between advice to ministers and advice to government, and the term 'adviser' does not sufficiently alert us to that differentiation. Indeed, the term 'adviser' is traditionally used to signify public servants, who are formally charged with the responsibility of advice to government. I have therefore elected to borrow the term 'minder', a term that is creeping into journalism and into the vernacular to refer to a member of a minister's staff. We can thus distinguish at once between minders (personal advisers) and mandarins (public servants).

There has been a tendency to use 'minder' to refer to a ministerial staffer who acts as a handler, carefully organizing and superintending the personal appearances of a minister and exerting influence to develop a favourable persona for that minister. There is, however, a countervailing tendency to apply it more broadly,[1] and taking my licence from the second passage quoted above, I wish to establish a wider provenance for it here. There is a good reason for this. The fact is that within ministerial offices functional differentiations (between, say, media handlers and an advisory élite) tend to break down: all staff may take an advisory role at some stage, and *all* staff are constrained to play the minder's role at *every* stage. That is to say, ministerial staff members are the creatures of their minister, and must always put the minister's interests first. Therefore, no matter how important they see their advisory role as being (and in chapter 6 it will be seen that ministerial staff increasingly rate policy advising as their most important function), and no matter how lofty their own aspirations are, they have no independent standing, and must couch their advice in terms of the minister's needs. The term 'minder', therefore, serves as a salutory reminder of their subordinate role. This is not, however, to underrate their importance: the personal adviser has a venerable history, as chapter 2 indicates, and the institutionalization of minders in the private offices of the political executive signifies an important stage in the evolution of contemporary leadership, as is demonstrated in chapters 2 and 3.

The uneasy partnership between bureaucrats and politicians in modern societies has generated this category of political activist: the partisan adviser or minder appointed to the staff of the political executive. Most discussions of policy-making, however, remain focused on what political science continues to assure us are the key actors — politicans and public servants — without attention to these new participants in the inner circle. It is the contention of this book that if we are to comprehend the nature of the policy process, we should try to understand the nature of the work of *all* participants in central policy-making institutions. Hence my attention to this neglected group.

This book is essentially a work of description, but in its course general arguments about the nature of political life are canvassed. First, it is suggested that there is a tendency for mainstream conflict politics either to attenuate, or to draw in those who lack, capacities for introspection, abstract thinking, acquisition of knowledge — even administration. Forced to be fighters and raiders, politicians have always had to rely on others to supply these capacities for them. Bacon long ago remarked upon 'the inseparable conjunction of counsel with kings'. This is the core of 'court politics' with its reciprocity between the leader's patronage and the courtier's provision of instrumental functions. And it explains the ubiquity of court politics even in modern polities. Second, the expectation that state bureaucracies could supply such needs, and so supplant earlier traditions of court politics has been disappointed — partly because the sociology of bureaucracy has never been adequately taken into account in the classic conception of the division of functions between executive and bureaucracy. In practical terms we are drawn to consider the circumstances under which political executives come to feel disillusioned with their 'official' advisers, and seek to establish 'counter bureaucracies' of loyalists in their private offices. Third, the complex imperatives of modern politics create a demand for people trained in the skills of information and communication in these partisan staff roles.

The outcome in all western democracies has been the institutionalization of private office staff who, though party loyalists, depend on personal patronage, and who are predominantly tertiary educated meritocrats rather than grass-roots activists. They have many of the qualities of the mandarin — except the ideological neutrality expected of the bureaucrat, or the critical detachment supposed to be characteristic of the intellectual. While they are highly educated (see chapter 5), and many of them bring to their work skills acquired through advanced training, these staff members are not (or have chosen not to adopt the role of) experts. They are generalists ranging over a number of areas dictated by political imperatives. Thus, they are distinct from the 'programme professionals',[2] such as the economists who take it upon themselves to advise governments (as happened in the depression — see chapter 3), the specialists who are brought in to consult only on their area (as for instance Deeble and Scotton in establishing Medibank in Australia — see chapters 3 and 6), or the academics contributing to commissions and enquiries. These programme professionals are an interesting manifestation of contemporary society and its demand for knowledge and are worthy of attention in their own right, but their contribution to policy is particular, not general, one-off rather than extended. No matter how influential, their contribution to the policy process is discontinuous and *ad hoc*, whereas the minders are now continuously at their ministers' elbows, nudging their deliberations. By extension, the programme professionals are recognizable less clearly as political operatives than the minders. Hence, they will not be considered here.

Putting the matter of expertise aside, clearly the minders are a subset of the intelligentsia. Survey work in Australia and in three parallel countries, as reported in chapter 5, reveals not only high levels of education, but also that they are increasingly drawn from professional or quasi-professional backgrounds — and from what some now call the 'semi-professions'[3] — where work depends on credentials and involves familiarity with institutions and their regulation, the generation or brokerage of ideas, articulation and organization. This does not mean that all of these people have the same skills, that they are any the less political operatives than earlier activists who were not of the intelligentsia, or even that they would see themselves as part of the intelligentsia. The categorization is important for us because it locates these people in the structure of contemporary society (including the class structure). The complicating factor, as shown in chapters 5 and 7, is that in modern societies ministers and mandarins are also part of the intelligentsia.

This book can be read on one level as a story of the way in which social and institutional change has opened an avenue for *some* members of the intelligentsia to the upper reaches of the political process which avoids the gatekeepers of party and bureaucracy. This is not to suggest a conspiratorial process at work. The intelligentsia itself is a formation of modern society. And the minder's role is a product of the discrepancy between political conventions and the demands made on leaders, rather than of the opportunism of new meritocrats on the make. Naturally, the story has been influenced here by more general discussions of the role of the intelligentsia in modern politics and society, and the psychology of the politically-engaged intellectual.

The psychosocial aspects of this story nevertheless are only lightly sketched here: as the first sustained study in the area attention has perforce been directed first to social and institutional changes associated with contemporary politics and policy, and this has dictated a largely descriptive and demographic approach. Yet once we broach questions about the contextual features of a modern social formation like the intelligentsia and the distinctions within it, questions about matters of psychological differentiation suggest themselves (see particularly the commentary towards the end of chapters 5 and 6 and in chapter 7). For instance, we are teased by the issues of why some of the intelligentsia become socially engaged and some become 'neutral' bureaucrats, while others insist on remaining 'detached' intellectuals; and why some of the engaged choose mainstream politics while others choose to work behind the scenes and become minders. The latter is of course a question about leaders and followers. Centrally, we are confronted with what it might be that creates the affinities and divergences between ministers and minders — distinctions upon which their symbiosis in the inner circles of politics depends. By extension, we must refer to the psychological dynamics of group life. Where psychologically informed speculation appears helpful in suggesting resolutions to such matters it has been utilized, while always remaining a subsidiary enterprise.[4]

At four points in the text (after chapters 2, 3, 4 and 6) brief biographies of particular advisers are introduced. These are intended to be no more than illustrations of the general discussion, which is to say they are designed to complement the argument, not to carry it. They provide a change of pace, and perhaps additional material for those with a more sustained psychosocial interest, but they can be skimmed or omitted by those who are so inclined without serious detriment to the rest of the book.

While it is strongly argued that personal advisers (minders) can be influential in politics, there is little attempt to assess the relative importance of their work against that of politicians (ministers) and bureaucrats (mandarins). It is considerably more important to recognize that political decisions are the outcome of group deliberations rather than of individual inputs. That is, it is necessary to attend to the dynamics of the policy-making group as a group containing ministers, mandarins *and* minders, rather than concentrate on the individuals who constitute the group.

This book is limited by controlling factors. It is limited by the obsessive internalization of decision-making in Australia, and the consequent restraints that policy-makers feel obliged to exercise against outside analysts of their work. There remains a secret history to every decision, so each remains beyond debate in important respects. Without more candour from policy-makers it will remain impossible accurately to map the processes by which we are governed. If one accepts the principle that responsible democratic choices can only be made by voters with full knowledge of how their governments operate, this must be accounted a significant impediment to democracy in Australia. As long as this impediment remains, books like this must remain suggestive rather than demonstrative, raising questions rather than answering them.

2

Advisers and Advisory Structures in the Modern Age

This chapter follows three themes. First, it is shown that leadership is essentially a group enterprise: a leader can only act on the basis of knowledge, and this entails a need for information, and negotiations with and between counsellors who supply that need. Such negotiations are at the base of 'court politics'. With the evolution of western bourgeois societies which emphasize rationalization and specialization of functions, there occurs the institutionalization of parliament (the forum for political leadership) and the bureaucratic civil service (the source of advice), and patterns of court politics seem outmoded.

However, a study of the sociology of organization reveals that bureaucracies have their own pathologies, and this is the second theme in this chapter. Bureaucratic organization and the methods appropriate to it inevitably entail limited responses to political demands. The political executive, which does not fully understand the nature of bureaucracy, perceives the civil service as resistant to its will and so turns to alternative advisers. At first these are more or less unofficial personal retainers, but eventually forms of personal secretariat become institutionalized.

Third, for a broad comparative understanding of the practical detail of this process we turn to western polities analogous to Australia: the United States, Canada, and Britain. In all three we see the growth in the quantity and complexity of demands on national leadership accompanied by the elaboration of bureaucracy, leading to the cry for sympathetic aides to push the executive's interests in the face of what is experienced as organizational inertia. In all three it can be seen that at a certain level this demand leads to the foundation of formal staff structures directly serving chief executives and ministers of state. In all three the characteristics of these staff structures can be surveyed. But the long term history of resort to cronies, 'kitchen cabinets' and the like, suggests that this is the formalization of something more ubiquitous: court politics remains integral in the modern state.

The business of government has never been the enterprise of individuals. Except in the most primitive tribal band, leaders of the body politic have not been able to rule alone. Even in feudal societies where hereditary monarchs and despots might appear entitled to have claimed individual rule, kings needed to negotiate with barons to ensure their continued co-operation, to maintain the loyalty of retainers who would act as their eyes and ears throughout the realm, to seek economic and political information from trustworthy counsellors, and to reward officials who acted for them, and in their name. That is, the king was at the centre of an institutional network, a group enterprise — the court. And the decrees issued in the king's name can be regarded not simply as the expression of his individual will, but as the outcome of court politics.

Court politics in its purest form was dominated by the monarch, who controlled his vassals through awarding or withdrawing his favour. Participants in the court could only achieve influence and power through the king's patronage. Yet he in his turn was dependent upon them to serve his needs, and in the political sense his most important need was for the information that would enable him to make the administrative decisions that would maintain his kingdom and facilitate his continued dominance of it. Thus, as Bacon noted, our most ancient myths show 'the inseparable conjunction of counsel with kings'.[1] But information is never neutral; data as apparently empirical as statistics are shaped by the preconceptions that govern their collection, and the way they are interpreted when presented. More importantly, in the arena of court politics, the information sought by the king could be utilized as a commodity by courtiers competing for his attention and patronage. His decisions therefore would be a register not only of his own will, his personal preconceptions and judgment, but also of who was winning and who was losing in the politics of the court, with the corollary that only certain information and particular interpretations of it would be favoured.

The politics of the feudal monarchy must be understood in terms of group dynamics and the centrality of information to power — as should all politics. In comparison with modern societies, however, the networks within the court were relatively fluid and *ad hoc*. As kingdoms became more extensive and more powerful, the informal networks of court politics gave way to new practices. The system of vassals serving the king's needs because of the ties of personal loyalty, fostered by direct favours, gave way to one of official advice tendered by ministers appointed by the Crown (the origins of executive government), and royal government implemented by salaried officials (the origins of administrative bureaucracy). The institutions of executive government and bureaucracy were to come to full flower with the evolution of parliamentary systems and the emergence of liberal democracy in western societies.

Though parliament in England had been conceived initially as a means for the king to consult his more significant subjects on policy, the preoccupation with how to raise money to support policy, and the concomitant evolution of the convention that taxation must have parliamentary assent, led to its eventual dominance. The political transformation of the nascent institution proceeded by way of recurrent clashes between parliament and (the king's) executive over the money to support policy, the eventual assertion by parliament that its privileges were not of royal grace but of inheritance and right, and the necessity by extension for the executive to find its power base within parliament rather than through the king's favour. The factional politics that had been fostered by the king's ministers lobbying to gain support for royal policy became dysfunctional as power swung in parliament's favour, and as it became imperative for the executive to maintain support in parliament, the basis of the more enduring coalitions that led to the modern party system emerged. In England and in some Commonwealth countries the fiction that the monarch remains the head of government, acting on the advice of the executive, has been preserved, but court politics, as an arena of importance, has long since been transcended by parliamentary politics.

These quite particular changes took place in a context which encouraged more widescale intellectual, ideological and social change. The transformation of parliament was only a part of this. If the intellectual underpinnings of the monarchy and the feudal system were challenged by radical ideas of acting on the basis of individual conscience rather than the church's direction or community orthodoxy, and thinking in terms of change and progress (self-improvement and society's betterment) rather than the stasis of social tradition, these were but manifestations of far more profound economic changes and a concomitant flow of power to new hands.

The agrarian and industrial revolutions of the period when parliament emerged disrupted and dispersed traditional communities, created demands for a mobile population which would not only move off the land, but also go wherever new industries dictated. More importantly, the people who controlled and developed the resources, finances, machinery — and ideology — of this revolution were not the hereditary nobility whose power was based on land, but an enterprising new class who needed to legitimate and consolidate their power. Protestantism (and its elevation of individual conscience) provided religious sanction for the impious transgression of the established order. Individualism with its assertion of rights and possibilities could be used to persuade a population to renounce received ideas of a natural order enshrined in tradition, and to move off in the restless search for self-improvement and better prospects elsewhere. Needless to say, material incentives drove the population to the factory towns. Economic individualism, with its implication that success was open to anyone who worked hard enough and that community progress depended on individual striving, was taken to justify the competitiveness and rapacity of the new class. At base, the ideology of the old order — the 'superstitions' of tradition and institutional religion linking church and state and justifying monarchy and the dominance of hereditary nobility — did not serve the interests of the ascendant bourgeoisie. As important as their assertion of the transcendent nature of individual rights was the idea that progress in all fields could be achieved through the application of mind rather than the exercise of faith. The concomitant was that progress could be achieved efficiently through the precise definition of rational goals and determination of the logical means for their attainment: this was profoundly to affect methods of social organization. And the importation of all of these ideas into the political realm ushered in the theory of liberal democracy,[2] whose terms dictated the decisive transformation of the parliamentary institution into its modern form as an elected 'representative' assembly and its dominance by the bourgeoisie.

The progressive institutionalization of executive government in parliaments, and the emergence of the modern executive dependent upon maintaining party support in these popularly elected assemblies, was accompanied by an equally significant trans- formation of the flow of information and advice to the execu- tive. In theory, representatives were meant to be the bearers of information and demands from their electorates, which would be taken into account by the executive in its decision-making. In practice, more and more of the responsibility for gathering, evaluating and advising on the matters about which the executive had to decide flowed to appointed officials in organizations designed to serve parliaments — the civil service or public service.[3] Bureaucracy, like parliament, had its origins in the needs of the court, but it burgeoned immensely and found its modern form in the political, economic and ideological transformation (and concomitant 'rationalization' of social processes) effected with the emergence of the bourgeoisie.

Organizations have proliferated in modern industrial society as a consequence of the increasing diversification and specialization of labour. The public service bureaucracies are just one instance of this. Max Weber, who believed bureaucratic organizations to be the dominant institutions of industrial society, saw them as the inevitable outcome of the social history of the bourgeoisie.[4] He defined bureaucracy as 'A hierarchical organization designed rationally to co-ordinate the work of many individuals in the pursuit of large-scale administrative tasks and organizational goals'. Weber isolated the characteristics of bureaucracy as a system of abstract formal rules, a staff of salaried administrative officers appointed on the basis of technical knowledge, a hierarchy of authority (where authority depends on office and function, not on person), an ethic of formalistic impersonality, and the systematic retention of organizational records. The drive by capi- talist companies to achieve 'rational' goals compelled them to adopt such practices, just as the efficient satisfaction of the requirements of an increasingly fragmented and complex society demanded that social institutions adopt like forms.

In the case of the public service, the logic of the specialization of labour suggested a split between 'political' tasks, proper to parliament and executive, and 'administrative' tasks which could be appropriately dealt with by the bureaucracy. In addition, the enormous technological advances of industrial society meant that government deliberations frequently depended on information that could only be gathered, understood and evaluated by special- ists — it was not accessible to laymen, or generalist politicians. The bureaucracy therefore was seen by the late nineteenth century as the device through which specialists and experts could be trained and mobilized in the service of government. Hence the bureaucracy was charged with responsibility for the advice upon which decisions would be made and for the implementation of those policy decisions. But the decisions themselves, the policy, were to remain the prerogative of the executive.

Much discussion of policy-making remains reliant on such notions of the executive and bureaucratic functions being comple- mentary. It will be necessary here to qualify that scenario. But first the leading characteristics of the evolution of political leader- ship and advice in western societies should be culled from this gloss on political history. The transition to more complex forms of social organization was matched by the transformation of the court's relatively informal networks, distinguished by shifting patronage relationships, into the reified institutions of parliament and bureaucracy. If there has been a perpetual conjunction in all societies between leadership and advice (Bacon's 'inseparable conjunction of counsel with kings'), in contemporary western societies advice has primarily been seen as the function of bureau- cracy. Where courtiers were in a dependent relationship with kings, bureaucrats serve politicians, but are not dependent upon them because of the career structure of the civil service. The process that started with the personal relationship between king and courtier has ended with the 'formalistic impersonality' of the relations between bureaucrats and their clients and political masters. The utilization of information as a commodity by courtiers competing for patronage and influence has been superseded by the employment of specialist knowledge and skill by career officials. The vagaries of court politics appear completely transcended by the 'rational' politics of parliament and bureaucracy. Yet it will be seen that contemporary politics offers some scope for group enterprises to function in ways analogous to court politics, and that bureaucracy has its own pathologies.

Many of the classical theorists of bureaucracy — for instance, Max Weber, John Stuart Mill, Robert Michels, Gaetano Mosca — have regarded it with suspicion and pessimism. For Weber, bureaucracy was the inevitable administrative response to the problems of order and organization in the large, diversified modern societies made possible by industrialism. At the same time he saw it as an 'iron cage' limiting individual freedom and happiness by its imposition of uniformity, hierarchy and order.[5] He saw dangers, too, in the bureaucracy's 'technical superiority' over all other forms of organization: 'bureaucracy has been and is a power instrument of the first order — for the one who controls the bureaucratic apparatus'. The question of who controlled the apparatus could not be left to chance: Weber believed danger could only be avoided by strong parliamentary control of the bureaucracy. Weber's contemporary, Robert Michels, however, threw into question the very possibility of effective outside control over bureaucratic organizations.[6]

Believing, with Weber, that 'democracy is inconceivable without organization' Michels nonetheless showed that democracy is inconceivable within organizations because the effective achievement of organizational goals demands a specialized division of labour with control and co-ordination at the top. Further, the larger and more specialized the organization grows, the more its operations become incomprehensible to all but direct participants, and matters are increasingly left in the hands of the élite at the top. Bureaucratic leaders, therefore, may come to be represented as so crucial to the operation of the organization that they seem to be irreplaceable. And since the privileges and status of their position depend upon being at the apex of the hierarchy, they become preoccupied with maintaining power. Which is to say, their concern with maintaining the organization itself (since that is their power base) takes pre-eminence over the stated goals of the organization. Preservation of the bureaucracy and its rights and privileges thus becomes an end in itself rather than a means to an end. This pathology of the organization has been called Michels's 'iron law of oligarchy'.

Remarkably, Weber and Michels achieved their insights over half a century ago when state bureaucracies were still relatively small. The period from about 1930 on has seen both a marked increase in the powers of central governments and a mighty growth in state bureaucracies — conditions appropriate for assessing the accuracy of their observations. Indeed, during this half century of growth and diversification, political executives have consistently expressed their frustration with the unresponsiveness and limitations of their bureaucracies. Reform governments and their supporters have tended to identify this unresponsiveness as evidence of the recruitment and encouragement of ideological conservatives by the bureaucracy — which can thus be read as itself the creation of the dominant anti-reformist class. Yet Weber and Michels have implied the possibility that it is as much to do with the sociology of the organization as with the ideological leanings of the bureaucrats, and we should be alert for this. In any case, even if reform governments have taken the lead in initiatives to assert a measure of independence from the bureaucracy, succeeding conservative governments have frequently followed their lead: there has been an increasing tendency for political executives of all complexions to resort to non-public service sources of information and advice to supplement that of their official 'advisers'. This has been apparent in the appointment of consultants, commissions, and committees of enquiry, as bodies to look into particular matters and report to the executive. More significantly, it is manifest in the growth of staff numbers, and the increasing sophistication in the structure, of the private offices of political leaders.

In this, France has led the field: there, each minister has a *cabinet ministériel* or personal secretariat, and the practice has a history of development over a century and a half.[7] Within each *cabinet* 'three roles are of capital importance; that of *directeur*, usually a high official with experience of the administrative machine and ability to co-ordinate; that of *chef de cabinet*, generally in political sympathy with the minister; and that of the technical advisers . . .'.[8] The French instance is worth noting not only as a manifestation of an early recognition of the dynamics articulated by Weber and Michels, but also because the model influenced consideration of advisory structures in Canada, and later Australia.

In general, it is this development of personal secretariats that shall particularly engage us, since it offers a third ingress to the policy process — that is, one neither through election nor entry to the career public service (and avoiding the gatekeepers of party and bureaucracy). This suggests a qualification concerning the received notion of interaction between the political executive and bureaucracy as being central to policy-making. It suggests inherent limitations in the process of 'rationalization', conceived as a value-free technical efficiency that somehow transcended politics, which the bureaucracy was seen to exemplify — and incidentally suggests the persistence of efforts to rend 'the iron cage'. This assertion by political executives of the need for subordinates who are directly responsible, politically responsive, and loyal appointees, also suggests the persistence of small-group enterprise at the heart of political leadership, with features perhaps analogous to court politics, even in the modern state.

An extensive literature on the 'invisible presidency'[9] — that is the proliferation of advisers and political functionaries around the office of the president of the United States — prompts the decision to look first to America for case materials on this modern development.

Despite the importance that has always been ascribed to the office of president in the government of the United States, reflecting the Hamiltonian doctrine that the unity and drive of the political system would only come from a strong executive, the president for a long time lacked institutional support in his bargaining with Congress and management of the bureaucracy.[10] It was initially deemed that his cabinet should supply him with all the advice he needed, and it was not until 1857 that Congress passed legislation that allowed for the provision of some personal staff — a private secretary, a steward and a part-time messenger. The first significant advance on this was not made until 1937, under the administration of Franklin Delano Roosevelt. Yet it is apparent that from Washington through to Roosevelt, presidents had been unable to act alone. A history of the presidency suggests that the reliance on intimates and confidantes, and the formation of 'kitchen cabinets' or 'inner circles', for advice and support had always been important.[11] Perhaps the best documented of these relationships was that covered by Alexander and Juliette George in their landmark study, *Woodrow Wilson and Colonel House*.[12] The development of White House staffing after Roosevelt was the result of the institutionalization of such practices.

Roosevelt was an activist president leading a reforming administration. Faced with the crisis of economic depression, he moved in the direction of expansionary economic policy and stronger central government control. As a corollary of this Roosevelt appointed a committee, chaired by Louis Brownlow, to consider how the presidency might be more effectively organized to manage and control federal administration.

The Brownlow report, delivered in 1937, insisted that 'the President needs help', and recommended the establishment of an Executive Office of the President and — most pertinent to our purposes — the appointment of administrative assistants to work directly with the president. Legislation enacting such proposals was passed by Congress in 1939 and this has been the point of origin for the development of the modern executive presidency.

The Executive Office of the President (EOP) has served as an umbrella under which have been created advisory mechanisms, in the form of special agencies or staff units, in areas that diverge from or supplement the established line-departments of the bureaucracy. But within the EOP, there have been particular staff attached to the White House, and the White House staff shall be the focus of attention in this chapter.

The number of staff assigned directly to White House roles has increased from dozens to several hundreds in the period since Roosevelt had Congress enact legislation based on the Brownlow report. More importantly, these staff, who were intended by the Brownlow committee to serve a largely functional role, have increasingly taken up a policy role. A number of contingencies have facilitated this.

There has, for one thing, been an accretion of powers flowing to the president, and an increasing emphasis on strong executive direction of policy. This has occurred in response to periods of crisis — the depression, and the Second World War encouraged the public to look to the national leader for decisive responses, and this continued through the Cold War (and the 'hot' wars of Korea and Vietnam), and specific incidents like the Bay of Pigs attempt to invade Cuba and the Cuban missile crisis. The emphasis has been accentuated by reform presidencies — Roosevelt's 'New Deal', Kennedy's 'New Frontier', Johnson's 'Great Society' — encouraging the belief that the presidency is the appropriate place for the resolution of crucial societal problems, and that the president should be helped in this by more staff, qualified experts and wise men with skills matching the critical issues they face.[13] Thus, the accretion of powers by the president has been matched by a parallel increase in the reliance on, and influence of, the White House staff.

It is significant, too, that the increasing sophistication of electoral politics has made an effective campaign team an essential resource for presidential aspirants. The group that succeeds in this high risk and critical enterprise possibly builds up an assumption of being an embattled group contending with others, and certainly develops internal patterns of interaction, influence, interdependence and trust. And naturally modern presidents have almost uniformly taken key members of their campaign team into office as members of the White House staff — for instance, Carter's 'Georgia Mafia' — and because of the continuation of relations of trust and interdependence these have exercised influence out of proportion to their experience, political skill or formal position.

The increasing focus on the president as the source of policy action, the growth of his powers, and the establishment by aspirants of a viable group before the assumption of office which is taken with them into power, have been factors underlying what Stephen Hess has described as a trend towards a 'personalized and centralized presidency'.[14] Being close to the person at the centre has served to accentuate the status of White House staff members — working with and for the president, they have access that is rarely enjoyed by cabinet members or bureaucrats. Equally significant, they are at the focus of the flow of information within the system, and in the game of advice and influence inside knowledge is the avenue to power. White House staff has been quick to recognize this as Bill Moyers, a key aide to Lyndon Johnson, notes:

There are two main sources of power . . . in Washington. One is information. The other is access to the President. The White House staff now has information more quickly, or just as quickly, as the Secretary of State or the Secretary of Defense, and they certainly have physical access to the President more readily than Cabinet Secretaries do. This tends to give the initiative to the White House staff operation.[15]

The particular ways in which White House staff members have been deployed have varied from president to president, but the unmistakable trend has been that of their increase and aggrandizement. The events of Watergate, in which the operation of Nixon's 'palace guard' and his interactions with his key aides were so crucial, seemed to underline once and for all the pivotal nature and inherent dangers of the modern White House staff. Yet even before Watergate, the trend had not gone uncriticized, as commentators noted that this new class of mandarins was unelected, unrepresentative, subject to no formal scrutiny, and yet exerted more influence than all but the most powerful department heads and members of Congress.[16] And even after Nixon, when Carter denounced big White House staffs as a symbol of the 'imperial presidency', he, like his predecessors, gradually came to rely more on his White House staff and less on bureaucrats and cabinet appointees. At the time of writing, President Reagan had seemingly marked the zenith of this tendency as commentators sought to explain his apparent decline in his second term as due to the loss of the team of advisers who had so deftly handled him during his first term:

It was the team of Michael Deaver, Edwin Meese and James Baker which made the man and resuscitated the Presidency. Advisers are more important to Mr. Reagan than perhaps any other modern President . . . . He is, and has always been, utterly dependent on his aides.[17]

The underlying dynamic of this trend relates to the relations between executive and bureaucracy. Presidents are charged with getting things done, yet they are constrained to negotiate with Congress and the bureaucracy to get their programmes accepted and implemented. The political and management problems this entails are considerable. It seems that most presidents, assuming office with an orientation to action and enthusiasm for a programme, come to experience these constraints as intentional impediments. The problem of dealing with the vast administrative network of the bureaucracy is a particular source of frustration. Presidents may come to power signalling their intention of relying on their cabinet secretaries and the bureaucracy: the shifts they are forced to make to avoid being drawn into bureaucratic battles not germane to their programmes, and their gradual distancing from cabinet secretaries as these become identified with their departmental causes, often lead to strain and distrust.[18] The sheer weight of bureaucratic procedures and the time these involve begins to show. And the implicit orientation towards cautious pragmatism by career bureaucrats — with their eyes not just on this administration but on their own long-term futures — may be read as resistance to the lead of the current White House occupant. In effect, the role expectations of the president and the practice of the bureaucracy may be incompatible, and this may have as much to do with the emergence of 'the personalized and centralized presidency' and the nature of bureaucracy, as it has with the intentions of either president or bureaucrats. Whatever is the case, Presidents Kennedy, Johnson, Nixon and Carter all complained bitterly about the apparent recalcitrance of the federal bureaucracy, and increasingly each turned to his personal White House staff for policy initiation and help in controlling the executive establishment, as his presidency progressed.[19]

In short, 'the tendency has been towards a strong and sizeable White House staff to protect the political interests of the President, to act as his principal policy advisers, and to direct (as opposed to monitor and co-ordinate) the implementation of his priorities by the bureaucracy'.[20] If the White House staff members have become influential policy advocates and power-brokers (Patrick Anderson quotes one of them reflecting: 'I had more power over national affairs in a few years in the White House than I could if I spent the rest of my life in the Senate'),[21] this has been an outcome of circumstances as much as intention. In fact, White House staffs have grown in power and influence because presidents have wanted it that way. Faced with a vast and unwieldy governmental apparatus, presidents have (as Brownlow recognized) needed help, and, as John Hart suggests: 'whatever the shortcomings of the presidential staff system, post-war presidents have believed that it has served their purpose better than the cabinet system'.[22] That presidential staffs have become important is critical to the purpose of this enquiry, for we see here an instance of the process by which unelected political irregulars can come to the fore in a modern system — the third ingress to the policy process mentioned earlier. Are such developments, however, peculiar to American politics with its centralization of executive power in the presidency, or can they also be recognized in the more diffuse system of executive management characteristic of Westminster parliaments?

Turning to Britain, it is apparent that the distinction between a polity with a chief executive (the president) and one with a collective executive (the cabinet) leads to manifold differences in politics and in administration.[23] The party politicians, with their own parliamentary power bases, who become British cabinet ministers, cannot be regarded as instruments of the prime minister's political will in the same manner as can the president's political appointees to the American cabinet. But nor is the prime minister isolated at the apex in the same manner as are American presidents: the cabinet as a collective entity[24] working together may be more cohesive and less fragmented than a system with a single executive. As a politically attuned team it may seem less at the mercy of the bureaucratic monolith, for the British minister — constrained to maintain credibility in party and parliament — would seem less prone to 'go native' in the face of bureaucratic pressure than the US cabinet appointee. The size of the team, its interaction, the nature of its experience and its constituency contacts, may suggest that it is the appropriate instrument for bringing political judgement to bear on official advice — at least ministers can look to each other and to party colleagues for opinion. A collective of politicians with long experience would seem, too, on the face of it, to have less need for political antennae than a chief executive reliant on appointees who may or may not be politically skilled.

On such grounds, it has been suggested that the Westminster system has not created such circumstances as lead to the demand for special advisers and advisory mechanisms outside the bureaucratic establishment in the same way as has the American system.[25] And certainly, in comparison with the EOP or the White House staff, the growth of central agencies and of numbers of policy-oriented personal appointees has been more attenuated in Britain than in America.

Nonetheless, some growth has taken place, and for reasons which appear on examination very similar to those which impelled the American developments discussed above. In Britain, as in America, there has been an increase in the quantity and complexity of the demands made on the executive, increasing attention to national leadership with respect to the resolution of societal problems, and complaint about the resistance and elephantiasis of the bureaucracy frustrating attempts at political control — all conditions conducive to the resort to special advisers. And in conjunction, there has been a history of use of more or less unofficial personal retainers, particularly by prime ministers, which has become increasingly institutionalized since the middle 1960s.

It can always be assumed that the perception by politicians of the bureaucracy's tendency to impede policy implementation by design or inertia plays a large part in their decision to utilize countervailing measures. Certainly, the emergence of special advisers as an institutional part of British political life in the mid-1960s coincided with a period of debate about and inquiry into the civil service. In 1966 the then Prime Minister Harold Wilson appointed a committee headed by an academic, Lord Fulton, to investigate the British civil service. But the reformist recommendations brought down by the Fulton committee two years later were never successfully implemented, and it has been argued that reform was successfully blocked by the civil servants themselves[26] — a substantial indication of their influence. Cabinet ministers have testified to their feelings of manipulation and frustration by the civil service. Richard Crossman, within days of taking office noted:

the sense of being isolated from the world. Every time I walk down those great steps outside the Ministry I breathe again, and feel I've entered real life again.

. . . At first I felt like someone in a padded cell, but I must now modify this. In fact, I feel like someone floating on the most comfortable support. The whole Department is there to support the Minister. In to his in-tray come hour by hour notes with suggestions as to what he should do. Everything is done to sustain him in the line officials think he should take. But if one is very careful and conscious one is aware that this supporting soft framework of recommendations is the result of a great deal of secret discussion between the civil servants below. There is a constant debate as to how the Minister should be advised or, shall we say, directed and cajoled and pushed into the line required by the Ministry. . . . Each Ministry has its own departmental policy and this policy goes on while Ministers come and go.[27]

Similarly, Barbara Castle wrote:

the Minister is cut off from every source of political activity that has given her life meaning and expression. Political activity continues to the extent only that it is authorised by the management of the Minister's life.

. . . I suddenly discovered that I was never allowed to take anything to Cabinet unless it had been processed . . . The departments did the horse-trading, and having struck their bargains at official level they then briefed their Ministers on it, and so in Cabinet I found I wasn't in a political caucus at all. I was faced by departmental enemies.[28]

Whether such impressions are entirely accurate, or in part influenced by a misunderstanding of the nature of bureaucracy and its potential for responsiveness, these notions gained such wide currency by the late 1970s that the BBC television series, 'Yes Minister', could proceed on the assumption that a mass audience could readily be persuaded that the bureaucracy controls government. The success of the series in Britain (and in Australia) perhaps indicates how readily this was achieved. Meanwhile academic observers typically identified the bureaucracy as 'the unloved establishment'[29] and identified the problem of control as inherent in the growth and complexity of the administrative structure in the post-Second World War period. Anthony Sampson, for instance, locating the origins of the development in the expansive and ambitious mood that followed war, argues:

After twenty years expansion was succeeded by contraction, optimism by pessimism . . . But the age of expansion and bigness . . . had left many relics which could not easily be dismantled . . . The bigger bureaucracies had added to Britain's inflexibility, when she needed to be more flexible than ever . . . While private companies were compelled to lose some of their fat, public institutions were much harder to reduce . . . The great bureaucracies were like pie crusts which had risen with the rising prosperity, and were now left as high superstructures while the rest of the pie subsided.[30]

It is instructive to cite these elements of the critique of bureaucracy in Britain in order to note how many parallels with the arguments of Weber and Michels are evoked: the 'technical superiority' of the bureaucracy making it unamenable to control by other institutions (Weber); the concern with maintaining the institution as an end in itself (Michels); the development by bureaucrats of their own interests, leading to 'departmental' policy while 'Ministers come and go' (Michels); the politicians' and observers' growing sense of the necessity for strong parliamentary control (Weber) undercut by the difficulty of really knowing what is going on because of the bureaucratic claim to expertise and control of information (Michels). Throughout all, key civil servants have continued to argue that the bureaucracy conforms to the nineteenth century ideal of rationality, competence, neutrality, and service,[31] and they have become resigned to ridicule: it was the special mark of the mandarin, noted Richard Wilding, secretary of the Fulton Committee: 'that he should feel that to be misunderstood by the ignorant is inevitable, and that to be traduced is our peculiar badge of honour'.[32]

If this sort of debate can be read as a manifestation of the tensions and frustrations that prove fertile in encouraging resort to countervailing sources of advice, it is salutory to remark that the developments of the 1960s and 1970s did have precedents in a long tradition of resort, by prime ministers especially, to cronies for support and advice. This reflects the utilization of kitchen cabinets and inner circles by American presidents before Roosevelt instituted the modern executive structure.

Before the 1900s the prime minister's private office was composed of both personal, political appointees and officials — and some of the latter had entered the civil service under political patronage.[33] During the early years of this century, the prime minister's principal private secretary was his personal and political appointee, not a permanent official. A trend after 1900 toward civil service monopoly of the office was reversed when Lloyd George, in 1916, organized a personal bureau or secretariat, housed in new buildings in the garden of Number 10, and hence known as 'the garden suburb'.[34] Headed by an Oxford academic, Professor W. G. S. Adams, these specialized secretaries were personally loyal to Lloyd George and took an interest in everything that required his attention and action. The secretariat wrote short memoranda to him, or snatched brief talks with him, and so circumvented unproductive use of his time and the floodtide of paperwork.

Though 'the garden suburb' did not survive Lloyd George's fall in 1922, and the burgeoning civil service (perhaps in reaction to Lloyd George's innovations) managed to exclude partisan and personal appointees from the prime minister's private office from the 1930s until the mid-1960s, Winston Churchill again established something very close to a personal secretariat during the Second World War. This unit, headed by Professor F. A. Lindemann (Lord Cherwell), was officially deemed a statistics unit but its staff of economists made policy recommendations on the basis of these statistics, and like 'the garden suburb' produced a flow of memoranda for the prime minister. The unit was:

essentially personal to the Prime Minister; it worked continuously for him; it had some idea of what was in his mind; it knew the sort of thing he wanted to know and how he liked to have it presented; its loyalty was to him and to no-one else.[35]

Just as Churchill relied on Cherwell as personal assistant, post-war prime ministers occasionally supplemented the private office with personal and political appointees: Clement Attlee made use of Douglas Jay, Harold Macmillan appointed John Wyndham, Harold Wilson had Marcia Williams (Lady Falkender) and Edward Heath had Douglas Hurd as political secretaries.[36] Everything indicates that personal and partisan irregulars remained a recurrent element in the circles around prime ministers, and that an issue was the sporadic attempt to establish personal secretariats. The perceived need for alternative and loyalist sources of advice has persisted.

In the 1960s and 1970s, however, came the most sustained attempts to put such developments on an institutional footing. The Wilson Labour government, 1964–70, made wider and more systematic use of special advisers than had any previous government, although they tended to be concentrated about the prime minister. Wilson's conservative successor, Edward Heath, reduced the political element at Number 10 — though he did, as has been noted, bring in Douglas Hurd, later to be elected a conservative MP, as his political secretary. But Heath conceived another potentially important innovation, the Central Policy Review Staff (CPRS).

The CPRS, with a substantial contingent of outsiders (including its head, Lord Rothschild), was intended to countervail the exclusive departmental or interdepartmental official advice ministers received.[37] It was seen as a monitoring unit which would act for cabinet as a whole, keeping a close watch on government strategy, and producing its own analyses to help ministers make independent policy decisions. Soon, because of the access granted the CPRS's head, it moved directly into the orbit of the prime minister. Yet, though cabinet retained the analytic capacity of the CPRS for thirteen years, it has been argued that it was soon effectively neutralized by the civil service.[38] After Rothschild, the head of the CPRS was appointed from within the civil service, and the number of significant outsiders on its staff declined. When in 1976 CPRS advice on nuclear reactors to the prime minister, James Callaghan, reflected that of the Department of Energy, with which the Minister for Energy, Tony Benn, was in dispute, Benn argued that the CPRS was being used to undercut ministers.[39] Thereafter, the impression grew that the CPRS was brought in by the bureaucracy as an allegedly quasi-independent body to give legitimacy to civil service recommendations. If a case can be made that the CPRS was effectively absorbed by the traditional Whitehall machine, it remains important to remember the motives which gave rise to it. Margaret Thatcher abolished the CPRS in 1983.

Returned to power in 1974, the Wilson Labour government formalized and institutionalized the system of special advisers. Though never a large group — some ministers chose not to appoint such advisers, others appointed one or two — they were an available resource, taking some of the load off ministers' shoulders, keeping political channels open, devising (or alert to) alternative means of reaching agreed goals, and insisting on the politicization of policy.[40] In addition, a special policy unit was created within the prime minister's office, headed by Dr Bernard Donoughue, an academic from the London School of Economics. Staff was appointed to the unit on the criteria of specialist expertise, Whitehall experience, and partisan sympathy.[41] The unit which was intended to be capable of its own analysis and critically alert to the implications of civil service advice, had regular access to the prime minister, to civil service papers, and to official committees. Its purpose was to give the prime minister an independent capacity to question both civil service advice, and the items put up by ministers. Its members, enjoined to concentrate on the political aspects of problems, were classed as temporary civil servants whose appointment lapsed with the fall of government. When James Callaghan took over as Labour prime minister on Wilson's retirement, he maintained the policy unit with Donoughue at its head.

Margaret Thatcher's Conservative government, elected in 1979, initially chose to reverse the development of partisan elements in minister's offices undertaken by Labour.[42] On the grounds that she could not preach economy in government while allowing her political bureaucracy to increase, Thatcher allowed only half as many special advisers to ministers as provided under Callaghan, and eliminated the Number 10 policy unit. Instead there was an emphasis on institutional resources, as Thatcher set the pattern by striking up good relations with her private office whose staff, reverting to tradition, was provided by the civil service. Nonetheless, three or four partisan advisers, heavily involved in issues that the prime minister followed, soon came to be seen as occupying the territory formerly covered by Donoughue and the policy unit. One of these, the monetarist economist, Alan Walters, drew considerable media attention when on joining Thatcher he commanded an unprecedented salary — far in excess of that paid to second permanent secretaries, his official rank — to compensate for sacrificing a senior US academic post and a lucrative consultancy with the World Bank. Thatcher's willingness to accede in this indicates the importance she attached to his service and belies the apparent downgrading of the partisan adviser role.

The way in which partisan advisers have been utilized in Canada provides useful contrasts with British and American practices that can be noted briefly.[43] The French heritage in Canada encouraged some attention to the French practice of the *cabinet ministériel* when advisory structures were being established. While having a parliamentary system based on the Westminster model, Canada is also a society in which there has been much discussion of the 'presidentialization' of the prime ministership. This has come about largely because of the concentration of resources in the Prime Minister's Office (PMO), which is large and entirely politically appointed, and indeed quite closely approximates a *cabinet ministériel*.[44] It grew from around twelve members in the 1930s to over 100 in the 1970s for reasons analogous to those adduced in the American and British cases already discussed. Intended to give its first loyalty to the prime minister, it has come to bear the largest responsibility in the Canadian system for the provision of partisan political advice.

The role of the PMO has fluctuated according to the predilections of prime ministers and their principal private secretaries. In the early 1970s its leading members were certainly part of the 'supergroup' of insiders who allegedly exerted the key influence in policy deliberations under Trudeau. In the mid-1970s, particularly because of the pressures of minority government, it became a political technocracy, involved with strategic decisions rather than with policy. In parallel, it was suggested that Trudeau's early secretaries, Marc Lalonde and Jack Austin, were more deeply interested in policy than their successor, Jim Coutts (1975–81), who stressed a switchboard role for the PMO. But later, again, there were instances of decisive contributions to policy, and the PMO structure passed essentially unaltered from Trudeau to Clark, and later to Mulroney.

Observers have not resolved the debate about whether the PMO is usefully regarded as having a policy-advising function, or should instead be seen as a switchboard, transmitting messages and managing the prime minister's routine. Yet it is clear that the PMO has been an important filter of information flowing from the bureaucracy and interest groups — and that this is a significant role in determining what policy demands are considered. Most important from our point of view has been the fact that the partisan PMO has evolved into a significant central agency which has the power — even if intermittent — to be a countervailing force to the mainstream bureaucracy.

As in Britain, there has been a resource available to Canadian ministers more generally in the form of partisan advisers on their staffs, but these have played a less significant role than the PMO.

Canada may be taken to reflect the pressures that have led political executives in Britain and America to resort to partisan personal staffs. The PMO, however, is now more extensive and more integral than any equivalents in Britain. In these three countries we note the centrality of the *chief* executive to the partisan staff structures that have emerged: in the Australian case, as we shall see, the more extensive system of ministerial staff can be regarded as important, though there too the prime minister's office has always led the field.

The influence of special advisers on the processes of government remains problematic, and will be taken up in detail below (see chapters 5 and 6). Here, the intention has been to elucidate the circumstances that give rise to the phenomenon of the emergence of partisan advisory structures within existing institutions. The discussion of America and Britain (and, by extension, Canada) indicates that political executives have been forced to contend not only with public service resistance to control (that may be endemic given the size and complexity of modern bureaucracy), but also with the 'bureaucratization' of politics — as the public service takes policy initiatives and 'turn[s] all problems of politics into problems of administration' (as Mannheim long ago noted).[45] In response, political executives have attempted to politicize bureaucracy by bringing their own partisan elements into the interaction between executive and bureaucracy, and in so doing have opened up the arena to a class of political actors who stand in an ambiguous position between elected politicians and career officials. In the process there are indications that dependence upon personally supportive partisan loyalists by political executives has been a continuous element — albeit a largely unrecognized one since the demise of the court — in political leadership. The trends common to both Britain and America, despite the systematic differences in their polities, are taken as indicative of trends common to all western democracies.

Another reading of these events suggests how inappropriate the nineteenth century ideal of a mechanistic exchange relationship based on the complementarity of executive and bureaucratic functions has always been in analyzing politics. For that ideal depends upon the possibility of rational definition of goals and the logical determination of means of realizing them, and yet politics is full of imponderables that *only* admit of such operations after value judgements and ideological assumptions have been made. As Henry Fairlie, a long-time observer of politics in England and America, has remarked:

The most important fact about politicians is that they do not know what they are doing. Their task is not to make a profit, like a businessman; to fight a battle, like a general; to win a case, like a lawyer; to ready us for salvation, like a priest; to write a book, like an author; to make a shoe, like a shoemaker . . . A politician must deal from day to day with what Bismarck called *imponderabilia*. He cannot even choose his materials . . . for these in the end are only two — people and events — and for the most part they are given in any situation . . . these force themselves on his attention, and he must deal with them in the arena he has chosen . . .[46]

And if giving such imponderables sufficient definition to act is a matter not purely of logic, but of values and ideological persuasion, bureaucrats cannot 'neutrally' stand aside from the process. They, too, will be involved in matters of definition and persuasion, to which they will bring their own assumptions. There is much to suggest that the values and assumptions of the bureaucracy come to be significantly influenced by the sociology of organization (as Weber and Michels predicted), and hence the frustration experienced by political executives in trying to exert their political wills, and the incentive for them to resort to partisan irregulars as countervailing advisers and functionaries.

Having entered these qualifications against traditional institutional models of policy-making (i.e., those based on the institutions of executive and bureaucracy, and their responses to parliament, pressure groups, etc.), it becomes important to complement these with a more accurate representation of decision-making at the level of the political élite. There have been compelling studies of events such as the Cuban missile crisis,[47] or the process of America's escalating involvement in the Vietnam war,[48] that suggest we would be best placed in analyzing policy-making at the top by regarding it as the outcome of shifting coalitions around political executives. Public service bureaucrats certainly continue to play a crucial role in these coalitions,[49] but so too do the political irregulars brought in as aides by political executives. These people, given access to the inner circles of policy-making by means other than the paths of public service or election, have never been the objects of sustained attention in Australian politics. Our understanding of how political decisions are made can only be enhanced by attending to these neglected actors on the political stage.

Illustrative Biographies

The following biographical sketches are intended to illustrate and supplement the discussion so far. By turning back to Tudor England and Thomas Wolsey, the longevity of the pattern of the adviser type is suggested. This point in history is important, too, as the moment when new patterns of leadership and administration, such as those discussed earlier, first emerged. And if Wolsey depended on the monarch's patronage in the traditional manner of the court, he also marked a break by capitalizing on skills and training appropriate to the new age (and not on lineage) to ensure his access to power. He stands as a transitional figure, the harbinger of the modern political age, in our story. Colonel House, on the other hand, suggests the persistence of court politics into the twentieth century: he is the classic *éminence grise* and emphasizes the durability of this element in political life. McGeorge Bundy, however, signals another transition, the rise of the professional and the man of ideas, politically committed but able to turn expertise to the service of more than one patron.

Thomas Wolsey

The career of Thomas Wolsey (c. 1475–1530) gives one instance of the manner in which court politics opened the way to power and influence for those who, lacking hereditary status, could only capitalize on intellectual and personal attributes. His career benefited from a development in the court politics of the time: the aggrandizement of the monarch's power had reached such a point that it encouraged a new royal ambition to shrug off such traditional constraints as the obligation to appoint councillors with hereditary status. Instead, kings sought to circumvent the hereditary nobility by promoting their low-born intimates to eminence, at the same time assuring strong ties of loyalty among such favourites who owed their position exclusively to the monarch's beneficence.[1]

Wolsey was the son of an Ipswich butcher and meat dealer. Revealing early natural talent, he was initially educated by Ipswich churchmen, before taking an Oxford degree at the age of fifteen. Wolsey took Holy Orders, and wasted little time in using his intellectual edge and the practical skills of literacy and education to gain notice within the church, and eventually an introduction to the court where, by 1507, he had become chaplain to King Henry VII.

After demonstrating his secular skills in successfully handling diplomatic missions for Henry VII, Wolsey was appointed royal almoner by Henry VIII on the latter's accession to the throne. As adviser and factotum to Henry VIII Wolsey gained access to power in church and state. When his rapid elevation through the hierarchy of the church was blocked by the inconvenient tenure of office of the incumbent archbishop of Canterbury, William

Warham, Wolsey gained prestige by being created a cardinal in 1515 — significantly, Henry VIII interceded with the Pope to gain this status for his protégé. He wrote that Wolsey's 'merits are such that the king can do nothing of the least importance without him and esteems him among the dearest friends'.[2]

Among the things of importance Wolsey had achieved for Henry VIII were the organization of an army for the invasion of France in 1513, and the negotiation of a treaty with France in 1514. Thereafter he was named lord chancellor. Henry VIII was happy to leave routine governmental business to this competent administrator. Wolsey engineered a treaty of universal peace among European states in 1518, negotiated an alliance with France — though this soon ran into difficulties — and undertook minor reforms of church and state. But all the time he added to his own power in church and state, to the extent that he became known to foreign envoys as *Alter Rex*: 'Never before had one man amassed so many important offices in church and state, and his wealth, like his power, was regal in scale'.[3] Wolsey built his own facsimile court, Hampton Court Palace, and lived there in great splendour with a vast retinue.

Wolsey's fall from grace, however, underlined the fact that he always owed his power more to the king's favour than to the tenure of any particular office. Having failed in elaborate machinations within the church to engineer Henry VIII's divorce from Catherine of Aragon, Wolsey was dismissed as chancellor in 1529 and forced to leave London. Then, having been found in correspondence with foreign powers against the king's order, he was arrested and ordered to London. However, Wolsey died a natural death during the journey, lamenting that he had not served God as well as he had the king. Thomas Wolsey rose because of his service to the king and the trust he enjoyed: he was destroyed when Henry VIII came to believe he stood in the way of the king's own grasp at power and sexual gratification. It is important to emphasize that Wolsey's success depended not on the trad-itional avenues to power that were the preserve of the hereditary nobility, but on the intelligent deployment of native talent, and of the skills of literacy and administration that were monopolized by the churchmen of the time. Changed social conditions, that fostered both new royal ambitions to transcend the constraints imposed by the nobility, and — in leading to larger and more complex kingdoms — gave a new importance to the administrative routine of government, provided the circumstances on which he could capitalize. But he prospered because he was accounted by the king '. . . among the dearest friends'.

Edward Mandell House

In the modern period, another whose influence and power rested entirely on his being regarded by a national chief executive as 'dear, dear, friend' was Edward Mandell House (1858–1938).[4]

House, the son of a wealthy Houston merchant, was a sickly boy who early developed an ability to manipulate others to compensate for lack of strength, or a robust physical presence. After an undistinguished academic career in eastern universities, he returned to Houston in his early twenties to a comfortable inheritance from his father, which he augmented through successful business ventures of his own. However, his real interest was politics, and having determined 'that I would fall short of first place, and nothing less than that would satisfy me',[5] he turned to satisfying his ambitions in less direct ways.

House worked assiduously at developing connections with leading Texas Democrats. Attracted by the populist idealism of state governor, James S. Hogg, House became the unofficial campaign organizer for the latter's 1892 bid for re-election, which was opposed by powerful business interests in the state. Hogg's upset win in the election was regarded as largely due to House's patient and efficient organization behind the scenes. When House subsequently played a major part in the successful campaign of three further gubernatorial candidates, his position as behind-the-scenes boss of Texas politics was consolidated. He described his role as 'playing with politicians', at the same time developing his preference for staying in the background.

Eventually the limitations of state politics became burdensome, and House began to look to the national arena. He disengaged himself from Texas politics in 1902, and saw his opportunity, when the Republican Party split in 1910 over differences between then Republican President Taft and his predecessor, Theodore Roosevelt. House, believing this would favour the chances of an eastern liberal as Democratic presidential contender, travelled east to look over the candidates. His final choice, of Governor Woodrow Wilson of New Jersey, owed as much to the fact that his first choice, Mayor Gaynor of New York, had offended him, as to the the urging of friends. However Wilson and House, on meeting, discovered they were congenial souls who 'agreed on everything'. In fact House readily perceived Wilson's tremendous vanity and delicate ego, and catered to both with carefully calculated attention and flattery. Rapidly an intensely close and sentimental relationship developed. House subsequently played a central part in Wilson's campaign, not as campaign manager, but as an intimate whose friendship invested him with broad authority.

When Wilson won the presidency, he offered House a cabinet post. House declined, preferring the wider brief of general adviser to being confined to a particular department. In fact, House concealed his manipulatory predilections by projecting the impression of being self-sacrificing and self-effacing, wanting nothing for himself.

During the presidential campaign, House wrote a curious novel, entitled *Phillip Dru, Administrator*, which gave expression to fantasies of absolute power (Dru became a beneficent dictator), and political ideas of sweeping reform. The novel was published anonymously, and ridiculed for its romanticism but perceptive observers noted the parallels between Dru's programme and that which the Wilson administration began to effect.

House, involved in every aspect of President Wilson's work, participating in cabinet meetings, acting as secretary — regarded by some as Wilson's 'ex-officio Primary Minister' — held no official position, and drew no salary. Wilson and House maintained a constant correspondence when apart. Eventually, House (reflecting Wolsey) became Wilson's diplomatic emissary to the wide world. In Spring 1914, House travelled to Europe to try to effect compromises (in Wilson's name) that might help avert war. Although he carried no official brief, he was accepted by Heads of Government everywhere as the President's personal representative. After war broke out, House became a strong partisan of the allied cause, and began as early as 1915 casting the seeds of doubt on the wisdom of America maintaining an isolationist stance. In parallel, he began meeting secretly with British representatives.

Although Wilson ran for re-election on what was effectively an isolationist platform in 1916 — and his campaign organization was again dominated by House — within six weeks of inauguration he announced the commitment of American troops to the European war. It is now apparent that this was but the culmination of a long term erosion by House of the commitment to neutrality: Wilson had been convinced that US participation could lead to a perfect peace. William Jennings Bryan, a pacifist, resigned from his position as Secretary of State in protest, and his replacement, Robert Lansing, was sent by Wilson to House for briefing upon assuming the office. House was to argue in the 1930s that his behind-the-scenes campaign for American participation in the war was 'the greatest achievement of his life'.

It was Wilson and House together who hammered out the fourteen points which were to be published as America's war aims and which incorporated the notion of the formation of a League of Nations to achieve a lasting peace. When Germany collapsed in 1918, House initially sailed to Europe as the US representative on the Supreme War Council that was to work out details of the armistice. It was the apogee of House's influence, as the *New York Times* reported: 'never in history has any foreigner come to Europe and found greater acceptance or wielded more power'. At the same time, the rupture from his patron occurred over the Versailles peace conference.

Wilson, who finally came to Versailles himself against House's urging, was a poor negotiator who found his obsessive zeal with the 'perfect peace' was not to be realized. Already injured by the US press, which praised House extravagantly at Wilson's expense, Wilson found his protégé had developed close relations with other allied leaders, and was prepared to entertain their compromises. The rift was played upon by Wilson's second wife, who intended to ensure her own primacy by distancing House. Wilson parted from House to return to America and seek Congressional ratification of the Versailles treaty with strained feelings.

The story of how Wilson fell apart in the battle to achieve Senate ratification of the treaty, and of how his compulsive refusal to compromise, and his campaign to take the issues to the people destroyed his health, has been told elsewhere.[6] House, now distanced from the executive mansion, could only write urging a more realistic course. After a time, he returned from Paris (without presidential authorization) and worked to effect a compromise with Wilson's Senate opponents. But Wilson's wife, on the pretext of keeping distressing news from him, censored his mail, and none of House's communications got through. Wilson in turn thought that in his hour of need his friend had failed him: the disillusion turned to the bitter conviction of betrayal. For House, all possibility of influence came to an end. When Wilson died shortly afterwards, House was advised not to attend the funeral. House thereafter could do little but devote himself to ensuring his own place in history. While in his seventies he tried once more to attach himself to the rising star of Franklin Delano Roosevelt, but though Roosevelt listened to his advice politely, neither he nor his campaign team took the old man seriously.

In just two careers, separated by 400 years, there are many elements that can be recognized as common to advisers and the advisory vocation. Wolsey and House can also be taken to limn the potentials and limitations of adviser roles. Both men were interested in influencing the course of events, but both chose indirect means because of impediments to their ambitions — Wolsey, not being of the nobility, could not expect to take the traditional path to power; House felt he lacked the attributes of a successful public figure. Both, therefore, had to work through influential patrons who were the publicly accepted repositories of power in their time. They had to turn their native talents to serving the needs of their principals. The practical services provided — counsel, administration, diplomacy — are clear. Evidence suggests they may have catered to the emotional needs of their principals; J. C. Flugel, for instance, suggests that as an older man performing the paternal function of priest, Wolsey 'was regarded by Henry with feelings originally connected with his father venerative tendencies';[7] George and George argue persuasively that House unctuously flattered Wilson, reinforcing a self-esteem that was precarious.[8] There seems scarcely any distance between the overt court politics of Wolsey's time and the way House worked on his patron in a modern democratic system. Both men became regarded as interpreters of the will of their principals — Wolsey seen as *Alter Rex*, House accepted everywhere as Wilson's representative and ex-officio prime minister — yet both clearly capitalized upon this to put into effect their own political ambitions. One distinction that can be made, however, and it foreshadows divergences in the careers of adviser figures we may be familiar with in more recent times, is that while Wolsey wished his increasing influence to be paralleled by the award of official positions (cardinal, lord chancellor) reflecting his prestige, House developed a preference for remaining in the background — only at the end, when influence was gone, wanting to assure his place in history. In Wolsey, we see the antecedents of the Kissinger style career; in House the forerunner of the grey gatekeeper, like Haldeman. In the end, though, the capacity of such men to satisfy their political ambitions is limited by their dependence upon a patronage system — their careers come to a sudden end when their principals turn against them.

If these two careers raise much that should be considered when looking at the personal appointees of contemporary politicians, there is still a missing element. The modern era is distinguished by a diversification of labour and an emphasis on specialist knowledge. While Wolsey and House were clearly intellectually equipped for their chosen work, they approached it as generalists, not as men distinguished by their ideas. Access to influence because of an intellectual reputation may be distinctive to the modern period.

McGeorge Bundy

McGeorge Bundy (born 1919) is the son of a prominent Boston family whose father, a distinguished lawyer, had had several stints of service at a senior level to American governments.[9] Politics, diplomacy, and the consciousness of being well connected, are the staples of his family background. McGeorge Bundy, after proving himself an academic high-flyer at Yale and enjoying a stylish career as an army officer in the Second World War, dabbled on the edges of political engagement. He served a stint working for the Truman Administration's Marshall Plan, then as junior foreign policy adviser on Governor Davey's presidential election campaign team, followed by a period as foreign policy analyst for the Council on Foreign Relations. But rapid elevation came after he joined the faculty staff at Harvard in 1949, where he rapidly advanced to full professorship and by 1953 (at the age of thirty-four) was being considered for Harvard President. Being thought too young, he was instead promoted to the number two post, Dean of Arts and Sciences.

Widely respected for his ability (if not always liked personally), Bundy came to the attention of John Kennedy, whom he had known casually before the war. Although Bundy played no active role in Kennedy's presidential campaign, Kennedy wanted him as part of his administration and settled on the job of Special Assistant for National Security Affairs. 'Kennedy considered Bundy the second brightest man he knew (. . . long-time friend, British Ambassador, David Ormsby-Gore ranked first) and he once said of Bundy's talents: "First you can't beat brains, and with brains, judgment. Then, he gets the work done. He does a tremendous amount of work. And he doesn't fold or get rattled when they're sniping at him".'[10]

Under McGeorge Bundy, and with his intellectual impetus, the National Security Council (NSC) within the EOP became the sort of 'counter-bureaucracy' that, as we have noted, frequently emerges when presidents become dissatisfied with their line-departments. As Kennedy became disenchanted with slow reactions of the unwieldy Department of State, and had strained relations with Secretary of State, Dean Rusk, power flowed to the intellectually fertile and decisive McGeorge Bundy. When Bundy managed to have a communications centre established in the White House (against State Department resistance) he became the president's primary source of official information. Where Secretary of State Rush saw Kennedy irregularly, Bundy saw him as much as four times a day. During such events as the Cuban missile crisis, Kennedy turned to an Executive Committee of the NSC (primarily Bundy and his staff) for help with the hard decisions. Kennedy also used Bundy and his staff as spies in the territory of permanent government. It was said at the highest levels that Bundy had more influence on Kennedy than did Rusk. Bundy's own facility for reaching quick, informed decisions helped Kennedy decide between the conflicting advice flowing in from various agencies, and so keep abreast of fast-moving world events. Eventually Bundy became the recognized conduit on foreign policy matters, deciding what issues did or did not reach the President.

After Kennedy's assassination, Bundy, believing in continuity in government, stayed on in Johnson's service. Significantly, Johnson kept him on though he did not like him. He kept him because, at least initially, he could not cope without him. Johnson did not like Bundy's independence — as an establishment figure, Bundy had a certain political independence, as an intellectual he asserted his own ideas and had a prestige Johnson needed to utilize, and in fact he had not owed his position to Johnson. Johnson liked his people to derive their power from him alone. Bundy in turn disliked Johnson's abusive and manipulative manner with his staff. Inevitably, Bundy's influence declined, and when it became clear that he could have no expectation of replacing Rusk — something Kennedy foreshadowed would have been done during his second term, but with which Johnson had no intention of complying — Bundy decided to return to private life, to the presidency of the Ford Foundation. But it was his decision, and occurred at the time of his choosing.

Bundy, in contrast with Wolsey and House, suggests the relative independence of the man of ideas. What he offers can be of service to more than one master, and so to some extent he can transcend patronage relations and resist the pressures to conform to the ubiquitous modes of court politics. Granted, he could not last with Johnson — who, as much as any modern leader, demanded his 'court' — yet since Bundy's influence did not come to an end with Kennedy and he managed to preserve a measure of independent decision, he can be taken to mark the distinctive potentials of the modern adviser. If Wolsey and House point forward to such advisers as Kissinger and Haldeman, Bundy is more closely linked with such advisers as Bernard Donoughue, who as Head of British Labour's special policy unit in the mid 1970s[11] was politically committed, academically trained, yet personally disinterested, and able to serve Callaghan as readily as Wilson. In Australia, the likely parallels would be Peter Wilenski, or David Kemp.

3

The Search for Structures in Australia

Labor Initiatives in the 1940s and 1970s

In this chapter we will see the themes established in chapter 2 played out in Australia with particular clarity. There have always been loyal operatives at the side of the chief executive in Australia, confirming the ubiquitousness of our central theme. What has changed has been the source from which such personnel have been drawn. At first there seemed little distinction between advice to government and personal support to the executive — and prime ministers commonly relied on the nascent bureaucracy for both. However, as the bureaucracy settled into an administrative service role, a new breed of personally appointed press secretaries emerged to specialize in the role of sympathetic political adviser. Still, little emerged to disturb the assumption of complementary roles between politicians and bureaucracy. Indeed, the 'classical phase' arguably reached its high point with the Second World War when, despite a bureaucratic explosion and departmental innovation, circumstances facilitated a congruence of aims between political and bureaucratic leaders — instanced in Chifley's 'official family'. The post-war period, however, saw the dissolution of such consensus and the emergence of a sophisticated career bureaucracy. This body began to be perceived as limited in political responsiveness, and conservative ministers began to experiment with personal appointees. In turn, Whitlam's determinedly reformist government took office with the expectation that the bureaucracy would impede its aims, and so commenced the institutionalization of personally appointed ministerial staff.

In the early years of the Commonwealth there was little pressure on politicians or bureaucrats to differentiate between the roles of advice to government and support for ministers. The federal bureaucracy was small and relations with the political executive were face to face: indeed, substantially, ministerial staff *were* the department. This can be seen especially clearly in the emergence of the Prime Minister's Department, and the careers of its first permanent heads.

Malcolm Shepherd, the first secretary of the Prime Minister's Department, had initially joined the NSW public service in 1890 and transferred to the Commonwealth public service with federation in 1901. He had been private secretary to the prime minister 1904–11, serving Watson, Reid, Deakin and Fisher, before being appointed by Andrew Fisher to head the new Prime Minister's Department in 1911.[1] While the emergence of the new department can be traced to sound functional reasons connected with changing demands on the prime minister's office, the close working relationship between Shepherd and his principal led to suspicions of court politics at the time:

Much comment was aroused by the contemplated promotion of Shepherd, particularly in view of Fisher's partiality for his services and the vigour with which he commented on Shepherd's integrity and self-sacrifice. There was a suspicion that an attempt was being made to confer on Shepherd a certain status without Parliament being told what was intended . . .[2]

More striking still was the relationship between Shepherd's successor, Percy Deane, and prime minister Billy Hughes. Deane had obtained the post of private secretary to Billy Hughes after having been invalided out of the AIF in 1916.

It was said that Deane came to live 'inside the Prime Minister's brain' and Hughes, at first irritated by Deane's 'smooth pink complexion, orderly hair and ivory smile' soon found irresistible his audacious humour, immense capacity for long hours and skilful organising, and ability to project and develop Hughes' own ideas.[3]

An invaluable aide at the Imperial conferences of 1918 and 1921, a member of and secretary to the Australian delegation to the Versailles peace conference where he was the irascible Hughes' ally, Deane gained the secretaryship of the Prime Minister's Department in 1921 (Shepherd moved to take up the position of Secretary for the Commonwealth of Australia in Britain). '[Deane] now became "unquestionably the most discussed of Federal Government officials", his "impenetrable nonchalance" and status as Hughes *alter ego* making him "the one everyone wanted to know"'.[4] Dean, though now a senior public servant, continued to play the role of minder rather than mandarin: he 'guided Hughes' diatribes . . . soothing the prime minister in agitated moments, and being "masterful in a cozening sort of way". The relationship, which aroused much jealousy, reached almost filial levels'.[5] He was evidently a figure in the tradition of Wolsey and House, and like them, his career depended on his patron: with Hughes' defeat in 1923 his star began to dim.[6]

If, at this early stage, there was little distinction between loyalist and mandarin, and court politics could be overtly played within the bureaucracy, there was nonetheless a parallel development which was to lead, informally at first, to distinct strands within the prime minister's private office. This was the introduction of press secretaries, and the consequent development of two groups within the office, namely departmental officers — bureaucratically organized and 'internal' to institutional politics — and press officers, loosely organized, usually personally appointed and 'external'. These two strands were to characterize staff organization of the Prime Minister's Office (and later ministerial offices more broadly) until the early 1970s. And as the bureaucracy grew and developed characteristics which would inhibit public servants from playing the minder's role so congenial to Deane, these press secretaries became the more influential political advisers to prime ministers.

The start of this line may be identified with Lloyd Dumas, a parliamentary gallery journalist who was released by his newspaper, *The Argus*, at the behest of Billy Hughes, to assist the prime minister in the conscription campaign of 1916. He toured the Commonwealth with Hughes and struck up a close working relationship with him. Later, he accompanied Hughes as press secretary to the Imperial Conference of 1918, where he was responsible for the published statements and press releases attributed to Hughes.[7]

In May 1918, Hughes invited B. S. B. Cook, a prominent journalist and one time general president of the Australian Journalists' Association, to organize the first federal press bureau in the Prime Minister's Department[8] — a recognition of the importance of the press, and the first of many attempts to give it an institutional locus within the chief executive's orbit.

Dumas had some notable successors, such as Cecil Edwards,

press secretary to (and later biographer of) Bruce; Irvine Douglas who worked for Lyons both as Commonwealth Government Publicity Officer 1934–38 *and* as private secretary 1936–38; Dick Dawson, press secretary to Lyons and later to Menzies; Don Rodgers, who as press secretary to Curtin was allegedly closer to him than anyone else in politics,[9] and as press secretary to Chifley was an influential member of the 'official family' (see below); and Tony Eggleton, press secretary to Menzies, Holt and Gorton, who rose to become federal director of the Liberal Party, was the special confidante of Fraser, and has long been one of the most influential behind-the-scenes figures in Australian politics.

Although permanent secretaries were less likely to play a loyalist role after Deane, and the provision of political advice fell increasingly to press secretaries, the patterns of relationships in the private office as described above did not change substantially until the 1930s and 1940s. The bureaucracy was small and was not encouraged to grow. Federal development of an administrative service had been initially impeded by the 'Braddon clause', a constitutional guarantee that the national government would return at least three-quarters of its revenue to the States for the first decade of federation. The conservative governments which were dominant between 1916–41 were reluctant to interpret their powers broadly, leaving citizens to look primarily to their State governments for services. In any case, until the 1940s the federal government was content to follow Britain's lead, and so long as Australia remained essentially a subsidiary, while important decisions were taken elsewhere, there was little incentive for the federal bureaucracy to develop as anything other than a clerical service — and thus it remained an attenuated and second-rate body. Certainly it was not of a character either to develop the awesome efficiency feared by Weber, or the oligarchical tendencies identified by Michels: it operated '. . . more as a string of independent side-shows . . . than as a coherent, self-propelling bureaucracy'.[10]

The 1930s depression did not involve any radical redirection: the Scullin Labor government capitulated to the expectations of the 'mother country' despite bitter dissension within cabinet, caucus and the party at large. However, this period did give rise to the first group of programme professionals — a group of economists led by L. F. Giblin and D. B. Copland — who publicized their own views on policy and sought to influence government.[11]

And the experience of the depression laid the groundwork for more decisive transformations in the 1940s. It profoundly influenced a rising generation of young intellectuals who came to believe that the conservative measures of Australian governments had prolonged and deepened the depression, and who began to look for new directions in economics and to propagate ideas of a new social order. These people were particularly attuned to the opportunities generated by the demands of wartime administration.

The Second World War provided the incentive for centralized planning and was the catalyst of a bureaucratic explosion. With new demands on civil administration numbers employed in the federal public service virtually doubled in the period 1939–45.[12] The accession to power of a reformist Labor government under John Curtin in 1941 seemed to provide an opportunity for significant social reconstruction, using the special powers flowing from wartime administration. The turn from Britain entailed in Curtin's 'new directions speech' (and appeal to the USA) in December 1941 promised a new autonomy. Hence, a significant echelon of academically qualified persons, their intellectual antecedents in the 1930s having prompted them towards central planning (and Keynesian economics), and their imagination caught by the opportunity for social reform offered by wartime administration, were recruited into government service. It is important for our purposes to note, however, that these people were usually not employed as *ad hoc* advisers or political irregulars, but as orthodox (albeit sometimes temporary) public servants — the rapid expansion of the bureaucracy, the proliferation of new fiefdoms through increased resort to interdepartmental committees, and the creation of new wartime departments (most significantly, the Ministry for Post-War Reconstruction), offered sufficient access to the policy process at a relatively high level *through* the public service for the committed intelligentsia.

If this was the general rule, there is an exception which shows one potential emerging from the special circumstances of war. Alfred Conlon (whose career will be considered in more detail later)[13] is a person who achieved a degree of influence without going through orthodox channels. An intellectual entrepreneur of some skill, he had the gift of making connections with the influential and selling ideas. He profited by tailoring his capacities to the new demands of war. It was said that he played an influential part in formulating the wartime manpower planning policy adopted by the Labor government and in conceiving the idea for the establishment of the Australian Army Education Unit. Certainly, through attracting the patronage of key officers in the army (including the commander-in-chief), he managed to secure a commission for himself as director of an unusual unit which was called the Allied Land Forces Headquarters Directorate of Research and Civil Affairs. Conlon attracted to this army research unit able and intellectually gifted men, some of whom were his protégés, and many of whom were later to have significant public careers in their own rights. While the concrete effects of the Directorate have been much disputed, it is evident that in his capacity as director, Conlon was consulted both by the commander-in-chief and by the prime minister. And it is conceded that the Directorate played an integral role in some practical matters, for instance, planning reforming policies for Papua New Guinea after the war, and establishing the Australian School of Pacific Administration. Conlon used his access to those in power and his ability to establish links between them to bypass the bureaucracy in pursuit of the ends he thought were correct. Like other 'irregulars', therefore, he created opposition, and after the war and his demobilization the bureaucracy effectively curtailed the possibility of further influence.

In general, as has been suggested, the generation of innovative ideas and the creation of 'brains trusts'[14] took place at the instigation of intellectual entrepreneurs, such as H. C. Coombs (who is also considered below), *within* the public service, though they might call for outside help as well as using the resources that had been newly attracted into the bureaucracy. It was the effectiveness of these processes that allows Coombs to say when referring not to politicians, but to academics and bureaucrats: 'It was among these men that the ideas were being formulated which were to make the conduct of the war when it came and the transition from war to peace exercises in the application of Keynesian economic theory'.[15] Because of the parity of ideas between the new bureaucrats and the administrations of John Curtin and his successor, Ben Chifley, the bureaucracy was not merely transformed from a clerical to a policy advising body, but took up the key policy role in Australian politics in the 1940s. There was little pressure to seek alternative advice. Ben Chifley, as prime minister, made use of a group which his biographer calls the 'official family'[16] — a collective brought together under Chifley's aegis whose members were primarily public servants rather than personal appointees. One significant exception can be noted: Don Rodgers, Chifley's press secretary, and a personal appointee, was one of the most influential members of the 'official family'. The pre-war practice of reliance on a loyalist press secretary for political advice was maintained.

The period 1941–49, with the transformation of the bureaucracy, the war-inspired consensus (for at least the initial part of the period) on central planning, and the ascendance of ideals of social equity and welfare in government and bureaucracy, was the closest Australia came to a 'New Deal'. The dominance of Labor at this time led to the emergence on the right of the first systematic mechanism for political advice that was affiliated with neither parliament nor bureaucracy. The Institute of Public Affairs (IPA)[17] instigated by Sir Howard Gepp of the Victorian Chamber of Manufactures, and its programme articulated by Gepp's economic assistant, C. D. Kemp, was to represent business interests in the debates concerning post-war reconstruction and to be a focal point for the reunification of non-Labor political forces following the virtual collapse of the United Australia Party (UAP) which had precipitated Curtin's accession to power in 1941. The IPA accepted the need for a greater welfare role for government, endorsed the full-employment objective that was central in Labor's post-war programme, and recognized the need for a broader range of planning activities. But it emphasized above all the imperative to encourage healthy private enterprise as the foundation for prosperity and progress. The IPA programme was seized upon by former UAP prime minister Robert Menzies as the means for rallying non-Labor forces in the grouping that was eventually to become the Liberal Party. The IPA not only gave articulation to the aims of the right, but also went on to play a functional role in the formation of the new party. By such means, politicians like Menzies found intellectual mentors like Kemp, while the IPA continued thereafter as skilful publicist and propagandist for the non-Labor cause. Yet, however significant its role in the 1940s, the IPA has remained a free enterprise pressure group outside the orbit of parliamentary politics when non-Labor governments have been in power — not strictly speaking the sort of advisory body in which we are interested. What has been more important has been the effect of the failure of the post-war reconstructionists.

Though Curtin was an effective and popular wartime leader, and Chifley was in many respects a successful prime minister whose government achieved significant extensions in welfare provisions, post-war rehabilitation, and important economic programmes, the aspirations of committed intellectuals towards a new social order were confounded. The unparalleled unity of purpose that could be rallied in war was not to be reflected in peace. As early as 1944 when the Curtin government appealed by referendum for a constitutional change that would extend the central powers assumed in wartime to post-war federal government, the measure was defeated. Denied this important means of policy co-ordination, the federal government faced significant impediments to its programme by State governments, intent on reasserting States' rights. Once the single-mindedness of the war commitment was lost, the community reverted to the diverse demands and pressures of particular interests intent on bettering their own positions. Chifley's insistence on maintaining wartime restrictions and rationing to facilitate post-war recovery was resented and seized upon by the opposition as a campaigning issue. Chifley's pursuit of controversial banking legislation — seeking first in 1945 to ensure continued control over private banking activities (which had been achieved by regulation in wartime) through the Commonwealth Bank, and, when part of that had been ruled unconstitutional by the High Court, introducing legislation in 1947 to nationalize the banks — aroused a fierce and polemical response in the business and financial community, and this was enthusiastically beaten up by the press. The Banking Act was ruled unconstitutional by the High Court in 1948. At the same time, cold war fears of 'communist conspiracy' led to conflicting pressures within the Labor movement, coming to a spectacular head when the Labor government, deeming coal mining an essential service, sent in troops against the striking miners of the communist-led Miners' Federation in the coal strike of 1949. All of these factors played their part in the defeat of the Labor government in the federal elections of 1949.

Just as the community's own unity devolved into plural competing interests after the war, the unity of purpose that had facilitated collaboration between politicians and bureaucrats was lost in the political defeats of the period. As a result, more traditional patterns of bureaucratic interaction based on self interest emerged and creative and innovative groups within the bureaucracy dispersed.[18] Some of the notable recruits of the late 1930s and early 1940s — like political scientist L. F. (Fin) Crisp, and economists Gerald Firth and Trevor Swan — returned to academic positions. Those who remained moved into new areas. The Liberal–Country Party (L–CP) coalition government, dominated by Robert Menzies, carried on some of the reformist measures initiated by Curtin and Chifley while scrapping others, but in any case eschewed the notion of consistent central planning — sometimes, it seemed, of any planning at all. While developments were allowed to occur in an *ad hoc* way, the L–CP government benefited from the effects of a fortuitous combination of circumstances that led to a period of unparalleled prosperity (and a contemporary description of Menzies identified his chief talent as that of presiding over events while looking as if he knows what they are all about[19]). Menzies' real interests were in the forensics of parliament and the public arena, not in administration. Accordingly, though L–CP governments were largely content to rely on their 'official' advisers, the field of action open to the bureaucracy was significantly narrowed. It was no longer attractive as an instrumentality for those with an intellectual interest in government and reform. On the other hand, now a large and sophisticated organization with policy capacities, it was precisely the sort of body we might expect to develop the sociological characteristics of modern bureaucracy discussed earlier.

It is not relevant to rehearse here the shifts by which the L-CP coalition retained government between 1949 and 1972. It is sufficient to note that, throughout, politicians and bureaucrats continued to maintain the impression that politics and administration were separate spheres, and that prime ministers and their cabinet colleagues were largely content to rely upon private secretaries chosen by and seconded from their public service departments. This is by no means to cast doubt upon the importance of the adviser-leader relationships we have seen earlier. Coombs, for instance, identifies a series of rich personal relationships between particular ministers and their officials at this time as contributing to the best ministerial performances.[20] Nor is it to suggest that the persistent demand for partisan loyalists in the private office was entirely subsumed by reliance on the career bureaucracy. There continued to be influential non-departmental appointees: press secretaries, like Tony Eggleton, aides like Robert Kennedy (who worked for Menzies), Keith Sinclair (who worked for Holt, Gorton, and McMahon), and Ainslie Gotto (who worked for Gorton). Gotto in particular attracted a great deal of public attention, and provides a telling instance of the persistence of our central theme. Only twenty-two at the time of her appointment as prime minister John Gorton's personal assistant, her previous experience was limited to having been secretary to the chief government whip, Dudley Erwin. She was allegedly privy to everything that came before the prime minister, and was consulted on everything that happened in the private office. Final policy determination was said to depend on the trio of Gorton, Gotto and Gorton's permanent head, Lennox Hewitt.[21] Some ministers other than the prime minister also made limited attempts to bring outside advisers into the established ministerial staff system: for instance, Allen Fairhall as Minister for Defence sought relevant expertise in bringing in Ian Marsh as a personal appointee, and his successor in that portfolio, Malcolm Fraser, employed Vivian Davidson and Ian Marsh in similar circumstances.

These cases, however, were *ad hoc* exceptions to the bureaucratic dominance of ministerial offices, 1949–72. Indeed, public service control may have been the corollary of a limiting view of government and its role: ministers did not need to look far to satisfy their circumscribed aims. Not until nearly the end of this period — by which time the coalition had lost its grip on events, and its disarray began to look like that of the UAP before its collapse in the early 1940s — did a conservative prime minister, William McMahon, publicly signal an attempt to broaden his options by appealing to H. C. Coombs '. . . as a kind of guiding philosopher'.[22] By then it was too late (and, significantly, Coombs was prepared to entertain a similar invitation from the ensuing Labor prime minister, Gough Whitlam). With the coming to power of an avowedly reformist Labor government in 1972, a new phase began in the innovative use of the bureaucracy and the first *systematic* institutionalization of personal advisers.

During the period 1949–72 the political and social conditions which prevailed led to the formation of a public service body that was oligarchical, relatively inflexible, and conservative in effect, if not in intent. More than two decades of serving a single political master, and one which exercised little in the way of policy direction or strong parliamentary leadership, allowed the bureaucracy to develop characteristics which would later impede attempts to assert political control.

There were many subsidiary factors to facilitate this. Recruitment and promotion played a part. If the bureaucratic explosion of the 1940s had attracted a group oriented to reform, the defeat of their hopes presumably led to more limited aims in those who remained thereafter. At the same time the bureaucratic explosion had enhanced the public service as an avenue of secure employment for those who had the requisite skills. Thus, it is to be expected that during the years of stability and relative prosperity — when there was a powerful body of argument that the good society had been achieved, making ideological battles over reform irrelevant[23] — recruits would be moved by personal, careerist goals rather than ambitions for social change. In addition, the skills appropriate to the meritocratic orientation of this now relatively sophisticated organization demanded a certain level of education, leading H. C. Coombs, as chairman of the Royal Commission on Australian Government Administration in the mid-1970s, to remark:

the people who compose the bureaucracy . . . are selected by processes which give the greatest weight to qualities most likely to be possessed by those with privileged social background and access to privileged educational institutions. The composition of the bureaucracy therefore reflects not the structure of Australian society as a whole but that of the already privileged sections of it. The unconscious presumptions which influence its patterns of thought tend therefore to lean heavily towards the preservation of the status quo.[24]

It was natural, too, that throughout this period L-CP governments encouraged the appointment of departmental heads whose sympathies they felt to be compatible with their own politics. The expectation implicit in western democracies that regular changes of government would limit such tendencies, and by creating different demands keep bureaucrats on their toes, was not fulfilled in these years.

More important than the probable political orientation of the bureaucratic élite may have been the practice of leaving policy direction in their hands, for, lacking strong parliamentary direction (which Max Weber warned was essential), the bureaucracy was allowed to develop a clear sense of its own policy interests — usually couched in the language of unassailable expertise and 'the right way' of doing things. So, a leading Liberal politician, Billy Snedden, was later to say:

I believe that in the twenty-three years of government we had concentrated more and more on the bureaucracy. It was easy to get advice from there. It was easy to get information. It was easy to communicate; and what happened is that we did drift away from the essential base that is our major cause of strength as a political party. Our national party.[25]

Twenty-three years had been long enough to build a tradition, a body of expectation and precedent, that any government attempting to assert a stronger managerial line, let alone to effect political intervention and reform, would find a formidable barrier. The Labor government elected in December 1972, therefore, had good reason to feel suspicious of the bureaucracy. Senior bureaucrats were not all politically antagonistic to the Labor Party, and some now claim there was considerable goodwill towards the new government.[26] But it did not take them long to decide that the government showed a lamentable lack of appreciation of 'the right way' of doing things, and this for them created the difficulty in working with Labor. Some observers of both politicians and bureaucrats saw things differently:

what has emerged over the past few years is that the Canberra bureaucracy has become increasingly arrogant in the use of the power that the institutional structure of Australian politics allows it, and it has developed a philosophical frame of reference which is no longer a reflection of the attitudes of the party elected to Government . . . The non-partisanship of the Public Service has developed a particular style of its own which makes nonsense of the suggestion that the bias is one of party lines. Instead . . . there is a distinctive bureaucratic philosophy that has been nurtured in Canberra. It is conditioned by the fact that the ACT is affluent, educated, and overwhelmingly middle-class.[27]

It is important to keep this history in mind in considering the flow of advice, understanding that the interaction between executive and bureaucracy may be less affected by the party-political sympathies of some bureaucrats than by separate considerations of bureaucratic politics (those negotiations by which bureaucrats preserve the 'accepted' practices which maintain their own influence and standing). Snedden's statement, and McMahon's belated appeal to an outside 'philosopher', indicate that it was not only on the Labor side that disquiet about the predominance of the bureaucracy was felt, and this will be taken up again in considering the way in which Malcolm Fraser's Liberal-National Country Party (L-NCP) coalition government adopted some of the alternative structures initiated by Labor. Nonetheless, it was the Labor government, 1972–75, which first attempted to effect a measure of public service reorganization and reform, and which initiated the institutionalization of alternative sources of partisan advice in ministers' offices. The history of attempts at change, and of reaction to change, in the bureaucracy in these years is discussed elsewhere.[28] Interest here is in the resort to alternative sources of advice, and in particular to this incorporation of advisers in the private offices of the political executive.

In the period between Chifley's innovative use of his 'official family', and the election of the Whitlam Labor government in 1972, L-CP governments had relied on traditional patterns of staffing ministerial offices (albeit, with a few exceptions, as noted above). The practice was to follow the British model, where (until the Wilson government's innovations) the private office was virtually an annex of the department, staffed by departmental officers. In the Australian case, however, these officers were rarely the 'high fliers' seconded to ministers in Britain. The typical office comprised two junior departmental officers as private secretary and liaison officer, a press secretary, and clerical staff. While the private secretary was not encouraged to exercise initiative on his minister's behalf, the press secretary, who was usually employed under Australian Journalist Association (AJA) awards and was not a career public servant, might be drawn on for political intelligence, advice, and sympathy — and press secretaries thus could become figures of considerable influence. Junior departmental officers of course suffered divided loyalties between the ministers they served on secondment and the departments in which they expected to pursue their future careers: it was not realistic to expect staff of this status and calibre to buck the departmental view. Indeed, few ministers tried to impose their own priorities, and few saw the private office as a potential source of political and policy advice.[29]

The Labor Party determined to change this on coming to power. The initiative has been said to have come from Whitlam himself,[30] but if this was so, almost certainly the detailed preparatory planning was carried forward by others.[31] With a general concern for strengthening the hands of ministers in their dealings with their departments, the idea of ministerial 'cabinets' along French lines was toyed with,[32] before it was decided to expand and upgrade the role of ministerial staff. Allied to the concern with enhancing ministerial power was the conviction that Labor's programme of reform and change would impose quite different demands upon the bureaucracy than those that had stemmed from the L–CP government's preoccupation with managing the status quo. Under such general heads, a series of specific reasons for staff changes have commonly been adduced:[33]

— there was strong suspicion of the public service élite, which was felt to have been conditioned in a policy sense by twenty-three years of working with the L–CP coalition.

— there was a wariness of entrenched bureaucratic and departmental interests which might be expected to conflict with government interests, and which had seemingly triumphed in the recent past.

— Labor had commitments to new departments in areas where no public service expertise existed; it was essential for ministers in these departments to be able to call on expertise and support from elsewhere.

— Labor's shadow ministers in opposition had drawn heavily on voluntary unpaid advisers. It was natural to repay that debt by appointment of such people to positions in ministers' own offices, and would ensure the continued availability of their advice.

— the ALP came to office with specific policy commitments articulated in the party platform, and it was desirable for ministers to have around them people who understood and supported that platform, and who were familiar with the institutions and machinery of the ALP.

— there was a belief that wisdom need not reside solely in conventional institutions, and that it would therefore be desirable to multiply the government's sources of advice.

— the prime minister led the ministry in pointing out the necessity of having politically sensitive staff in their private offices in order to minimise the involvement of public service officers in the party political work those offices would inevitably have to handle.

After considerable debate, and a deal of wrangling with the Public Service Board, which found it difficult to move away from the traditional pattern, a new format for the private office was agreed. Essential to this was the new staff category of ministerial officer, which would cover all private secretaries, advisers, and research officers in ministerial offices. Though there were to be three levels in the category,[34] the gradings given to these ministerial officers were more senior than those that had applied to ministerial staff in the traditional system, indicating the enhanced significance that was intended to attach to the private office. The normal entitlement for each office was fixed at four ministerial officers, two assistant private secretaries, one secretary/typist and one steno-secretary. There was provision for one of the four ministerial officer positions to be filled by a press secretary, employed in the traditional way under an AJA award. It was also expected that at least one of these positions would be filled by a public servant, serving as departmental-liaison officer. Normally the two highest level officers were the private secretary, the head of the minister's staff, and the press secretary, but ministers were free to select their own staff from wherever they chose and to place them in an appropriate grade. Ministers could seek the approval of the prime minister to vary the numbers of the classifications of their staff. (The prime minister was entitled to a much larger staff, and could appoint ministerial officers at two grades above those fixed for the rest of the ministry.) Some time later, after it had been alleged that some public servants on secondment had been subjected to departmental pressure, it was made clear that all ministerial staff (including public servants) were under the direct and exclusive control of their ministers for the duration of their service in the private offices.[35]

Under the new system, the numbers of staff employed by ministers rose rapidly from 155 in April 1972 to 209 by December

1974 and 219 in November 1975 (just before the government fell).[36] Despite the new freedom of ministers regarding recruitment, about one-half of all staff came from the public service, most on secondment.[37] Of those staff in the ministerial officer category (who constituted less than half the total), about one-third were seconded officers (and most of these were designated as departmental-liaison officers). In short, despite the growth in numbers, the group of people who saw themselves or could be designated as advisers was relatively small — estimates range between 20[38] and 35 or so,[39] though one might add, say, a dozen more in consideration of some whose policy role was *ad hoc* and irregular.[40] Further, these advisers were deployed in an uneven way — in some offices there were no advisers at all; in others they were of comparatively low status; in yet others, those classed as advisers were permanent public servants.[41]

The limitations of this experiment are easier to see in retrospect — at the time it was difficult to pick which of these staffers were 'political', and one newspaper expressed what was undoubtedly a common view in speaking of '. . . an influx of rough-haired young "ideas" men — more than 100 of them at latest count, many of them graduates — who have been hired as ministers' private advisers beyond the control of the monolithic Public Service Board'.[42] Not only did the ALP government's change in established staffing practices attract attention, but also some of the appointments created controversy, and some of the advisers were outspoken about their views of their roles, and so this became a visible group, the most prominent members of which readily gained media attention.[43] It is also the case that these innovations provided the means by which a politically engaged group with strong network ties was drawn into the parliamentary political process. One commentator, John Edwards, gives expression to this:

I suppose when I walked into Parliament House earlier this year [1973], I would have known half the personal staffs who had already arrived, through nothing more conspiratorial than a left-liberal history in the local Labor party, the Sydney and NSW Fabian Societies, the anti-Vietnam movement and three years on the *Financial Review*. It was as though a part of a whole generation had marched through Kings Hall and filtered through to the various ministers' offices. It's in the discovery of so many connexions that one realises just what a small country this is, and how important face-to-face groups are.[44]

The network relationships made for swift communication and promoted like-minded attitudes and responses to events. These people were activists, wanting to play a part in what one of them described to me as 'a great reform government'. Like their predecessors who, in the 1940s, had sought a similar end through the bureaucracy, their hopes were to be confounded by the unprecedented fall of the Whitlam government in 1975.

The Prime Minister's Office, larger than those of his colleagues, and with a more pronounced policy capacity, might be taken as prototypical of the intentions behind these innovations. Before the election, thought had been given to the structure of the office and to its role, and a paper had been prepared at Whitlam's request, by Dr Peter Wilenski,[45] a public servant then on leave who was to become Whitlam's first principal private secretary after the election. Whitlam, therefore, was prepared to swing his personal staff into office and into action immediately, whereas the arrangements for staffing the other ministerial offices were not agreed until June 1973. Wilenski himself describes how, in 1973 and 1974, there was an attempt to make the Prime Minister's Office into a driving force in government, not only supporting and advising the prime minister, but also overseeing and co-ordinating the implementation of Labor's platform across the board. After some early success, the task of keeping track of increasingly complex programmes became too large for such a small group, and it was decided instead to transform the Department of Prime Minister and Cabinet so that it might more vigorously assert the prime minister's policies and priorities. Thereafter the influence of the Office declined.[46]

If the Prime Minister's Office itself experienced declining influence, how successful was the scheme at large? Many commentators (including Wilenski) have rated it only a modest success:[47] indeed a study commissioned by the Royal Commission on Australian Government Administration concluded: 'The work done by ministerial advisers varies considerably, but their part in the policy process has been essentially limited and confined'.[48] It is commonly pointed out that advisers were essentially dependents, not only appointed and disposable at a minister's whim,[49] but serving only in the manner he or she allowed: they had limited scope for entering the political process in their own right.[50] It has been argued that such staff were eventually neutralized, circumvented, or co-opted by the public service.[51] In the event of visible clashes between public service and ministerial staff personnel, the latter seemed to lose: for instance, in January 1973 Clem Lloyd, long a trusted ALP adviser and then press secretary to Defence Minister, Lance Barnard, resigned after he had been excluded from a meeting with the British Defence Secretary on the instructions of the head of the Defence Department, Sir Arthur Tange. In July 1975, Dr Jim Anthony, private secretary to Social Security Minister, John Wheeldon and a man who had advocated an activist role for ministerial staff in a paper published only a month before,[52] resigned his post, citing obstruction from 'yesterday's men', his description of the senior departmental officers.[53] In addition, there were appointments of family members and of controversial personalities — treasurer Jim Cairns' appointment of Junie Morosi is often cited — which were used by opposition and press in attempts to bring the scheme into disrepute. It is clear that some ministers deployed staff ineptly, and some staffers took up an unproductively combative role in relation to the public service. In fact, a major defect in the system 'was that there was no external vetting of ministerial selection, so that good ministers tended to appoint good ministerial staff and become better ministers, while some mediocre ministers tended to appoint bad ministerial staff and possibly become worse ministers'.[54]

Against these limiting views, however, other material can be cited. In a long article on the erosion of treasury influence over economic decision-making in 1974, Robert Haupt argued that the Treasury 'believed itself to be done in by the new style of administrative arrangements adopted by the Labor government'. The ministerial advisers in particular are cited as having a decided advantage over the department — control over what finally goes to a minister. It was felt that Treasury had lost its pre-eminence 'in the vital information game':

now the Treasury's up-to-the-minute submissions have had to meet the view of ministerial advisers who have . . . been overwhelmingly hostile witnesses.

There is feeling within the Treasury that the balance has been rather lop-sided: that ministerial advisers get to make comments to ministers entering Cabinet upon the Treasury submission, but that the Treasury does not get anything like a fair chance to reply.[55]

Indeed, in another dispute about the role and influence of advisers late in the term of the Fraser Liberal-National Country Party government, the head of Treasury referred back to the allegedly adverse outcome of these 1974 events as a warning.[56] Beside this instance of advantage in bureaucratic in-fighting might be placed some evidence of political effectiveness within the parliamentary party. In correspondence with this author, one Labor cabinet minister of the period has argued:

at the prime ministerial level . . . staffers regard themselves as being more powerful than ministers or private members of parliament. Indeed, they almost invariably *do* have more influence with their prime minister than do the ministers. . . . in all cases, the staff can, and do, influence a minister's relationships with his peers and senior public servants. This is crucial in the case of the prime minister. It is my firm belief that Crean, Cairns, Cass, Connor and Cameron were demoted or dismissed at the prompting of Whitlam's ministerial staff together with the influence of senior public servants. I believe the reports that Gough's disastrous decision to recall parliament for a one day sitting on 9 July 1975, germinated in the mind of a staffer; and that Hawke's . . . decision to hold a Royal Commission into certain aspects of his own government was made without the approval of Cabinet.

If influence is assessed not in terms of specific policy decisions put in place at the instigation of a specific adviser (although there *were* some of these;[57] albeit largely peripheral), but in more general terms, the question of effectiveness and of the viability of adviser roles for the politically interested remains more open. To the extent that the 'smooth' functioning of government that had prevailed under the L–CP coalition was disrupted, the inner workings of the public service were opened up to ministerial scrutiny and challenge. The public service was gingered-up, forced to argue for and justify its case in an unprecedented way.[58] While staffers were dependent upon their ministers, many of them were left free to define their own roles, and did this in ways that gave them considerable scope for action. The staff in the offices dealing with new areas (such as Urban and Regional Development) did essential work in early days. Most importantly, in emphasizing the limited scope for action by advisers in their own right, the limiting views we have considered take insufficient account of the

extent to which the new system promoted the emergence of the
'group enterprise'[59] (rather than the minister alone) as the basic
unit on the 'political' side of the policy-making equation: participation in the group (no matter how difficult it is later to discern
individual contributions) constitutes involvement in, access to, the
policy process. I have argued elsewhere, in studying backbenchers, that for the politically attuned access to and dealing in
'inside' information may be at least as important a reward as
'power' more crudely defined:[60] certainly ministerial staff take the
short road to where 'the action' is. These matters demand the
more careful and considered treatment given in chapters 5, 6 and
7. For the moment it is enough to establish that the matter of
whether or not opportunity exists for influential participation in
the political process through adviser roles remains an open
question.

In this discussion of Australian developments there is much that
parallels the pattern established in chapter 2. Where bureaucracy
remains limited and government seems relatively simple (or
subsidiary to larger decisions taken elsewhere), personalized face-
to-face interaction of the policy élite remains feasible. With institutional and societal growth, and its attendant complexity,
relations have to change. As well as changes dependent upon
contingencies (the bureaucratic explosion engendered by the
imperatives of war), there occur developments particular to
specific demands made on the bureaucracy (for example, the
Curtin and Chifley governments' preoccupation with effecting
reform through increasing the powers and central planning capacities of government). Perhaps the peculiarity of the Australian
case is that the circumstances of the bureaucratic explosion in the
1940s served at that time to facilitate a community of views
between political and bureaucratic elements: thus Chifley created
his 'official family' of special advisers from within the bureaucracy. Our lesson, however, is that all activist political leaders are
prone to create something like Chifley's 'official family', wherever
it is drawn from. When the bureaucracy no longer seems a
productive stable other measures will be taken.

The flowering of the modern bureaucracy in Australia is late:
it is essentially a development of the post-war years. And with

it we see that familiar increase in the political executive's experience of frustration with the apparent resistance or unresponsiveness of the bureaucracy, along with the suspicion that the bureaucracy is not a neutral instrument. Whether this is so or not (and top public servants continue to argue that it is not), political executives conceive the idea that they need help in managing and co-ordinating administrative machinery, along with a source of fresh ideas. While conservative leaders (like McMahon and Snedden) gave voice to this, Whitlam's reformist government acted on it, bringing in both bureaucratic change and a system of personal advisers to the political executive. In this, Whitlam followed the precedents of other reform leaders (like F. D. Roosevelt and Harold Wilson), not because he looked to them as models, but because his aims, and the circumstances in which he came to power, were conducive to the resort to such innovative measures. Whatever qualifications are entered about the Whitlam government's changes in the operations of the policy-making élite (and despite the ensuing conservative government's apparent down-grading of partisan advisers), the system is here to stay in its essentials. The Fraser L-NCP and the Hawke ALP governments have built on these foundations.

Illustrative Biographies

Three figures are considered here. Alf Conlon, while relatively unimportant in the larger historical scheme, nevertheless stands as characteristic of the political irregular, capitalizing on fortuitous circumstances, and foreshadowing what was to come. 'Nugget' Coombs, on the other hand, represents the highpoint of the 'classic' phase of complementary roles between bureaucrat and politician. He is important not as an external adviser, but as the exemplar of intellectual entrepreneurship and innovation within bureaucracy, and of the recognition of the potential influence this offered to the intelligentsia. His experience, however, signifies the frustration of that potential. Peter Wilenski stands here as representative of the modern adviser, or minder.

Alfred Conlon

Alfred Austin Joseph Conlon (1908–61)[1] was a child of Sydney's lower-class inner city. Born at Paddington, he lived later behind a shop in Newtown with his widowed mother (a seamstress) and two brothers. A child of lively intelligence and curiosity, who early developed a preference for reading and conversation rather than sports or outdoor games, he had the advantage of attending the notable Fort Street Boys' High School, 1922–25, although the family's straitened circumstances forced him to leave at the end of his fourth year, and he only matriculated later by private study. Conlon took an Arts course at the University of Sydney, graduating with mediocre honours in philosophy in 1931.[2] At the university, he came under the influence of the philosopher, Professor John Anderson, then avowedly Marxist, and this may have contributed to Conlon's own idealistic reformist views although he was never a Marxist. After graduation, there was a brief period of employment in the personnel section of the Shell Oil Company,[3] but Conlon had not yet determined his life course, nor had he finished with the business of education.

Conlon returned to university in 1932, joining the Medical Faculty, but after first year medicine, he went to work for a firm of solicitors as an articled clerk and read law, 1933–36. In 1937 he returned to medicine and completed the second and third year of the course before, in 1939, taking on a new role as a notable student politician. In 1938 Conlon was involved in the University Union and played a part in the newly formed National Union of Australian University Students. In 1939 he stood as student representative for the Senate of the university, challenging the sitting student senator. He was seen as candidate for the left, although his low-key campaign only contained commitments to the establishment of a Music Department, support for freedom of speech, and opposition to compulsory lectures. Election to the University Senate was to represent a turning point in his career. It was the forum where he first began to establish connections with members of the establishment. More importantly, the contingencies of the day made his a strategic position for advancement. As student representative, he was appointed to a Senate sub-committee established to investigate the deployment of students on the outbreak of war. As a result of this committee's deliberations the post of university manpower officer was established and Conlon was appointed to the position in 1940. As manpower officer he played an intermediary role between students, army, and civil and university authorities. The job brought him into contact with Major-General Victor Stantke whose appointment as Adjutant-General in mid-1940 included responsibility for army manpower. In late 1940 Stantke appointed Conlon to a committee investigating an army education scheme. As a member of this committee, Conlon enlarged his contacts at the highest levels of army and government, and travelled frequently to Melbourne and Canberra where in 1941 he came in touch with Labor leader and (by late 1941) prime minister John Curtin. The Army Education Service was established in 1941 and in February 1942, Conlon emerged as chairman of the prime minister's Committee of National Morale.

In parallel, Conlon had been working on Stantke to persuade him of the army's need for its own research unit, pointing to the army's lack of advisers competent to assist in the delicate inter-action with civil authorities on such complex issues as mobiliz-ation following the Japanese threat to Australia. Subsequently, Conlon was commissioned a major and appointed director of the Army Research Unit, under the Adjutant-General. In early 1942, therefore, a man who had hitherto looked like nothing so much as a perpetual undergraduate suddenly issued forth in the dual role of Army Director of Research, and chairman of the Committee on National Morale. The latter, despite an impressive member-ship, achieved little of importance, but it did give Conlon regular access to the prime minister. Out of such contact issued sugges-tions that Conlon played an influential role in some of the initi-atives of the new Labor government: for instance, that the manpower scheme effected by the Labor government after the start of the Pacific war emerged from a blueprint he had put up to Curtin.[4] In comparison with the Morale Committee, however, the Directorate of Research presents a more interesting and prob-lematic case.

What the Research Directorate actually did, and the extent of its influence, have always been subjects of dispute[5] — Conlon's preference for anonymity gave the operation a perhaps spurious secrecy. It has been said that the Directorate prepared contingency plans for rural administration and the partial evacuation of northern Australia in the event of a Japanese landing; was involved in supporting medical research and plans for a national university; supported wasteful military campaigns in New Guinea; attempted to influence allied plans for military government; and argued for

an Australian takeover of Borneo.[6] There is evidence of a close
association between Conlon, the Directorate, and the Labor
Minister for External Affairs, Eddie Ward — and in conjunction
the Directorate was closely involved in planning for the post-war
government of the territories of Papua and New Guinea, and
influenced the foundations on which civil goverment there was
resumed.[7] Certainly when it came to the appointment of the post-
war administrator for these territories, Conlon's influence —
against powerful opposition — appeared decisive.[8] The Directorate was also the instrumentality behind the establishment of the
School of Civil Affairs, out of which emerged, in the post-war
period, the School of Pacific Administration.

These achievements are of less interest to us than the way in
which Conlon could use the Directorate to his strategic advantage
for purposes of promoting ideas and participating in policy deter-
minations. Just as the Morale Committee provided avenues of
access to the civil powers, the Directorate was important because
it brought Conlon into regular working contact with General
Thomas Blamey, commander-in-chief of the army. This was not
achieved all at once: Conlon depended first on the patronage
of Adjutant-General Victor Stantke, and when Stantke was
succeeded in this position by Major-General C. E. M. Lloyd (no
enthusiast for Conlon's work) in January 1943, the future of the
research unit looked precarious. Conlon, however, capitalized on
his good relations with Brigadier Eugene Gorman, a Melbourne
barrister and K. C. who was close to Blamey, to preserve his
position, and subsequently succeeded in having the unit transferred to the Directorate of Military Intelligence, and thus out of
Lloyd's control. Then, by playing on his relations with prime
minister Curtin, and calling on the support of Gorman, Conlon
managed to bring the unit directly within the orbit of the
commander-in-chief, with whose support (and given a very broad
charter[9]), it became thereafter virtually unassailable. From a small
foothold, utilizing personal networks, and playing off powerful
connections against each other, Conlon managed to establish
himself as adviser to the most powerful authorities in wartime
Australia.

If on the one hand Conlon sought the attention and patronage
of those in the seats of power, once he was established as a 'fixer'
and a conduit to influence, his organization became attractive to

those who, in the circumstances of the day, had convictions about the way the war effort could lead to reform and sought an avenue to give effect to their ideas. Conlon was able to recruit not only academics of established reputation, but also a series of younger protégés who were to have notable public careers after the war (among these were James McAuley and John Kerr). Within the Directorate, something of the atmosphere of a renaissance court was said to prevail — Conlon, at the centre, was no administrator, but insisted on the importance of ideas, dialogue, inspiration. He seemed intent on finding, preserving and fostering talented minds, bringing them together and directing them towards a concern with the future of Australia. He used his networks to bring people with ideas into contact with those faced with actually dealing with the daunting contingencies of the day. But he was both an intellectual entrepreneur and an enthusiast who, seizing on promising ideas, took them straight to the top.

With the end of the war, the death of John Curtin, and the stepping down of Thomas Blamey, the conditions which facilitated Conlon's influence ended abruptly. He left the army in January 1946 and the Directorate was disbanded shortly thereafter. Conlon returned to his medical studies, interrupted only by a brief (and disastrous) term as principal of the Australian School of Pacific Administration in 1949. He graduated MB, BS in 1951 (more than two decades after he had first entered university), and practised as a general practitioner and later a psychiatrist until his death in 1961.

Alfred Conlon left ripples behind which would later serve the makers of myths and purveyors of conspiracy theories, perhaps because he was such an unusual figure on our political scene. He was interested in power and in reform, but not in the public domain or in personal recognition. He was unusually intent on the pursuit of information and ideas, and indeed, can be regarded primarily as an ideas broker. With this, he had a genius for creating interstitial organizations, a '. . . capacity to see gaps between existing organizations and weaknesses in informal networks, and to propose that some body under his control be used to plug gaps and restore links'.[10] But he was impatient of the constraints of *realpolitik* and the formal channels of bureaucracy, and his personalized mode of operation could only succeed in the vacuum created by wartime conditions, as has been suggested in this chapter. He was frozen out with the 'normalization' of bureaucracy and politics after the war. Conlon can stand as the limiting case of the political irregular in Australian politics — at least until the early 1970s. The alternate path for those of his generation interested in ideas and impelled towards reform, was through seizing the opportunities which opened up with the burgeoning of established institutions in those years. Chief amongst these was Dr H. C. Coombs. If Conlon, who created his own role and invented organizations to serve it, was the doyen of inside manipulators, Coombs showed the potential for intellectual initiative within established institutions. Significantly, Coombs, while paying tribute to Conlon's capacities, was suspicious of his pushiness and felt that he was less effective than he might have been had he followed more conventional practices.[11]

'Nugget' Coombs

Herbert Cole Coombs[12] was born in 1906 at Kalamunda, Western Australia, the eldest of five children. His father was railway stationmaster there — a position of some prestige in such small country towns early this century, but nonetheless a position of little account from broader perspectives of class and power. After early schooling in another small town, Bridgetown, to which the family moved in 1913, Coombs won a scholarship to the Perth Modern School in 1919. On completing schooling, he returned to live with his family, now in Busselton, where he began work as a pupil-teacher in the local state primary school in preparation for entering teachers' college. He describes this career decision as occurring almost by default: his school performance had been moderate and did not encourage thought of higher achievement, his parents were not affluent and could not support his entry to the professions: only teaching offered both easy access and professional training.

In teachers' college he found the conditions (small classes, close contact with staff, stimulating discussion) which encouraged him to become a successful student for the first time, and became aware of the intimations of social and economic crisis already in the air in the late 1920s. After teachers' college, therefore, he enrolled as an external student of the University of Western Australia, as he went out to teach in country schools. Two years later he managed to transfer back to a metropolitan school, to combine teaching with the demanding study for the third and fourth years of an honours degree. Coombs took a BA (Hons), and then an MA degree, from the University of Western Australia in 1930 and 1931. With a distinguished academic record in economics, he won a Hackett Scholarship to the London School of Economics.

By now the depression was starting to bite: a period of conflict between the Commonwealth Bank and the government, and Niemeyer's controversial visit to Australia, had occurred in 1930; the major events Coombs notes in 1931 were the collapse of the State Savings Bank of New South Wales, and the failure of the Commonwealth Bank to support it. Coombs was much exercised by this political dissension and economic distress, and convinced that the interface between economic and financial management offered work of critical importance. He therefore decided to study the role of central banks while at the LSE. During his period of postgraduate work, he took vacation jobs teaching in London County Council Schools, and through this gained some insight into social conditions broadly: 'I had never been outside Australia before, and to see a highly industrialized country like England in the grip of a depression was . . . horrifying.'[13] While at the LSE, he discovered Keynes, whose *General Theory of Employment, Interest and Money* he was later to describe as the seminal intellectual event of our time. Coombs believed Keynesian doctrines provided the means by which banking policy could become a matter of reasoning rather than intuition.[14] He completed his PhD thesis on central banking in the minimum period of two years, and returned to Western Australia to resume his school teaching career, now combined with some part-time lecturing on economics and economic history at technical college and university. However, while in London he had met Leslie Melville, economist for the Commonwealth Bank, and this contact, his own reflection on the problems of the depression, and the interests stemming from his postgraduate research, combined to suggest new possibilities. In 1935 he resigned from the Education Department to become assistant economist with the Commonwealth Bank.

There was probably an element of that extraordinary Australian capitulation before presumed expertise that impelled Coombs' career now, armed as he was with his LSE doctorate on central banking. Once in Sydney with the Commonwealth Bank as assistant to Melville, he rapidly moved into its central policy-making circles, and established contact more informally with a wide group of economically trained and strategically placed academics, bankers and public servants — people equally excited by Keynes, who would, claims Coombs, 'make the conduct of war when it came, and the planning of the transition from war to peace, exercises in the application of Keynesian economic theory'.[15] In late 1939, almost immediately after war had been declared, economic adviser and Commonwealth Statistician Roland Wilson negotiated for Coombs' release from the bank to act as economist to the Treasury, and to collaborate with Wilson. When Labor came to power in 1941 Coombs' ideas were sympathetically received by Labor treasurer, Ben Chifley and he became a close adviser to both Chifley and later prime minister John Curtin. Indeed, having sought Coombs' advice about the practicalities of introducing rationing, Curtin established a Rationing Commission and appointed Coombs its director in 1942.

Confronted with a task of considerable complexity, and with no prior executive experience (his contributions had been essentially analytical and advisory), Coombs set out to plan and recruit the decentralized administrative organization that he felt the situation required. Sceptical of the ability of the bureaucracy to provide resources, Coombs — armed with a prime ministerial directive asking for all possible help — set about drawing on his contacts within banks, the universities, and the professions. Thus was born the first 'brains trust' associated with Coombs. This successful exercise foreshadows later innovative initiatives identified with the Department of Post-War Reconstruction. Throughout this period, Coombs remained a senior adviser to Chifley and in 1941 he was nominated by Chifley to the Board of the Commonwealth Bank.

Coombs, with others, was involved during 1942 in advising Chifley, and, through him, Curtin, on the nature of an agency which was to be concerned with planning for the post-war period. When the projected Department of Post-War Reconstruction had been approved under Chifley's control, Chifley asked Coombs to become its director-general. Under Coombs, the Department of Post-War Reconstruction became a 'brains trust' on a significant scale. Still a young man (thirty-six at the time of his appointment), Coombs was receptive to people with ideas, and built up a team of talented enthusiasts whose age was below that of the traditional departments (Chifley joked of them as 'long-haired men and short-skirted women').[16] Coombs, like Conlon, was an effective intellectual entrepreneur:

Between them, these two pickers of brains had acquired a corner in Australia's young, non-combatant and often rather radical intelligentsia. In combination, their protégés . . . [later would] occupy an extraordinarily large number of the top positions in our universities and the Civil Service.[17]

The Department of Post-War Reconstruction was, for a time, an exciting milieu, moved by notions of equity and reform, centrally involved in landmark white papers on the economy and full employment, hammering out the details of a rehabilitation that would produce a new and better Australia.[18] Its rehabilitation work did contribute to an improved economic situation after the war, and parts of its programme were put into effect between 1945 and 1949. But the highest hopes of the reconstructionists were not to be realized, and the Department was conceived all along as having a limited life span. It was phased out in 1948, and Coombs was appointed governor of the Commonwealth Bank from 1 January 1949. The return to the bank, even as its governor, was in effect a move away from the policy mainstream, but Coombs believed his training in central banking left him with 'something to contribute to that art' and saw the reform of a conservative institution as a challenge.

Though Coombs's appointment was opposed by the private banks, and the Chifley Labor government lost power in December 1949, he was known to Liberal prime minister Robert Menzies (with whom he had worked, 1939–41), and his obvious integrity and belief that a public servant should serve the government of the day served to counter any initial hostility. Indeed, he served a distinguished term as governor of the Commonwealth Bank, and (from 1960) the Reserve Bank, under Menzies. In these positions he was, of course, a regular and influential economic consultant to the prime minister and to successive treasurers. But Menzies, despite a respect for Coombs, was not primarily interested in economics, and the circumstances were not conducive to reform. Coombs became increasingly involved in broader social and cultural activities, for instance, as pro-chancellor of the new Australian National University (in whose inception he, along with Conlon, was closely involved), and as chairman of the Elizabethan Theatre Trust.

In 1967 he resigned from the bank, to become — at the invitation of Menzies' successor, prime minister Harold Holt — chairman of both the Council for the Arts, and the Council for Aboriginal Affairs. In 1968 Coombs was elected chancellor of the Australian National University. In 1971 he came back into the policy process, as personal adviser by invitation to prime minister William McMahon — ironically, the first of the new breed of 'outside' advisers! The relationship was somewhat strained, however, by the manner in which McMahon referred to him in public as a sort of 'personal guru', and in any case McMahon did not last long. After McMahon's government fell in 1972, Coombs agreed to play a similar role for Labor prime minister, Gough Whitlam. Though a sort of senior statesman whose view was respected, it was clear that Coombs was not part of Whitlam's inner circle, and that his advice was ignored when it conflicted with what Whitlam wanted to do.[19] Coombs agreed to head two task forces for the Whitlam government, and in his last major governmental role was appointed in 1974 to head the Royal Commission on Australian Government Administration which conducted the first comprehensive review of the Australian public service in fifty years. His own distinguished career did not prevent him from voicing criticisms of some aspects of the public service in this role.[20] In 1976 Coombs retired from the chancellorship of the Australian National University, but continued research and writing (as a visiting fellow at the ANU's Centre for Resource and Environmental Studies), and his involvement in the Aboriginal movement (since 1979, as chairman of the Aboriginal Treaty Committee).

As has been elaborated earlier, conditions between the late 1940s and the early 1970s were not conducive to such irregulars as Conlon, nor to those who saw opportunities for innovation within bureaucratic institutions, like Coombs in the 1940s. Such figures were not to become features of the political landscape again until the Whitlam government came to power with new demands which created new openings in 1972.

Peter Wilenski

Any one of a number of people who played a part in the advisory process for Labor in the 1960s and early 1970s might be taken as representative of the contemporary potentials of the adviser role, and its links with future career opportunities. Race Mathews, a school teacher who became Whitlam's secretary in opposition, performed essential service as intermediary with academics and others in Whitlam's development of policy initiatives, was elected a Federal MP in 1972, and after defeat in 1975 returned to his home state of Victoria. There he was to become adviser to successive State Labor leaders, then a State MP, and eventually a minister in John Cain's Labor government. Jim Spigelman, lawyer and author, worked for Whitlam in opposition, then in government, and was appointed secretary of the Media Department during the term of the Labor government. John Menadue, Mathews' predecessor as Whitlam's secretary in opposition, was also an effective facilitator of contacts with possible contributors to policy. He contested unsuccessfully the federal seat of Hume for the ALP in 1966 and left Whitlam in late 1967 for a managerial career with Rupert Murdoch's News Ltd, then was appointed by Whitlam to the key position of secretary of the Department of Prime Minister and Cabinet, yet was able to translate his talents to the service of the new government after Whitlam's fall in 1975 and to continue his career in top public service positions. Perhaps the most protean of these figures however, constantly on the move between advisory positions, the public service, and academia, and a continual commentator on public administration and agitator for public service reform, is Dr Peter Wilenski. Review of Wilenski's career also brings us to consider developments involving the federal Labor government elected in 1983.

Peter Stephen Wilenski was born at Lodz in southern Poland on 10 May 1939, four months before the outbreak of the Second World War which would cause his wealthy Jewish family to become refugees.[21] While his father escaped to Britain to join the free Polish forces in the British army, Wilenski's mother, after a period in a Soviet internment camp, fled south with her child, travelling overland to India and eventually, by sea, to Australia. Wilenski's father joined them in Sydney after the war. With experience as an engineer in textiles, Wilenski's father joined the

Feltex company in Sydney. The family established themselves in comfortable circumstances in Sydney in the post-war years.

After completing secondary education at Sydney High School, Peter Wilenski entered Sydney University in 1956 to study medicine, at the urging of his parents. He was sixteen. He was soon disenchanted with the intellectual torpor of Australian university life in the mid-1950s, and began to discover politics. He developed strong general political interests, with a central concern for individual freedoms, but was naive about party politics, and speaks of having joined the Liberal Club, the ALP Club and the rival Labor Club, and then the Liberal Party.[22] He remained active in the Liberal Club and Liberal Party branches until the age of twenty. During that period he was also active in student politics, and claims that this led him to a more sophisticated understanding of politics and society, and eventually to disenchantment with the Liberal Party. In particular a trip to a student conference in Ghana in 1960, and knowledge of African freedom movements and human rights issues, has been said to have had a catalytic effect.[23] Thereafter he became increasingly active in student politics, and was elected president of the Student Representative Council, then of the National Union of Australian University Students, and later a student member of the University Senate. The year after graduation, he became president of the Sydney University Union. He was issue-oriented and visible, challenging, for instance, the White Australia policy, and speaking out against apartheid and relations with South Africa. In 1962 he graduated in medicine, and at about the same time, joined the ALP. However, like Conlon, he had not yet done with the business of education.

After eighteen months residency at Sydney's Royal North Shore hospital, Dr Wilenski decided to abandon medicine in favour of his central interests in politics and society — a move which he believed entailed a return to university. This decision took him first to Oxford University, where he took an MA in politics and economics. In 1967 he returned to Australia and joined the Australian Foreign Service — a decision he saw as a continuation of his interest in international affairs and human rights. Posted to Saigon at the time of Australia's increasing military escalation in Vietnam, which he opposed, his foreign affairs career started inauspiciously. After Saigon he was posted to Ottawa (where, coincidentally, he studied for an MA in international affairs at Carleton), then in 1969 he won a Commonwealth Fund Scholarship and a year's leave to study at Harvard, where he took an MPA degree. Wilenski returned to Australia in 1971, and in 1972 transferred from Foreign Affairs to Treasury to work in Treasury's overseas economic conditions and aid and development sections. After only six months, during which time Wilenski clashed with the Treasury's deputy secretary, John Stone (later to become secretary of the Treasury under Fraser, and to be retained for a time in that position by Hawke), he took leave to become an Honorary Fellow at the Institute for Advanced Studies at the ANU. His object was to write a paper on medical care in China. In fact, during this period he was to do essential preparatory work for the transition to power of the soon-to-be-elected Labor government.

After returning to Australia, Wilenski, through his friendship with an ex-Foreign Affairs officer, Stephen Fitzgerald (who had resigned in protest at the L-CP government's policies on China and Vietnam, and was to be appointed ambassador to China by Whitlam), became acquainted with the floating group of advisers around Whitlam. Wilenski had met Whitlam briefly in 1963 (as President of NUAUS), and again in 1968 when Whitlam had visited Saigon. Now Whitlam's advisers, impressed by Wilenski's commitment, his knowledge of the public service, and his academic credentials, instigated another meeting. One of the advisers, Dick Hall, suggested that Wilenski become principal private secretary after the election. After an encouraging meeting (but one from which Wilenski came away feeling that no firm offer had been made), Whitlam asked Wilenski to prepare some papers along quite specific lines, concerning a reorganization of the public service, a draft administrative arrangements order for the new ministry, and the organization of the prime minister's personal staff. Wilenski agreed to undertake these tasks, but — with an eye to his ongoing public service career — said that he would not provide the materials until the day after Whitlam had won election. He was therefore centrally involved in the blueprint for transition: Whitlam's government was the first to come to power so prepared, and Wilenski's work here may be regarded as analogous to that of Richard Neustadt with his paper for John Kennedy on organizing the transition.

Wilenski assumed the role of Whitlam's principal private secre-
tray after the election (after some initial awkardness as he waited
for someone to tell him clearly and officially that he had been
appointed, while the office apparently expected him simply to
start work). During the early period, when the PM's office served
as the crucial policy dynamo and facilitator, Wilenski was one of
its central figures. He also gained public attention, particularly
when sent to Washington for discussions with then secretary of
state, Henry Kissinger, on Whitlam's behalf. During this
exchange, Whitlam referred to Wilenski as 'My "Kissinger"
. . .'.[24] Wilenski was one of those who had some influence with
Whitlam in a number of areas including child care, women's
programmes, establishment of the Australian Development
Assistance Agency, condemnation of Nixon's Christmas bombing
of Hanoi, and the establishment of the Royal Commission on
Australian Government Administration. But in 1974, in the hurly-
burly of a double dissolution, Wilenski stood for ALP preselection
for the federal seat of Fraser in the ACT. He failed to obtain ALP
endorsement by only one vote, but his campaign meant that he
was unavailable to Whitlam at a crucial stage in the run-up to the
elections. To compound this, Wilenski then fell ill and could play
little part in the government's fight for survival. This introduced
some tension into Whitlam's relationship with his principal
private secretary, and it was decided shortly afterwards that
Wilenski would leave the PM's staff to become special adviser to
the newly established Coombs' Commission on Government
Administration. Then, in 1975, Wilenski became a departmental
head, appointed by Clyde Cameron as secretary of the Department of Labour and Immigration.

Wilenski's was one of the appointments exploited by the opposition and the press as 'jobs for the boys'. After Whitlam's defeat
in 1975, Wilenski was unable to counter the hostility that these
circumstances created, and the L-NCP government contrived to
get rid of him. It is reported that Fraser asked Wilenski to go to
Hanoi and that Wilenski refused.[25] Wilenski then returned to the
ANU as a visiting fellow, and in 1977 was appointed foundation
professor of the Australian Graduate School of Management at the
University of New South Wales. His involvement with government and public service, however, was not finished.

The most significant achievements of Wilenski's career came after 1975, and hence are not strictly germane to our interests, except insofar as they represent career potentials that can be achieved with a period as ministerial adviser (and see chapter 7). It is worth noting that Wilenski's ideals were bound up with public service reform, and that his advance in pursuit of those ideals was predicated on networks that had little to do with patterns traditional to public service, politics or academia. At one level, Wilenski remained a public servant — albeit on leave or on the unattached list — for most of the period 1975–83. In fact he engaged with extraordinary intensity in a diversity of activities as a consultant to educational, welfare, public administration and governmental bodies.[26] Of interest is the way he straddled academic and political fields: on the one hand, foundation professor of the Australian Graduate School of Management at the University of New South Wales 1977–81, then professorial fellow in the Social Justice Project in the Australian National University Research School 1981–83,[27] and on the other simultaneously holding an appointment as commissioner into New South Wales Government Administration 1977–80, acting as an adviser to an ALP task force on government administration, to the team planning the transition to power (see chapter 4), then to Hawke's Ministerial Staff Advisory Panel (see chapter 4), and throughout a polemicist and educator in the causes of public service reform and social welfare.

He was in effect in exile from the public service mainstream. Yet he was engaged in activities that brought him influence and attention, and was able subsequently to persuade the Hawke government to move him back into the upper echelons of the public service — despite strong resistance from the most highly placed public servants, John Stone and Sir Geoffrey Yeend, respectively secretaries of Treasury and of Prime Minister and Cabinet.[28] Thus he became, first, secretary of the Department of Education and Youth Affairs, then in October 1983 attained the position crucial to his ambitions for reform, chairman of the Public Service Board.

What is important for our purposes is that in Wilenski's career we see an instance of the way modern political developments have opened up avenues for achievement which pay no regard to the received wisdom of electoral politics or bureaucracy. Wilenski has always been on the move between institutions. He has never been elected to a mainstream political position. While he has always kept one foot in the public service, every major advance in his career has been opposed by the career bureaucracy — he has not come up through the ranks. Yet by the end of 1983 at the age of forty-four, he came to occupy one of the most influential positions in Canberra, at the nerve centre of the federal bureaucracy. On one hand, his career has been built on intellectual facility and acquired expertise — the long involvement in public service review can be seen on one level as a process of self-education and preparation. On the other hand, while there can be no question of his merit, his career has been advanced by political patronage: he has never been a neutral 'expert' but a politically committed activist whose service clearly advanced the cause of Labor governments. He has reached the top because they have wanted him there, and his achievement has been in apparent defiance of institutional norms. In part his achievement signifies that such norms should be reassessed (which has always been one of Wilenski's arguments): his appointment serves as the clearest indication of a political influence on senior public service appointments that has become increasingly open since the Whitlam years.

There are repeated patterns in these stories: the mobility from the relatively marginal socio-economic status of Conlon's and Coombs's families of origin and the ethnic marginality of Wilenski's refugee parents; the pronounced interest in ideas and intellectual pursuits that precedes political commitment; the restless search for knowledge — particularly with the prolonged student careers of Conlon and Wilenski (and the humanism that perhaps motivates their choice of medicine); the importance of academic 'credentials' and reputation to their ascendance. For all three there is a moratorium at the time when most young adults choose careers: Coombs dallying as a student teacher, Conlon and Wilenski repeatedly sampling the different offerings of the student world and trying themselves out (and establishing contacts) in the arena of student politics. At one level the careers of all three reaffirm the ubiquity of court politics: Conlon wholly reliant on powerful patrons, but also creating his own personalized organization and fostering protégés; Coombs a member of Chifley's 'official family', but also a builder of 'brains trusts' that gave impetus to the careers of his protégés; Wilenski the aide to one of the most princely prime ministers and part of one of the most person-centred PM's staffs of our time.[29] Wilenski's case indicates a specifically modern advance, and one dependent upon the changes wrought in both ministerial staff and public service by the Labor government of the early 1970s. He has been able to sidestep the sort of bureaucratic opposition which ended Conlon's influence by leapfrogging from contested positions within the public service, to political advisory positions, to academia, and back to the public service at the behest of ensuing Labor governments. If Conlon and Coombs indicated alternative paths — political engagement and service to strategically placed patrons versus initiative and innovation within institutions — Wilenski has been able to suggest a third line of advance by capitalizing on both: a tactic that can only succeed with the alternation of governments of different complexions, and with the admission that a level of partisanship inevitably plays a part in the public service.

4

Following the Whitlam Government's Lead

Ministerial staff under Fraser and Hawke

This chapter traces the elaboration of the ministerial staff structures introduced by Whitlam. It will become clear that the distinction between advice to government (the preserve of the public service) and advice to ministers (the bailiwick of minders) has become reified, and that subsequent governments have continued to place high value on the latter. At first, the Fraser government publicly signalled a repudiation of Labor initiatives in developing the private office, but there was soon a resurgence in ministerial staff numbers, testifying to the need of ministers for such resources. More importantly, under Fraser there was a considerable augmentation of the PM's office such as to make it a significant policy resource. Hawke's government inherited the advantages of an institutionalized ministerial staff, and of the sophisticated prime ministerial office structure developed under Fraser. To this it added a mechanism for scrutinizing the appointment of ministerial staff, thus avoiding the accusations that had plagued Whitlam, and made provision for ministers to amplify their private office resources through the appointment of consultants. The theme, then, is of increasing recognition of the importance of politically and philosophically attuned minders, and the progressive subordination of the bureaucratic element, in ministerial offices.

After twenty-three years in government, the coalition parties regarded their relegation to the opposition benches in December 1972, with considerable rancour: it was frequently noted in the period 1972–75 that they acted as if the ALP government was illegitimate, and the coalition parties were 'the government in exile'. Defeat, however, forced a period of reflection and rethinking of direction and policies. At one level, this had its issue in negotiation about the nature of the coalition relationship, manifest in the bickering between the Liberal Party and the

Country Party about their respective dues in forming the shadow ministry (and particularly about whether CP leader Doug Anthony should assume the position of deputy leader of the Opposition, when the deputy leader of the Liberal Party, Phillip Lynch, felt he had a claim). In 1974 the Country Party itself made a bid for more universal appeal by retitling itself, with much publicity, the National Country Party. Then there were the changes of Liberal Party leadership — McMahon succeeded by Billy Snedden after the 1972 election, Snedden challenged by Malcolm Fraser in 1974, then defeated by him in a second challenge in March 1975[1] — as the Liberals sought not only a 'winner' but also a leader who promised a new direction for the party.

At a less public level, deliberations concerning policy and philosophy impelled conservatives to look for ideas and philosophical input in new areas. Deprived of the back-up service of the bureaucracy, upon which they had become reliant over two decades (to their cost, as Snedden suggests), they were forced to develop new resources. A start was provided by the Labor government which as a complement to the upgrading of ministerial staff, provided an enlarged establishment for leaders and office holders of the opposition — by 1974 there was an increase of 58 per cent in staff numbers over those with which Labor had been provided in opposition in 1972.[2] A major policy review during 1973–75 called on all levels of the Liberal Party in an unprecedented way.[3] A policy research unit was established within the national secretariat of the Liberal Party, and after the 1974 double dissolution election in which Labor retained power this research unit merged with the secretariat, and the director of the research unit, Timothy Pascoe, became federal director of the Party. Part of the research unit's role was as a conduit, bringing together shadow ministers, backbenchers, and outside experts for seminars on major policy areas.[4] In short, just as Labor was establishing institutional channels for partisan advice in government, the coalition parties were building networks of advice and advisers in opposition. Indeed, some observers remarked that these networks were more highly developed than had been those of the Labor opposition at a comparable stage prior to 1972, and assumed that if conservatives returned to government they would take advantage of Labor's initiatives to bring their support personnel in with them.[5]

Malcolm Fraser built the skeleton of a staff group which he was to take into government with him. In 1973 he had engaged a public relations firm, John Royce Public Relations, to advise on his image, and the operative they assigned to him, Alistair Drysdale, went on to assist him in policy development relating to his shadow portfolio of industrial relations, and in the challenge that was to topple Billy Snedden.[6] In 1974, Fraser began to call on the services of a Melbourne academic, Dr David Kemp, as a speech writer. Kemp (son of C. D. Kemp, see chapter 3), had clearly defined views on liberal philosophy and leadership, expounded in what was to become an influential article, 'A leader and a philosophy',[7] written after the defeat of the L-CP in 1972, and clearly serviceable to Fraser in his bid for power. Kemp had been brought to Fraser's attention by Liberal MP, Tony Staley, a former academic who had worked with Kemp in the University of Melbourne Politics Department, and had been Fraser's lieutenant in the challenges to Snedden. After Fraser became Liberal Party leader in March 1975, he brought in Dale Budd as his principal private secretary to run his office of leader of the opposition. Budd had worked for him once before, as private secretary, when Fraser had been Minister for Defence in Gorton's administration. Similarly, in 1975, Fraser's office had engaged the then director of the Australian Associated Press's Canberra bureau, David Barnett, as press secretary. Barnett had expressed his sympathy for Fraser's cause to Tony Staley after the first challenge to Snedden, then offered his services — via party director, Tony Eggleton — to the office of the new leader when Snedden was toppled. These four were integrally involved in Fraser's 1975 campaign and were to form the nucleus of his private office when he became prime minister.

Yet despite this, the first moves of the L-NCP government on returning to power in late 1975 appeared to repudiate the initiatives of the Labor government on development of the ministerial staff structure. Fraser was said to have been suspicious of the way ministerial staff had worked under Labor,[8] and to have rejected the extra-bureaucratic advisory system.[9] In any case, he had come to office with a commitment to cutting back government spending, and the ministerial staff system — particularly given its criticism fostered by the conservative parties when in opposition — seemed one of the obvious targets. It has also been argued that the new

L-NCP ministers were 'duchessed' by the public service, which effusively flattered them, rapidly provided staff for their private offices and effectively usurped the electoral and office staff some of them had been planning to bring with them from opposition.[10] Certainly staff numbers in the private offices fell, from around 220 in the final year of the Whitlam government, to 138 in early 1976 under Fraser.[11] Commentators at the time suggested that 'apart from a vestigial Prime Ministers Office, little remained of the new ministerial staff system . . .'[12] It was also noted that staffers of the Fraser government were less 'visible' than their counterparts had been under Whitlam.[13]

Although this curtailment of ministerial staff was noted, not much was made of the changed constitution of private offices under the Fraser government, in which a higher *proportion* of officers were of senior status than those who had served the Whitlam ministry — the cutbacks operated primarily at the lowest grade of the ministerial officer scale.[14] Conceivably, this retention of more senior personnel may have resulted in offices with an undiminished capacity to influence their ministers; though there is the counter-argument that since advisers and research officers were frequently employed at the lowest grade, these may have been offices which were less policy oriented. Whatever was the case, there was in time a significant resurgence in ministerial staff numbers, so that by May 1981 there were again in excess of 220,[15] which amounted to a restoration of the *status quo ante*. It might be said in summary that, in general, the L-NCP governments of 1975–83 had an initially ambivalent attitude towards the sort of ministerial staff arrangements introduced by Labor and that the public service capitalized on this ambivalence to reassert the bureaucratic element. In consequence, there was a rolling-back of the Labor initiative at first. Yet, faced with levels of complexity and demands for action (rather than simply management) foreign to the long period of conservative hegemony before 1972, Fraser's ministers came to realize the value of, and the need for, private staff. So the private offices grew once more. In the main, the system was not developed, but nor was it (as early commentators had feared) again minimized under the L-NCP coalition. In short, like many conservative governments, the L-NCP carried on the initiative of their reformist predecessors. To restrict comments to this general level, however, obscures one area where the Fraser years saw a significant extrapolation from the foundation established by Labor: the evolution of the prime minister's private office.

In fact, not only did Fraser bring into office with him the nucleus of a staff developed in opposition, as had Whitlam, but his staff entitlement as prime minister was not cut from the level enjoyed by Whitlam, and this *despite* pressure from the department of Prime Minister and Cabinet for a reduction. Indeed, Fraser foreshadowed the pattern to be followed by Thatcher (noted in chapter 2) where the rhetoric of suspicion of reformist initiatives, trust in the permanent bureaucracy, and responsibility entailing cut-backs, is belied by the importance attached to his own advisers. As the only minister to retain an extensive staff, Fraser enjoyed an even greater measure of policy dominance over his colleagues than had Whitlam. There were, of course, other means by which Fraser ensured his pre-eminence, but the retention of an extensive staff also had to do with quite clear views developed within the private office of what its purpose should be, and with Fraser's own growing conviction of the value of ministerial staff. By the end of 1977, in the Garran Oration, Fraser was arguing in terms of:

the valuable role being played by ministerial staff in strengthening ministerial control. The ministerial staff provide an important support to the minister in carrying out those functions which cannot be delegated to departments without handing over responsibilities which must be his alone. The ministerial staff have become an important increment to the resources available to the elected government in carrying out the task for which it was elected.

The experience of the present government shows that it is possible for the ministerial staff and departments to work harmoniously together in carrying out their respective functions. Provided it is recognised that the functions of these two groups of staff are distinct, it is possible to avoid the damaging competition which arose in the past. I have no doubt that the system can continue to develop in a way which strengthens the principle of ministerial responsibility in our system of government.

These views, however, were not to give rise to significant changes in his office structure until 1981, after what may be regarded as a period of prolonged fencing with the bureaucracy.

During the latter half of the Whitlam administration, and partly at the prompting of his private office, the department of Prime Minister and Cabinet had developed an enhanced policy and co-ordination capacity. When Fraser was elected, it was PM and C which urged ministerial staff cutbacks and further development of its own policy role.[16] By and large Fraser accepted that advice, except in one particular — the reduction of his own private office was resisted. Nonetheless, the advice was taken to the extent that Fraser's office was initially set up in a fairly conventional manner — albeit with his successful staff from opposition, Budd (principal private secretary), Kemp (senior adviser), Barnett (press secretary), and Drysdale (press officer), at its core — while Fraser worked closely with PM and C on policy and co-ordination.[17] There was no attempt, then, to make the private office a policy dynamo in the manner that had been first attempted by the Whitlam office in 1973.

In 1976, David Kemp left Fraser's staff to resume his academic career; his role as senior adviser was taken up by another Melbourne political scientist, Petro Georgiou. Then, in 1978, Dale Budd left the office to establish a consultancy business. At that point, there was an attempt, influenced by the federal director of the Liberal Party, Tony Eggleton, to make the office more politically attuned and closely in touch with the party organiz-ation.[18] Eggleton's personal assistant from the national secretariat, Darcy Tronson, took Budd's place as principal private secretary. The office may have gained in political sensitivity but at the cost of administrative effectiveness: the move was not a success. And it was strongly resisted from the first by the secretary of PM and C, Sir Geoffrey Yeend. Hence, when Tronson left the staff in late 1979 to return to a job at Liberal Party headquarters, a new phase was ushered in with the appointment of a permanent public servant, Michael Cook, who had been a career diplomat, to the newly titled position of chief executive.

If at this point Fraser had been successfully persuaded of the centrality of the bureaucratic element to the private office, before the year was out he was to be profoundly dissatisfied. Cook provided competent administration of the office, but tried to preserve a public servant's 'neutrality' when it came to the inevitable political decisions and actions the private office had to take. The problem came to a head with the October 1980 election campaign. Cook's resistance to any involvement in the political aspects of the private office's work in effect precluded him from participation in the campaign. So Fraser's office lacked leadership and co-ordination at a crucial time, and Fraser was forced to campaign without an effective personal staff. Fraser retained power, but the difficulty of the campaign, when for the first time since 1975 the L–NCP government looked seriously threatened, and the abundant criticism of the way in which the campaign had been conducted, compounded his conviction that the private office had seriously let him down. Determined not to face future difficulties of this sort, Fraser instigated the moves which were to lead to significant revamping of the private office, developing it beyond the structure that had been inherited from his Labor predecessor.

His first move was to turn back to the personnel who had served him well in 1975 and 1976. Dr David Kemp, now a professor of politics at Monash University, was invited to return to the staff. Kemp had begun to argue for a more far-reaching policy and political role for the private office during his earlier period of service with Fraser, and the invitation to return was tantamount to a recognition of the force of that argument. On Kemp's acceptance of this invitation, Michael Cook resigned to return to the public service, as director-general of the Office of National Assessments. With Kemp's return, the office was both expanded and upgraded.

At the senior level, the office was strengthened by moving away from the ministerial officer gradings initiated by Labor, and bringing in advisers on consultancy fees. Professor Kemp was appointed director of the private office, and was paid $50,000 on a consultancy basis, a level significantly above that which would have been accommodated under any of the previous ministerial officer gradings. The intention behind this controversial move was that by bringing the salary of the director of the PM's office within the public service permanent head range, the importance of the position and the calibre of its occupant would be signalled clearly. Further, the director's position was now to be the apex of the whole ministerial staff structure, the point of direction and co-ordination, and the fulcrum for a stronger and more independent structure. With the emphasis on policy overview and co-ordination now attached to the director's role, the work of office administration passed to another new position, that of senior administrator (somewhat akin to the former position of principal private secretary) and Dale Budd was invited to return to the office temporarily in that capacity and charged with tightening up office functions and helping to find and train his successor. Budd, too, was paid on a consultancy basis, as were some high-level part-time academic advisers: Professor John Rose, an economist from the University of Melbourne, and Professor Cliff Walsh, an economist from the University of Adelaide. (At the same time, the treasurer John Howard, brought another academic economist, Professor John Hewson of the University of New South Wales, on to his staff on a consultancy basis.) The prime minister also called on the advice of foreign affairs specialist Professor Owen Harries of the University of New South Wales, who had initially been brought into government service at the instigation of the then foreign minister Andrew Peacock in 1977, and situated in the department of Foreign Affairs, but had gradually been taken up by the prime minister, and now moved into the department of Prime Minister and Cabinet to work at Fraser's behest.

These initiatives were popularly represented as 'a triumph of academia over bureaucracy',[19] or hailed as the 'return of the eggheads',[20] and (more significantly) one newspaper headed its report 'Private team moves into PM's realm'.[21] By late 1981, the PM's private office under Fraser had become a more powerful policy resource than any enjoyed by his predecessors. Tables 4.1 and 4.2 give a comparison of senior prime ministerial staff under Whitlam (in 1974) and Fraser (in 1981) and underline the structural and qualitative changes.[22]

Table 4.1   Prime Minister's staff, 1974: Mr Whitlam

Designation	*Name*	*Salary* (1981 level)
Ministerial Officer 5	Mr J. Spigelman	$32 250
Ministerial Officer 3	Mr G. Blunden	$24 954–25 821
Clerk Class 11	Ms E. Reid	$29 096
Ministerial Officer 3	Mr M. Delaney	$24 954–25 821
Ministerial Officer 1	Ms C. Summerhayes	$17 718–18 879
Press Secretary	Mr E. Williams	$29 792
Public Relations Officer	Mr D. Solomon	(no 1981 equivalent)
Public Relations Officer	Mr E. Walsh	(no 1981 equivalent)
Media Secretary	Ms P. Warn	(no 1981 equivalent)

(Total staff of PM's private office = 21)

Table 4.2   Prime Minister's staff, 1981: Mr Fraser

Designation	Name	Salary/Consultancy
Director	Professor D. Kemp	$50 000
Senior Administrator	Mr D. Budd	$46 950
Senior Adviser (part-time)	Professor C. Walsh	$ 8 183
Consultant to PM (part-time)	Professor P. J. Rose	$ 9 900
Senior Adviser (MO 4)	Dr D. N. White	$32 228
Senior Private Secretary (MO 4)	Dr D. Rosalky	$32 228
Press Secretary (JA 4)	Mr D. F. S. Barnett	$29 792
Press Officer (JA 1)	Mr O. Lloyd	$23 694–24 581
Ministerial Officer/Cabinet (Clerk Class 9)	Mr R. Bagley	$23 224–24 083

(Total staff of PM's private office = 23)

By late 1981 the PM's private office was a body of senior status and impressive credentials. Within the government, the partisan, political and policy role of the office (and by extension of other ministerial staffs) was now recognized. The bureaucratic element was subordinate, as the value of a politically attuned staff was asserted. It was accepted that any advice entailed certain values and assumptions, that the values of the public service might not necessarily complement those of the government, and that it was therefore essential to have a mechanism for evaluation staffed by those who clearly shared the government's aims and philosophy. Indeed, the PM's office laid considerable stress on its concern with the philosophical consistency of the government's actions — evaluating in these terms both the advice it was receiving, and the initiatives put forward by different ministers. The object was to encourage the government's unity of purpose as well as broader party unity. The intention was not for the office to use its own expertise to generate alternative policy advice, but rather to call on its resources of technical competence combined with political sensitivity, to evaluate the advice that was being put forward. The aim, therefore, was not to compete with the public service, but rather, by commentary and consultation, to stimulate it to work along lines that took cognizance of the government's political purposes. In other words, the private office was not designed primarily as a source of policy initiatives, but to extend the prime minister's directive and controlling capacities with respect to the public service and the generation of policy. Coincidentally, of course, it gave Fraser a considerable capacity to overview the work of his ministerial colleagues.

After the experiences of 1980, it was also felt that the office must play a more direct role in liaising with the party more generally; facilitating contact between cabinet and backbench, and communication with the party secretariat, State branches, and organizations such as the Young Liberals.

Arguably, Fraser's private office might have been expected to take up a role akin to that originally intended for Whitlam's priorities review staff. Unlike that ill-fated body, it could not be shunted aside as a peripheral oddity — located in parliament with the prime minister, the private office was the strategic point where the flow of information from both party and public service institutions came together, and for the first time, it had the personnel and facilities to take advantage of this. Yet events were to prevent the new structure realizing its potential.

The evolution of the PM's private office was a late development in Fraser's term, impelled by 'the smell of defeat'[23] around the 1980 campaign and Fraser's conviction that a more effective office was essential to his resurgence. The L-NCP coalition remained embattled throughout 1981–82: Fraser's office had neither the time, nor sufficiently settled circumstances, to reach top gear. Changes of key personnel played their part. Speech writer Alan Jones left the staff in early 1981, commenting 'it's no career being speech writer to a prime minister'. Special adviser on foreign affairs, Owen Harries, left Fraser's service late in 1981 to take up the plum appointment of ambassador to UNESCO. David Kemp, out of whose discussions with Fraser the new office structure emerged, and a key figure in its implementation, returned to his academic post at the end of 1981 following a family tragedy. He was succeeded by Dr Denis White, a political scientist and colleague of Kemp's from Monash University who had been brought into the office as an adviser by Kemp early in 1981, but who had neither the political nor the intellectual gifts of Kemp. Dale Budd's chosen successor as senior administrator, Keith Witney, an economist from the ANZ Bank, stayed with the office less than a year, and was in turn succeeded by Ron Harvey, a public servant from PM and C who reverted to the title of principal private secretary. After seven years heading the prime minister's press staff, David Barnett resigned to join a consulting business in 1982. A senior staffer was moved to remark in retrospect: 'These things tend to be built around personalities, and if a personality is removed and is not adequately replaced . . . the system changes'. Indeed, by the end of 1982, the urgency of 'restocking' the PM's private office, and the possibility of new procedures as a result of this was a matter of public comment: one report referred to 'the power vacuum behind the throne'.[24] The experiment came to an end early in 1983 when Fraser gambled on calling an early election and lost government.

If the PM's private office was not as effective as had been hoped in realizing the intentions that had impelled its restructuring, it was nonetheless a significant advance on the groundwork established by the Whitlam government. What is more, the potential for policy influence of 'the private team' began to be recognized, and their names began to appear in the press, just as had those of Whitlam's team when these operations were more novel. The controversy surrounding the level of Kemp's reappointment to the office sparked speculation about the 'power' that would attach to his position.[25] As the new office settled down, the names of economic advisers Rose, Walsh, and Hewson (the latter attached not to the PM, but to the treasurer) began to figure frequently in commentary on economic policy.[26] Indeed, when a business magazine commenting on the making of the 1982 budget, referred to the 'troika' of Walsh, Hewson, and Mr Ed Visbord (a deputy secretary in PM and C) as the government's most influential economic think-tank, the secretary of Treasury was provoked to a stinging reply, attacking 'meretricious players of the advisory stage', and warning of 'what happened to [the Whitlam] . . . government' in 1974 when it 'stopped listening' to Treasury.[27] Walsh later spoke of this response as a defence against Treasury's loss of power over a budget the strategy of which it found unpalatable, but asserted in unabashed terms 'that advisory staff will very much have the role of trying to educate the bureaucrats . . . to the direction the government wants to go in'.[28] It is evident that Fraser's advisers did not, finally, cast themselves in the low profile, service role that many commentators had predicted for them in the early months of the L-NCP government. Indeed, seized with the importance of their work, they might be argued to have pushed the limits of the adviser role further than any of their Labor counterparts in 1972–75. The legacy of the Fraser years was a prime ministerial office system that could serve as a significant political and policy resource for subsequent governments.

The Labor Party in opposition, December 1975–March 1983, benefited from the Whitlam government's 1973 initiative in introducing staff entitlements for the shadow ministry. Fraser's L–NCP government cut back the opposition establishment in 1976,[29] as it did ministerial staff, but in line with the subsequent resurgence in ministerial staff, opposition staff entitlements also grew. By late 1982, the Labor Party had an establishment of 47 staff (L–NCP leaders had had 41 staff when in opposition).[30] Probably in excess of 30 per cent of these staff were secretarial and clerical,[31] and most of the rest were lowly paid, their salaries pegged to the lowest level of the ministerial officer scale. Nonetheless, there was a pool of experienced and dedicated staffers who had worked in parliament at the side of the shadow ministry developing policy, and this was a significant augmentation in comparison to the tiny band that had been available to the Labor government elected in 1972. Despite the introduction of a considerably more elaborate and formal procedure for the selection and appointment of ministerial staff when a Labor government was elected in March 1983, most of these staffers succeeded to ministerial staff jobs after the election.

The Labor Party, especially after the resignation of E. G. Whitlam from the parliamentary leadership after the election defeat of 1977, set about drawing the lessons from its reverses. Whitlam was succeeded by Bill Hayden — cautious, pragmatic, conciliatory, and hard-working, but not as it turned out, gifted in communicating his grasp of issues to the electorate in an accessible way, nor in overcoming a basic suspicion of others' motives to establish close working relationships with colleagues. He was, however, the sort of low-key leader necessary for a period of regrouping and consolidation. In 1978, the ALP national executive established a committee of inquiry into its own structure, organization, policies and programmes. The outcome of the committee's activities was a series of discussion papers, disseminated first throughout the party to inform the deliberations of

State and national conferences on matters of reorganization and policy, and then published to encourage broader debate.[32] In 1979, the parliamentary Labor Party turned its attention to the matter of the transition to power of a future Labor government, and a caucus task force produced a report which was endorsed as a model for the transition shortly before the 1980 elections. In 1981, a second such task force was established, and by late 1982 another and more extensive report was produced, which was to provide the guidelines for the actual transition which took place after the elections of March 1983.[33] While Whitlam's preparatory planning for government had been a trail-blazing effort,[34] and the Liberal and National Country parties, in opposition, had followed his lead, no Australian federal government has been more carefully prepared for the transition than the Labor government of 1983. It took office with a detailed plan covering cabinet organization, internal arrangements of the public service and public authorities, relations with caucus — and the establishment of ministerial staff.[35]

One of the factors behind this preparatory work was a desire to avoid the mistakes of the early Whitlam period — the rush to assume power of the Whitlam/Barnard duumvirate,[36] and the lack of oversight in the appointment of ministerial staffs were among these mistakes. This time, Labor's parliamentary leaders were concerned to ensure an appearance of proper deliberateness and due process, and to avoid any suggestion of nepotism or political jobbery in the appointment of staff to ministerial private offices. It happened by coincidence that Bill Hayden was forced to stand down from ALP party leadership in favour of Bob Hawke — long the most highly rated figure in Australian public life according to opinion polls — on the very day that Malcolm Fraser announced the calling of an early federal election. Thus, Hawke, who had played no part in the caucus task force (while Hayden had), was quickly able to benefit from the outcome of its planning, by holding a press conference early in the campaign to discuss a document on Labor's plans for administration which reproduced much of the task force report.[37] The team planning the transition continued its work during the campaign. It was led by Senator Gareth Evans, who acted in effect as Hawke's principal private secretary and chief adviser on these matters for the course of the campaign, although he did not travel with Hawke during the day-to-day politicking.

On the issue of ministerial staff, it was now a matter of arriving at practical procedures which would guard against 'cronyism' and would encourage applications from candidates of calibre in the event of a Labor victory. Advice was sought from a consulting firm, Chandler and Macleod, which had given effective guidance to the recently elected Victorian Labor government on such matters. A memorandum from Chandler and Macleod noting the most common roles and functions of ministerial staff [38] was circulated to shadow ministers to start them thinking on these matters, and some discussions were held. Two weeks before the election, Hawke wrote to shadow ministers 'to draw [their] attention to — and indicate my own thinking on — some matters relating to ministerial staff appointments'. His most important points were that *all* ministerial staff appointments would be subject to his approval as prime minister, and that ministers' autonomy on staffing matters would be circumscribed: 'where a ministerial staff member has brought the government into disrepute or caused it serious embarrassment, the staff member's resignation may be required'. He specified that all such staff would be required to disclose their financial interests to him, and that none would be given access to sensitive or classified material without a security clearance. And he suggested that professional search agencies might be employed by ministers to 'search out persons for key appointments'. [39] While these comments suggested clear parameters to the shadow ministry, there was yet to be found the device by which Hawke's commitment to oversight could be made workable. Consultation between Hawke and the transition planning team (via Evans), and discussions with outsiders sympathetic to the party and experienced in the public service, gave rise to the idea of an advisory panel on the selection of staff which would vet applications, prepare short lists for the ministry, and transmit recommendations to the prime minister. It has been said that Gareth Evans was 'really the father of the thing,' [40] but Hawke readily saw that it was a means to carry out his commitment, and (as shall be seen) a source of concomitant political benefits.

On 6 March 1983, the day after the ALP had been returned to power in the federal elections, the Ministerial Staff Advisory Panel (MSAP) was set up. Its members were: Dr Peter Wilenski, who had been attached as an adviser to the caucus team planning the transition; Mr Bill Butler, a former public servant of extensive experience, a party member, and now a Canberra businessman;

and Mr Terry Moran, a ministerial staffer 1972–75, a former operative with Chandler and Macleod at the time of their consultation with the Victorian Labor government on like matters, and now employed with the Victorian Public Service Board. Wilenski remained with the MSAP only during the initial weeks of its operations, and in that time was much involved in discussions concerning his own future with cabinet members and the Public Service Board: he left the panel on being appointed secretary of the department of Education and Youth Affairs, and was replaced by Concetta Benn, a prominent Melbourne social worker, active in the migrant community and in the ALP. Moran's participation was also partial, his time being divided between his duties with the Victorian Public Service Board and the panel. Thus, while all the members of the panel were concerned in initial deliberations on how it would operate, it was Butler who did the bulk of the ground work following those guidelines, with back-up spot-checking, and discussion, by Wilenski (and later Benn) and Moran.[41]

In the week following the election, advertisements were placed in the major metropolitan newspapers nationwide seeking applications for staff jobs with the new ALP ministry. There were some 2000 applications. The panel set out to assess every applicant:

People were first classified on the basis of assessment of their general ability, intelligence, experience and, given that they were to work closely with Ministers, their likely sympathy with the objectives of the Government's programme. Suitable people were sought out both among those who might provide innovation and policy ideas and among those who would have the administrative capacity to run a Minister's office.[42]

In time, the panel sifted through the applications to produce a list of about 300 who were regarded as possible appointees, and this was circulated to all ministers. Ministers were also invited to make known their specific requirements: many did not respond. Where needs were transmitted, or could be assessed, the panel prepared short lists of likely candidates for particular positions — though each minister was free to choose from the complete list. Ministers were free in turn to nominate anyone they chose, whether on the list or not, but in the latter case details had to be provided to the panel for assessment under its criteria. One extra criterion that was announced in the form of a prime ministerial directive on 7 April (though it was influenced by an MSAP recommendation) was that no person who had recently worked for a coalition minister could be appointed to a senior staff position unless a minister could produce 'compelling reasons' to waive the rule.[43] The MSAP was not involved in interviewing candidates: ministers and their staff were responsible for that once choices had been made. Each nomination made by a minister went back through the panel, which transmitted it with a note of its recommendation concerning suitability and salary level to Hawke for approval. On 27 July 1983, by which time most staff positions had been filled, it was announced that the MSAP operations had concluded, and any future appointments would be made through reference to the Special Minister of State, whose department would arrange security clearance and seek prime ministerial approval.

As a practical selection and appointment procedure there are grounds for arguing that the MSAP was most inefficient: as a political operation it might be regarded as a success. Among ministerial staff, there was widespread criticism of the panel (in conversations with senior staff from twenty-one of the twenty-seven ministerial offices in August 1983, I found only three staffers who spoke positively of the MSAP). Their criticisms fell into four areas. First, it was often said that it was a profligate expenditure of time and energy in terms of the people it actually placed. In fact this is a qualification the panel would concede, suggesting that of the approximately eighty senior staff positions, perhaps only twelve to fifteen were filled through the MSAP — and that from the first the panel was unaware of how many of these positions were 'really' open (that is, in many cases ministers already had nominees in mind, many from their opposition staff). Thus, the operation did not introduce much new blood nor strictly speaking did it open up the process to appointments purely on merit. Nonetheless, every nominee had to go through the MSAP scrutiny, and though for many already in the ALP staff pool this involved no more than the provision of a curriculum vitae and no contact with the panel; arguably, the very provision of this procedure served to discourage the unreflective appointment of cronies that had been a minor (through much commented on) feature of the Whitlam ministry's appointments. Second, it was suggested that the panel was unwieldy and slow: 'If we'd waited for its suggestions, we'd still be missing half our staff'. Clearly logistics account for that: a three person panel, one of whom did the bulk of the work, sifting 2000 applicants for at best eighty (and perhaps considerably fewer) positions is bound to take time. But it has also been suggested that slowness was precisely what was needed: it was the unthinking rush to appoint which allowed errors under the Whitlam ministry; this barrier gave Hawke's ministers time to settle into office, to reflect on their needs and the types of persons who would best fulfil them, and perhaps to weigh political imperatives against past obligations. And where expectations, or a sense of obligation, had been built up, these could be offset without embarrassment by referring individuals to a compulsory selection process. Third, critics pointed to a lack of co-ordination between the ministry and the panel, a gap between the criteria for selection and the information provided (particularly information about political affiliation) in the MSAP schedule, and the ministers' requirements. Against this, the panel could point to failure of ministers to respond to requests for definition of their needs, and the sort of information that would help them, so the panel was forced to make its own judgements. In addition, the public advertisements, in appearing to emphasize qualifications and experience, perhaps gave insufficient encouragement to applicants to address the issue of political affiliation: the panel was left with little to go on in some cases. The fourth criticism, usually related to the third, was that the MSAP schedule according to some views was biased towards formal qualifications and public service experience rather than party experience and knowledge of the party policy-making process. Certainly all three panel members had public service experience, but it would seem odd for that to dominate — Wilenski had also built a career on trenchant criticism of the established bureaucracy, both Wilenski and Moran had been ministerial staffers, and all three had demonstrated Labor sympathies. It seems more likely that this perceived bias was another reflection of the limitations of the information the panel had to go on, shaped as it was by advertisements that appeared to call for demonstration of merit rather than party experience.[44] A fifth qualification, raised not by staffers but by the panel, was that: 'in a few cases, we were totally opposed to appointments, or strongly queried the salary rates suggested — we never won any of those battles'.[45] In such cases, however, ministers were forced to think deeply about appointments, were usually required to make personal representations to the prime minister, and implicitly forewarned that in the event of future embarrassment as a result of this decision the repercussions would rebound entirely on them since the opposition of the prime minister and his panel was on record.

However much these qualifications weigh against the MSAP as a selection process, it was an operation with evident political pay-offs. It defused the sorts of criticism levelled at the Whitlam government's appointment of staff, and even at Fraser's 'eggheads'. It introduced an element of formality and due process into what had previously been, under every government, an entirely idiosyncratic operation, and thus stimulated greater public confidence in the probity of the system and the quality of those appointed. By extension, it represented a further degree of institutionalization in the ministerial staff system, signifying that such personnel are here to stay: the private office advisory system is no longer 'irregular'. Finally, it placed Hawke at the end of the line as arbiter, while protecting him from the adverse consequences of negative decisions. His attention was drawn to nominations likely to prove contentious, and he was forewarned of possible future problems which enabled him to remind ministers that they could be called to account for their choices: yet where hostility or dissatisfaction was aroused this was directed at the MSAP rather than at the prime minister.

Hawke himself had to appoint a new staff, and one not subject to the deliberations of the MSAP. As party leader for such a short time before the 1983 elections, he had no opportunity to build up a team. But as prime minister, with all the pressures of leadership and the concomitant need for support staff, neither could he afford to wait on the services of the MSAP — personal choice had to be the prerogative of the leader. In fact, he drew heavily on operatives who had been advisers to successful State Labor leaders during the election campaign, and these were persuaded to stay on as his key advisers in government. Hawke's staff had to undergo security clearances, and most as a matter of form provided curriculum vitaes to the MSAP — but most were in position and in operation before the MSAP was.

The MSAP was the main innovation introduced by the Hawke government: an operation designed to benefit from the staffing system introduced by the last Labor government, but to counter the problems it experienced. With respect to the structure of private offices, the Hawke government initially followed closely the pattern that had been inherited from the Fraser government. The numbers of staff and conditions obtained under Fraser were closely looked at: the new government wished to avoid any suggestion of extravagance or special perks. Thus the staff establishment after the transition remained relatively constant.

There were, however, some modifications in four areas. First, the appointment of press secretaries to individual ministers had proved contentious under the Whitlam government: it was said they frequently promoted their own minister's interests at the expense of his colleagues and the government as a whole. Fraser's senior ministers had, however, retained press secretaries. John Cain's Labor government in Victoria suggested an alternative by establishing a collective press pool for the Victorian ministry soon after its election. Under the Hawke government it was decided that the prime minister alone should have a personally designated media group, that the leader of the government in the Senate and the treasurer should have press secretaries, and that the rest of the ministry should rely on the services of a pool of press secretaries, the Ministerial Media Group, operating under its own director. In practice, that modification soon broke down: the other parliamentary leaders mounted cases for having their own press secretaries, which were conceded, and by late 1983 many of the media group operatives were working out of individual minister's offices. By Hawke's second term (his government was re-elected at an early poll in December 1984) it was generally conceded that the press pool model had failed, and more traditional patterns of press secretaries working for senior ministers re-emerged.

Second, the Hawke government, acting on the recommendation of the MSAP, moved away from the ministerial officer gradings initiated under the Whitlam government and developed under Fraser, to salaries tied to specific job designations.[46] This was an attempt to reduce categories (thus, for instance, a private secretary would not be classed, for salary purposes, ministerial officer grade 3, but paid the rate now designated for private secretaries). This was not only a matter of clarification, but it gave ministers broader options: for instance, a private secretary could now be paid at a rate equivalent to the top of the MO 3 scale under Fraser, but might also be appointed at a rate lower than the old MO 1 grading.[47] (Actually, ministers ignored this option — most, believing their nominees to be exemplary, recommended appointment at the top of the scale, to the frustration of the MSAP.) At senior levels, the practice was to tie ministerial staff positions to what were regarded as positions of equivalent importance in the public service. Thus, the salary of a senior private secretary to a minister not in cabinet was equivalent to that of an assistant secretary in a department not designated a major policy department (for example, Defence Support), while the salary of a senior private secretary to a minister in cabinet was equivalent to that of an assistant secretary in a major policy department (for example, Treasury). The senior officers in the Prime Minister's Office: Hawke's principal private secretary, principal adviser, and senior adviser, were all paid salaries equivalent (in 1983 terms) to that negotiated by Kemp when he returned as director of Fraser's office. That is to say, they enjoyed a status in the lower reaches of the permanent head range. Salary details have no relevance to this discussion — the exercise is significant because of the way gradings are used to signify the calibre of ministerial staff and to register the importance of their work in ways recognizable to the public service. In such a manner the relative importance of ministerial staff was determined by the new government: there was to be no amelioration of the gains won under Whitlam and Fraser.

Third, while Hawke maintained a prime ministerial staff exactly the size of Fraser's, reproducing the advantage Fraser had enjoyed over his colleagues, he gave pre-eminence to different sorts of skills and organized his office differently. There is some evidence that overall co-ordination of ministerial staff was intended to flow from the senior levels of Hawke's private office,[48] a recognition of the doctrine Kemp had articulated under Fraser. The political and party elements were accentuated in the organization of the office: a public service officer, Graham Evans, with extensive experience in Foreign Affairs and Treasury, took the principal private secretary role, Hawke's principal adviser, Peter Barron, had been a key figure on NSW Premier Neville Wran's team, and his senior adviser, Bob Hogg, had served remarkably successfully for six years in the difficult position of State secretary of the Victorian Labor Party. Hawke also drew in people of academic expertise and used the consultancy system much as Fraser had. But while academics and experts had a role, they were far more subsidiary than such intellectuals as Wilenski under Whitlam or — more importantly — Kemp, Rose and Walsh under Fraser. Hawke was less interested in ideas than Whitlam, and while sharing Fraser's drive to win at all costs, less interested in philosophical justification than Fraser. 'Hawke saw politics as a contest of men rather than a battle of ideas . . . he made too few concessions to the idealism of the ALP . . .'[49] The staffing of his private office reflected this: Barron, a ruthless and intelligent pragmatist tutored by the distinctively hard-nosed NSW machine, assumed the central role that Kemp had been called on to play under Fraser.

With the emphasis on the practical, Hawke's office showed more functional rationalization than had Fraser's. It was divided into three groups: the administrative and secretariat group, the advising group, and the media relations group, with staff roles specifically designated within each group. Hawke's office perhaps appeared an administratively more effective unit than Fraser's. Nonetheless, it remained, like its predecessors, a sprawling political unit where there was little attempt at effective co-ordination — perhaps as a result of the working practices of ministerial staffers (see chapter 6). It is important to note here that Hawke's office was clearly developed on the basis of arrangements introduced by Kemp under Fraser, and arguably represented a more pointed recognition of the argument which motivated Kemp's modification: namely, the importance of the elevation of the partisan and political elements (as opposed to the purely administrative and functional roles) of the private office.

The fourth modification to staffing patterns in ministerial offices by the Hawke government was the legislative provision in 1984,[50] for ministers to appoint consultants on top of their established staff entitlement. Previously it had been possible to appoint consultants for specific tasks within departments, through departmental machinery, but this did not satisfy demands for consultants to work directly for ministers. Fraser had introduced consultants into the office of prime minister and treasurer, but the 1984 legislation gave a statutory basis for the entire ministry to take up this practice. This was, then, another augmentation of the personal advice resources of ministers, as opposed to the formal advice of the bureaucracy. Nonetheless, with an eye to the strategic value of the MSAP exercise, formal approval of the appointment of consultants was vested in the prime minister, and a somewhat cumbersome mechanism was instituted to vet appointments and to restrain hasty decisions. Cabinet decided to establish a merit panel to review requests for appointment. Its members were Alan Rose, a deputy secretary from PM and C, Roger Holditch, a deputy secretary from the department of the Special Minister of State (SMOS), and Clem Lloyd, an ANU research fellow and long-time adviser to Labor governments who was then on foreign minister Bill Hayden's staff. The procedure adopted was for a minister wishing to appoint a consultant to put a proposal to the Public Service Board (PSB) for preliminary advice on appropriate terms and conditions of appointment. On receiving PSB advice, the minister would forward the proposal along with that advice to the merit panel for review. As a result of its review, the merit panel would write a short report for the prime minister. The proposal, along with the PSB advice and the merit panel's report, would then be taken to cabinet for consideration. Once granted cabinet approval, the minister could apply to the PSB for a formal determination of terms and conditions, and then sign a contract with the consultant which would be forwarded to SMOS for implementation. Each minister could appoint up to two consultants. Like other ministerial staff, the tenure of consultants depended entirely upon the fortunes of their minister.

At the time of writing the effects of this initiative were difficult to assess. It appeared that much the same sort of people (see chapter 5) were being drawn into ministerial staffs through this avenue as had entered through the established route, though as consultants they were wearing a specialist hat. There was some tendency for existing staff to attempt to transfer to consultancies in order to obtain more lucrative contracts. The important point here is that the Hawke government extended still further the ramparts of the 'counter bureaucracy' at the minister's side.

In summary, the early period of the Hawke government manifests a consolidation of staffing trends under both Whitlam and Fraser. Hawke's ministers had the benefit of some continuity of the staff that had served them in opposition — a core group of people who were not simply enthusiasts, but experienced in the ways of parliament, and in matters of policy development. Careful transition planning took account of the lessons of the past. The establishment of the MSAP served as a constraint on the autonomy of ministerial choice, a public signal that these personnel were not simply idiosyncratic 'irregulars', and a move towards a new emphasis on objective merit and professionalism. Yet staff members were not to be simply technocrats: the MSAP panellists themselves were characterized not only by their public service experience, but also by their party commitment, and would seek a similar blend in applicants. If the Whitlam staffers had been represented as political enthusiasts, the later Fraser period had seen Kemp's emphasis on blending professionalism with party loyalty, and the Hawke transition showed a serious attempt to institute a formal mechanism for achieving that end. As ministerial staffing becomes more clearly institutionalized, there are signs of it serving as another mechanism[51] to assure prime ministerial pre-eminence: the moves towards co-ordination of the whole system from the prime ministerial office under Fraser and Hawke; the augmentation of the prime minister's personal resources under Fraser, which proceeds unchanged under Hawke; and the establishment of Hawke as final arbiter on ministerial choice, can be read in this way.

Illustrative Biographies

Chapter 4 discussed the extension under Fraser of a staff structure influenced by, and providing access to inner circles of government for, the contemporary intelligentsia. This development reflected the work of David Kemp, himself a representative of what he called 'the knowledge élite'. But Hawke's predilections allowed for the resurgence of more traditional political operatives in the inner circle — exemplified here by Bob Hogg and Peter Barron — which reminds us to be alert for the ubiquitous analogues of Wolsey and House.

David Kemp

David Alistair Kemp[1] was born in October 1941, a week after John Curtin had become ALP prime minister, at a time when Australia's conservative political forces had reached their nadir. His father, Charles Denton Kemp, was to work closely with those whose influence and ideas contributed to the renaissance of the conservatives under Menzies, with the new banner of the Liberal Party. C. D. Kemp was an economist who worked at that time as personal assistant to Sir Howard Gepp, managing director of Australian Paper Manufacturers Ltd. He was instrumental in the formation of the Institute of Public Affairs under Gepp's aegis. In 1944 he left APM to become economic adviser to the IPA, and in 1948 became director of that organization. As a man who worked with and through significant business men and business interests to articulate and publicize a particular policy position, C. D. Kemp might be regarded as a model of the committed activist utilizing channels of influence other than the familiar ones of institutional politics.

The Kemps lived in comfortable circumstances in the solid establishment Melbourne suburb of Kew. David Kemp followed in his father's footsteps, to one of the 'greater public schools', Scotch College, and then to the University of Melbourne. To the observer the process appears one of smooth socialization: Kemp early developed an interest in the politics and preservation of 'a free society', and saw libertarianism as a central value — his father through the IPA had long been a public exponent of just such values. David Kemp was very active in the Liberal Club at the university. He became its president and organized study groups focusing on the politics, policy and philosophy of liberalism. He was also influenced by the Moral Rearmament Movement.[2] Kemp joined the Liberal Party in 1960. As an undergraduate, he studied for the arts/law degree — his arts major was in politics — and showed himself a gifted student. For his honours thesis in politics, he chose to study the Institute for Public Affairs.[3]

Kemp graduated as Bachelor of Arts and Bachelor of Laws but never practised law. Instead he took a position as a tutor, then as acting lecturer, in international relations in the Melbourne University politics department. His next move — and one that involved declining an invitation to be John Gorton's speech writer — was to Yale University to study for his PhD. While at Yale his interest changed from international relations to electoral politics. On his return from America, Kemp rejoined the politics department at Melbourne University. At this time, in the early 1970s, the conservative parties were once more losing their impetus.

Although Kemp renewed his activity in the Liberal Party

branches when he returned to Australia, he never seriously considered running for office in his own right. Nevertheless, he had firm views about the government of Australia, and about the threat to sound government represented by the Labor Party in the 1970s. When Whitlam's ALP ministry won government in December 1972, Kemp set out to point out in what respects the Liberal Party had failed. The resulting article, 'A leader and a philosophy'[4] was not only descriptive but also prescriptive. Kemp pointed to the loss of purpose in the Liberal Party, and, with this, the divisions in its leadership. He proposed that a leader must be found who could draw on the sources of authority in the party to unify it once more — and particular stress was laid on liberal philosophy as one of these sources of authority. The authoritative articulation of liberal philosophy and its distinctions from ALP practice, then, was to be the foundation for the return to power. But in proposing a particular interpretation of liberal philosophy, the article stood in effect as the *speculum principis*[5] for whichever prince might emerge, and Kemp by implication as his potential mentor.

Such ideas played their part in the Liberal Party's reconsideration of policy and philosophy during its years in opposition. But what drew Kemp more decisively to the political centre of the conservative revival was the contingency of friendship. Tony Staley, a student leader in the early 1960s, then lecturer in the Melbourne University political science department, had won the seat of Chisholm for the Liberal Party in 1970. He had become parliamentary secretary to the leader of the opposition, Billy Snedden, in 1973. In the same year he began sharing a house in Canberra with fellow Liberal MPs, Malcolm Fraser and Tony Street. Staley became an enthusiast of Fraser as party leader, and transferred his loyalty from the then leader Snedden. In 1974 and early 1975, he acted as Fraser's lieutenant and organizer in the two party-room challenges which brought about Snedden's defeat.[6] Staley brought his long-time friend and former faculty colleague David Kemp into Fraser's service, initially as a part-time speech writer (Staley and Kemp are credited with drafting the 1975 ANZAAS speech which boosted Fraser's prestige in the party), and then, after Fraser had won the party leadership, as a senior adviser. Kemp continued as senior adviser to Fraser after the latter had become prime minister, though always intending to resume his academic career. This he did towards the end of 1976, when he returned to the University of Melbourne as senior lecturer in politics.

During the initial term of his work for Fraser, Kemp was credited with a considerable input into Fraser's articulation of philosophy and ideas. John Edwards has analyzed the speeches of this period to show how Kemp's contribution transformed Fraser's preoccupations to give him 'the elevated moral tone which distinguishes the leader of stature'. Indeed, Edwards argued at that time 'all the rubrics of the Government's present philosophy stem from Kemp'.[7] Kemp himself felt that Fraser was the best approximation of the sort of leader he had pointed towards in the 1973 article, 'A leader and a philosophy'. He undertook to work for him because he saw it as a way of realizing his own ideas concerning good government: Fraser was the person best able to express the values Kemp deemed essential. The administrative trivia and the day-to-day grind of the Prime Minister's Office as it was then organized, however, served as an impediment to the clear-sighted pursuit of philosophical consistency in political practice. Kemp's return to academia represented his belief in a more specialized division of labour, and the pursuit of his interests on another front. Significantly, however, Kemp, who remained a member of the Liberal Party's policy platform committee, was publicly identified as the man who provided the blueprint for the Liberal Party's successful election strategy in 1977.[8]

In 1978 Kemp published *Society and Electoral Behaviour in Australia*.[9] The central theses of this work were foreshadowed in a 1977 article[10] and were presumed to have been influential in determining Liberal Party strategy in the elections of that year.[11] Kemp's argument was that the correlation between class and voting patterns had declined to the point of no longer being significant:

the traditionally important cleavages of Western industrial societies — class, religion, region, and the urban-rural cleavage — are of decreasing significance politically because of structural trends in the societies which are altering the bases on which perceptions of political interest are formed.[12]

The appeal to class interests by political parties was redundant: people instead chose on the basis of their assessment of a party's principles in terms of their own values and beliefs. While allowing that Liberal voters incline towards a stable structure of authority in society, and Labor voters incline towards concern for the under-privileged, Kemp argued that this only happens *within* the terms of a broad value consensus. Key features of this value consensus were said to be an individualist ethos — Australians are socially egalitarian, but believe everyone has the right to get ahead by hard work and are not sympathetic to intervention which might limit the potential to achieve success in this way — and an acceptance of strong leaders: 'Australians generally believe that it is the outstanding individual who is a significant source of social progress . . . a huge majority accept that ultimately a few strong and able people are necessary to run *everything*'.[13] Kemp argued that trade union affiliation to the ALP locked Australian parties into an outmoded party contest, perpetuating the illusion of class-based interests relating to particular parties, depriving unions of influence over the L-NCP, and consequently driving corporate interests closer to the coalition since 'they are certainly not among friends in the alternative government'.[14] The dissolution of these links would reveal both major parties to be keen to seek union as well as business support and mitigate the unhealthy polarization of our politics. Essentially, each grouping should reach towards the middle ground, and their support would be fluidly related to broad attitudes within the community.[15] A subsidiary part of the argument was that both major parties had yet to accommodate to a shift in power towards the new element of tertiary educated professionals who, having no affection for the special interests of business, bureaucracy or unions, tend to support alternative parties.

In practical terms, Kemp's arguments supported the primacy of the articulation of principles and strong leadership — themes which he had been pushing since the early 1970s. They gained considerable coverage[16] and generated some controversy.[17] Certainly they suggested that the ALP in particular, with its structural linkage to the unions, was outmoded. In terms of coalition campaign strategy, it has been suggested that in 1977 voters' anxiety about the chances of getting ahead in an uncertain economic climate were triggered by references to the chaos allegedly engendered by the Whitlam Labor government, while the coalition offered firm leadership and confidence about stable authority in the future.[18]

In 1979, David Kemp left the University of Melbourne to take up a chair in the politics department at Monash University.

In 1980, the Liberal Party appeared to have difficulty in projecting conviction even on the grounds Kemp had defined. After the shock of the campaign, Malcolm Fraser prevailed upon him to join his inner circle once more. Professor Kemp came back with a message — the government must *do less*,[19] and a condition — the private office must be restructured to ensure that those at the top, who should be occupied with political considerations and philosophical consistency, were not diverted by administrative trivia. The first amounted to a reassertion of the importance of affirming principles and recognizing that the Australian ethos supported individual initiative and small government. The second led to the major reorganization of the prime ministerial office on terms agreed upon between Kemp and Fraser. In effect this initiative augmented the importance of personal advisers on the political stage. Unfortunately its full potential was not to be achieved by its chief architect: after the death of his wife and two of his three children in a Canberra road accident in late 1981, Kemp left political service to return to Monash University.

He remains, however, an engaged commentator on the political scene,[20] and one who might be expected to move to positions of direct influence in the future.

Robert Hogg and Peter Barron

Kemp, like Wilenski, signifies the pre-eminence of intellectual and administrative concerns in the new class with which this book is concerned. These two also indicate the importance Whitlam and Fraser conceded to such concerns. As prime minister, Bob Hawke has not wholly followed the lead of Whitlam and Fraser, despite the high placing of analogous figures in his own inner circle: his economic adviser, an ANU academic Ross Garnaut, and his principal private secretary, a former lecturer, and experienced Foreign Affairs and Treasury officer Graham Evans, spring to mind. But Hawke has placed greater emphasis on party politics than his predecessors, and has elevated party machine-men Peter Barron (NSW) and Bob Hogg (Victoria) to the highest levels in the private office. Of these two, Bob Hogg has long pursued a career in the public eye,[21] but has been less influential with Hawke than the backroom operator, Peter Barron.

Robert Hogg was born in Melbourne in August 1937. From a working-class background, he was educated at State schools and at the Caulfield Institute of Technology (where he studied for, but did not complete, a diploma of mechanical engineering). He worked at various levels as a project engineer in the food industry, then as a layout and paste-up artist and a draughtsman in the printing industry. His longest and most sustained interest was in the politics of the labour movement. In the mid-1960s, like many trying to establish his credentials in the party, he contested an unwinnable seat for the ALP. Then in 1967 he was appointed a State organizer for the Victorian ALP. The Victorian branch of the ALP was then defiantly left-wing, and Hogg was regarded as a promising young radical within it. When the Federal Executive of the ALP intervened in the affairs of the Victorian Branch in 1970 to overturn what was regarded as the electorally detrimental dominance of the left,[22] the Victorian State Executive was dismissed, and so Hogg lost his job.

Hogg then became a founder member of, and a full-time (though unpaid) organizer for, the socialist-left faction of the ALP. Later, he again held positions as a layout and paste-up artist, then as electorate assistant to a Labor MP. In 1976 his unremitting activism within the party paid off: he was elected State secretary of the Victorian ALP. This, however, was a difficult position: the internal politics of the Victorian ALP had been divisive and bitter for two decades, and Hogg was elected unopposed only because the warring factions could agree on no other candidate. Yet Hogg, himself abrupt and aggressive, proved adept at political brinkmanship — 'It never worried me that I might be removed, I was not going to be intimidated by that possibility and it never inhibited me'[23] — and he secured his position by convincing the contending factions of the necessity for co-existence. In the context of the Victorian ALP this was a considerable achievement and Hogg gained great respect for his firmness and his organizational abilities.

As an electoral strategist, Hogg gained kudos from the 1980 federal election results, when Victoria's ALP vote reached its highest level since the Second World War. This then became the springboard for the Victorian State elections of 1982. In the run-up to these elections, the then ALP leader, Frank Wilkes, was toppled by John Cain. Hogg, as State secretary, is credited with a major role in engineering Cain's elevation. Subsequently, after a campaign largely directed by Hogg, the ALP won the State elections and assumed government in Victoria for the first time since 1955. Although retaining the position of State secretary, Hogg then became in effect premier John Cain's closest adviser.

Impressed by Hogg's success, Federal ALP leader Bill Hayden tried to woo him with the 1983 elections in mind. Hogg had come to Hayden's assistance previously, working closely with him at the 1979 ALP conference to draft changes in the party's economic platform which countered the intentions of the aspiring leader Bob Hawke, then chairman of the Economics Committee. But Hogg, pursuing the theme of co-existence, had also sought to heal the rift between Hayden and Hawke, without success. After Hayden's failure to consolidate his leadership following Hawke's first unsuccessful bid for leadership in July 1982, Hogg became disenchanted, although he promised to work for the federal election campaign team in 1983. When Fraser called an early election, and Hawke coincidentally took the leadership from Hayden on 10 February 1983, Hogg readily transferred his allegiance to the new leader, and entered the campaign with gusto.

Hogg had by now moved some distance from his radical origins. Hawke, who as ACTU and ALP president had emphasized pragmatism and consensus, had long been out of favour with the left, and the Victorian socialist-left in particular. Hogg himself had become more strategist and tactician than ideologue during his six years as Victorian State secretary, and began to see the left's opposition to Hawke as perverse and unwise. When, in a spirit of *realpolitik*, Hogg drew up and moved an amendment to the ALP uranium policy at the 1982 federal conference which allowed existing mining contracts to continue, he was barred from the socialist-left (for whom the cessation of uranium mining was an article of faith). In effect, Hogg was ever moving closer to Hawke. Hogg confirmed his reputation as an electoral strategist as one of the core group travelling with Hawke and advising him on tactics throughout the 1983 campaign.

After the poll victory of 5 March 1983, Hawke felt a strong incentive to take his successful campaign team into office with him. Having been leader only for the duration of the campaign, he had no long established staff group to call on. Within days, it was rumoured that Hogg, now described as 'a key architect of the Labor Party's new dominance of federal and State political spheres',[24] would be offered a top job in the prime minister's private office. Behind the scenes, Hogg was negotiating with Victorian premier John Cain who was reluctant to lose his services. Shortly thereafter Hogg's appointment as Hawke's senior adviser was announced, and he relinquished his position as State secretary of the Victorian Party.

Hogg's appointment represented the realization of the importance of the party political element in the PM's private office. His strengths were not those of the intellectual, the ideologue, or the technical policy consultant. He was instead a person with deep knowledge of the party at all its levels, with extensive contacts and with evident capacity in assessing the electorate. He was attuned to assessing the ramifications of decisions in the party and the electorate, and thus advising on policy implementation. He was responsible for negotiations within and co-ordination of the parliamentary ALP, the party organization, its State levels, and the unions. He agreed that he could accurately be described as a 'trouble-shooter'. In a sense, however, it is clear that Hogg had a political standing and a career independent of Hawke — he was involved in his own right in factional groupings around the 1984 conference, for instance, albeit pursuing ends which he thought to be in Hawke's (and the party's) interests. As the party *apparatchik*, Hogg was less clearly placed to play the minder's role than Peter Barron who saw himself not as an activist, but as a professional, and in time Barron emerged as the most influential figure in Hawke's office, and one of the most influential advisers of recent times.[25]

Peter Barron was born in 1946 in the working-class Sydney suburb of Bass, where his father was a carpenter. His was a Catholic family. He had no tertiary education, leaving school in 1963 at seventeen to become a journalist with the *Sydney Sun*, an afternoon tabloid with a racy style and a sensational approach to politics. After some years of hack work, he moved to the *Sun's* Canberra bureau, and then to Murdoch's *Daily Mirror*. He was a federal political reporter until mid-1975, when he resigned to work for the Whitlam government's media department — a badly timed decision given the demise of the Whitlam government in November 1975.

However, during his period as a political journalist Barron had come to know John Ducker, then controller of the NSW Labor machine, and in early 1976 he was offered a job with the party's advertising agency — allegedly as a result of head office patronage. Although paid by head office his job in fact was to be the agency operative for NSW ALP parliamentary leader Neville Wran. He had not met Wran until offered the job. It was another precarious move, since the job was guaranteed only until the election held in May that year. In the event, however, Barron became part of the campaign that brought Wran to power in 1976.

Barron was then placed in charge of the State government's ministerial press pool. That initiative was eventually abandoned, and Barron went on to Wran's personal staff in an indeterminate role. Nonetheless, he maintained close relations with John Ducker, and with the then State secretary Graham Richardson, who became a close friend. Never far from Wran, in effect Barron became the conduit between the premier and head office. In 1981, when Wran's long-time press secretary, Brian Dale, left his staff, Barron replaced him and became Wran's senior staff adviser. He was, thenceforth, an ever present shadow at Wran's side.[26]

Bob Hawke had a long acquaintanceship with Graham Richardson, and in February 1983, when as newly elected party leader he needed staff support to fight an immediate election, he was advised by Richardson to take Barron on to his team.[27] Hawke approached Wran, asking to 'borrow' Barron for the duration of the campaign.[28] Barron rapidly established his credentials as a media handler — persuading Hawke to modify an aggressive style which was proving counter-productive, and as a strategist — convincing Hawke, for instance, to change the nature of tax cuts promised in the campaign in order to appeal to middle class voters.[29] Hawke was pleased with Barron's work and persuaded him to stay on his personal staff after he became prime minister.

In power, Hawke adopted the Wran office model, as advised by Barron, in which all press problems, advice, strategy and tactics were channelled through Barron between Hawke and his press officers.[30] This of course made Barron the fulcrum, and facilitated his ascendance.

His influence was accentuated by three other factors. First, by the time he joined Hawke, he had spent thirteen years as a journalist, seven of them as a political journalist, and then seven years working for Wran. He may not have been a party activist (in fact he did not join the Labor Party until he was thirty, and already working for it), and he appears not to have been an idealist (some descriptions stress his cynicism about politics[31]), but he knew about the uses of the media, and he was intimately acquainted with the dynamics of power and of winning through his apprenticeship with Wran's machine. This experience, allied with his intelligence and ability, made him a consummate professional in the role of minder. This was a role particularly important to Hawke, given the unique path by which he had reached the prime-ministership and his relative lack of experience in parliament and associated institutions. It was a role that Hogg may have been more ambivalent about playing.

Second,. Barron's emphasis on pragmatism rather than on ideological commitment accorded with Hawke's own predilections. Not only this, but Barron signalled that his primary loyalty was to Hawke: '. . . I work for Hawke. He's the boss . . . and my job is to satisfy him by the quality of what I do. Not anybody else'.[32] Hogg, though increasingly pragmatic, still tended to talk in terms of the broad interests of the party (which might, by implication, not always be identical with Hawke's own). This may have been more realistic, but must have given Barron the edge in the court politics of the private office. Not surprisingly, relations between Barron and Hogg were reported to be cool.[33]

Third, Barron's position was reinforced by his close ties with the dominant figures in NSW Labor, since these became a significant force in the Hawke government. Graham Richardson, friend and mentor to Barron, was elected to the Senate in 1983, and although holding no ministerial post was rapidly recognized as Hawke's confidante and power broker.[34] Hawke came to rely on the NSW right in the perennial factional struggles within the party, and Barron was of that group and kept Wran's ear. Paul Keating, another acolyte of the NSW machine and associate of Barron, used the Treasury portfolio to good effect to become perhaps the most influential voice in the Hawke ministry. These figures were said to be integral to the style of the Hawke government:

The great authority Hawke has as the nation's most popular political leader gives him a degree of personal power that is unique in Labor Party politics. Hawke has used this authority to build an informal power structure on top of the formal mechanisms.

It is at this level that the New South Wales influence has worked and the style and character of the Hawke government has largely been determined . . .

The four key figures are Hawke, treasurer Paul Keating, Hawke's key political adviser Peter Barron and New South Wales Senator Graham Richardson, referred to by some as 'the Gang of Four'.[35]

Barron has thus arrived in the inner circle of government. His story is not one of idealism or of activism but of hard-nosed professionalism and of capitalization on networks. Where Wilenski talked of reform, Kemp of preserving and maintaining the hard-won attributes of a good society, and Hogg of pursuing the party's interests, Barron simply talked of winning: 'Satisfaction? I like winning. I'm very keen on that. I try hard not to be seduced just by being around the centre of power, although you probably wouldn't be truthful with yourself if you didn't concede that's an element of it.'[36] But of course this is a story of power and of being close to power — and Barron may most closely approximate Colonel House, who made a career as a personal loyalist because he enjoyed 'playing with politicians'.

In some respects, Kemp and Wilenski present telling similarities. Both are high achievers whose advance depends on their being part of (what Kemp identified as) the 'knowledge élite'. Both have pushed consistent messages throughout their careers and their advance also has depended on their being able to persuade politicians of the appropriateness of these messages. That is, they have not, primarily, been party-political workers achieving recognition through sterling contributions within their respective machines, nor have they tempered their ideas to changing winds. But they have been able to move into and out of the political realm — because of maintenance of academic bases elsewhere — to suit their purposes. They are not politically ambitious in what might formerly have been regarded as the conventional sense. Rather, they are ambitious to see the realization of their ideas through politics. In important respects, their loyalty is first to their own

110 *The Ministers' Minders*

beliefs and values, and to their respective parties (seen as vehicles for implementing those beliefs and values) second. The growing awareness of these members of the intelligentsia of the necessity for admitting the 'party-political' back to the heart of the policy process, however, has been paralleled by the resurgence of machine-men like Peter Barron and Bob Hogg at the side of the elected politicians. Not surprisingly, the machine-men have regarded the intelligentsia as politically inept. It is also true that such political operatives have always been able to exert an influence, as shown by the long history of 'kitchen cabinets'. Still, it should be recognized that the institutional transformation of ministerial staff has been engendered by such as Wilenski and Kemp, allowing more traditional operatives like Barron and Hogg a new access to the political and policy heartland.

5

Who are the Minders?

To this stage there have been three underlying constituent themes. First, that modern societies, with their complex demands on leadership, create the conditions for the emergence of particular sorts of institutions to serve leaders. For if even the kings in simpler monarchical structures were unable to cope without counsel, how much less ability will the political leaders of modern states have to balance the imperatives of their primary concern — 'combat politics'[1] — against the minutia of organization and administration, the uninterrupted time to grapple with complex and specialist information, or the abstraction necessary to think things through?

In time institutionalized 'civil' services are formed to service these needs. It is unlikely however, that these bureaucracies will entirely supplant the cronies on which many leaders rely — presidents and prime ministers have a long history of forming 'kitchen cabinets'. And at a certain point in the evolution of modern societies it seems, inevitably, that political leaders begin to doubt the tractability of their bureaucracies: this is the second theme. This arises because *none* of the participants in the policy process can be 'value neutral', since policy deliberations are full of imponderables which can only be given definition when facts are interpreted in the light of assumptions, and these assumptions will incorporate values. If politicians believe bureaucrats share, or can simply take on board, their values this will not be a problem and in such circumstances the myth of the bureaucracy being value neutral will be preserved. This will only occur when organizations (legislative and bureaucratic) are relatively small and decisions are relatively simple. When the bureaucratic element becomes large and complex itself, demanding abstract relationships and a sophisticated organizational structure, the sociology of organization has taught us that it is likely to develop its own politics and its own values which may not be in concert with those of the political leaders.[2]

At this stage the political leadership will perceive a tendency on the part of bureaucracy to impede its policies, if not by design then by inertia. There will be a call on the one hand for reform of the bureaucracy to make it more responsive to the political will of elected representatives (*vide*: the work of Wilenski *et al*. in the Australian instance). On the other hand, there will be much greater resort to 'irregulars', and eventually the institutionalization of systems of partisan advice around political leaders: this has been the third theme.

In Australia, the work of both mainstream politicians and of the bureaucracy has been studied,[3] but the emergence of advisers, or minders, in the policy process has not been considered. Now that the evolution of ministerial staff structures has been discussed, the following questions should be asked: who are the people who are drawn into, and who devote part of their careers to, these new structures? What characteristics, what skills, and more importantly, what values, do they bring to the policy process?

Some of these questions have been considered in the bio-graphical sketches at the end of previous chapters. Looking back, a cluster of elements emerges. First, these people are formed by and capitalize on changing social conditions (note particularly the careers of Wolsey and Conlon). Their success depends on intellectual and administrative skills in every case, usually fostered by particular forms of institutional training specific to their social context (Wolsey, for instance, turned the church's monopoly of the capacities of literacy and administration to political advantage; Barron translated his journalistic experience and acculturation to machine politics into skills as a leader's handler and organizer). Reasons for not entering mainstream politics may be important (House reasoned that he could not attain first place, and nothing less than that would satisfy him): certainly there is a preference for remaining in the background. Career success, indeed the career itself, depends on patronage rather than occupancy of a particular role. (House demonstrates that recognized links and intimacy with the political leader confer more authority than a particular role, and even avoids precise role definition since that would narrow his sphere of activity.) In modern times, patronage has been attracted by those with specialist knowledge, or those who can act as ideas brokers. Advanced education, intellectual networks, and a marked interest in self-education have become characteristic (and note the prolonged undergraduate careers of people such as Conlon and Wilenski). The man of ideas has been able to be independent of particular leaders and hence of patronage based on particular interpersonal relationships (Bundy and Wilenski). Capacities for intellectual entrepreneurship in forming 'brains trusts' have become important (Conlon and Coombs), and these seem based on native curiosity (Conlon in particular). Along with curiosity and a drive for knowledge is sometimes seen a peculiar naïvete (Conlon's apparent innocence regarding the way bureaucrats would reciprocate for his incursions; Wilenski's joining of political parties of every complexion while an under-graduate). With the commitment to ideas goes a sense that in some circumstances certain ideas might transcend the parties and persons chosen to implement them (see Kemp's attitude to Fraser as the best exponent of libertarian ideas; Wilenski's commitment to the ALP as the party best able to achieve reforms). Yet these people are not intellectuals or critics working at a remove: they are engaged polemicists concerned to assist in the imposition of a political will on the nation's development. Everything points to them being meritocrats ambitious to realize a particular vision of society but reluctant to enter the fray of 'combat politics' (or perhaps impatient of its constraints). So far, however, these are impressions garnered from only a few cases. How do they stand up to more sustained analysis of the staffs of the private offices of political leaders?

Studies in the mid-1970s of the staff groups of American presi-dents identified consistent patterns.[4] It was found that the White House Office was an overwhelmingly white male world, peopled by city-bred staffers who were middle-aged or younger (the median age was forty-two, but one in three were appointed in their thirties). These men were considerably more highly educated than the population at large and predominantly trained in ivy league or private universities, suggesting that they were the chil-dren of middle-class families. The northeast and south of the country were overrepresented in terms of places of education, and the east coast was the major location for jobs immediately prior to appointment to the White House staff. More than half had previously pursued a career in the private sector, but the single largest category — nearly one-third — had been in non-elective government positions. Typically, White House staffers had chosen the occupations of government administration, law, business or academic life. They were distinguished from mainstream politicians by having come to White House service through other than the usual political channels, and were distinguishable from business leaders, labour leaders and civil servants in age and education. Looking at the evolution of the staff groups between F. D. Roosevelt and Nixon it emerged that all of these characteristics were becoming increasingly concentrated, particularly youthfulness and high education. One observer described them as

not just ordinary or regularly mobile individuals but people who have been catapulted to a position at the peak of a political pyramid. These are men 'on the make', who have positioned themselves strategically, to ensure that they will be at the right place at the right time.[5]

There appear to have been no further comprehensive studies of White House staffers since the mid-1970s, but there has been increasing journalistic attention to White House and congressional staff and a scan of this literature[6] suggests nothing to modify these patterns.

In Britain, there has been no sustained analysis of the characteristics of recruits to such policy advisory bodies as the CPRS, or of the staff who have moved into ministerial private offices since Wilson's innovations opened up the terrain (see chapter 2). Nonetheless, in reading through more general commentaries on special advisers one notes references to the specialized pool — with a narrow Oxbridge base — from which they are drawn, the predominance of middle-aged or younger people, and the emphasis on academic expertise combined with party sympathy, with the proviso that Labour special advisers are mainly former academics while Conservative ones are drawn from party headquarters[7] (but note Margaret Thatcher's reliance on academic monetarist economists, chapter 2).

In the Canadian case, where the well staffed Prime Minister's Office[8] consists primarily of political appointees, personal advisers came to particular prominence during the long tenure of office of Pierre Trudeau — his immediate circle was called 'the Supergroup'.[9] 'The Supergroup' contained career public servants and elected politicians as well as personal appointees (and indeed some of the career officials were regarded as personal appointees). Often its members came from privileged backgrounds, they were usually sophisticated political operatives, or ambitious and highly qualified professionals and academics with policy ambitions. 'They . . . were technocrats . . . They were smart, successful, self-confident, as few Canadians are.'[10]

In all three countries,[11] then, despite different political practices, there is a congruent pattern attaching to political advisers: the pattern of relative youth, middle-class origins, high education, specialist credentials, and the leap from academic or governmental — but rarely political — backgrounds into the inner circle of leadership. It is, of course, a pattern illustrated by the biographical sketches. Against this data can be placed studies of Australian ministerial staff from the mid-1970s, which are supplemented by an analysis of the Hawke ALP ministry's staff in 1983.

Surveys of ministerial staff under Whitlam and Fraser by Roy Forward in 1975 and 1977 have described the population of private offices in terms of indices of gender, age, geographical origins, education, careers, and 'public service' or 'political' typologies.[12] This groundwork was taken as a basis for comparison in analyzing the ministerial staff of the Hawke government in 1983. In August 1983, I interviewed representative senior staffers from as many as possible of the private offices of ALP ministers: 23 people (most at senior private secretary level) from 21 of the 27 ministerial offices were interviewed. In September 1983, a postal questionnaire was sent to *all* staffers in the categories of assistant private secretary and above: the response rate was 56.5 per cent.[13]

The Hawke government's concern to avoid controversy over the issue of ministerial staffing is reflected in its care to maintain a rough parity with the staffing establishment inherited from the L-NCP government. Under the ALP government in 1983, 224 staff positions were provided for, while under the L-NCP coalition in 1981, there had been 217.[14] Fraser and Hawke maintained offices of almost exactly the same size (27 and 28 staff respectively), and the normal establishment allowed to ministers under each administration was seven.

Gender

In total, women outnumber men in ministers' offices. In 1983, 59 per cent of staff were women,[15] while in 1981 the proportion was as high as 66 per cent.[16] Yet the ratio between the sexes rapidly reverses as one ascends the hierarchy within these offices. Forward found that senior staff under both Whitlam and Fraser remained in the proportions 84–5 per cent male to 15–16 per cent female. Means of classifying staff positions have changed several times since the publication of Forward's article in 1977, but analysis of comparable categories in 1983 reveals a slight change in the ratio, with 80 per cent of senior staff male, and 20 per cent female.[17] If one looks at only the highest position in the normal ministerial office (senior private secretary) and adds those in higher gradings reserved to the offices of prime minister, treasurer, and deputy prime minister, in 1983 there were only three women among the thirty-five holding such jobs (i.e., 8.6 per cent). In 1981, there had been no women at all in such categories.

Age

The age spread of those staff members relevant to this discussion[18] which had been found to remain relatively constant under the Whitlam and Fraser governments, manifests a change in the Hawke government staff sample. Under the earlier governments 30 per cent of staffers were in their twenties, 54 per cent in their thirties, 10–12 per cent were in their forties, and 4–5 per cent were in their fifties. Under the Hawke government, the proportion of those in their twenties has dropped (to 15 per cent), while there has been an even more conspicuous bunching in the thirties bracket (which now constitutes 65 per cent), a rise in the group in their forties (to 15 per cent): only the fifties group remains constant (at 4 per cent). In terms of the Australian population of employable age, those in their twenties are slightly underrepresented in the group, those in their thirties are massively overrepresented, those in their forties are overrepresented, those in their fifties are underrepresented, and those in their late teens and early sixties are unrepresented. Mainstream politicians (members and senators of the federal parliament) also deviate from general population figures in terms of age groupings but in their case the most conspicuous bunching and overrepresentation occurs with those in their forties (41.27 per cent of the group, compared with 10.51 per cent of the general population), and fifties (32.81 per cent of the group, compared with 10.14 per cent of the general population).[19]

Birthplace

The earlier studies pointed to the care with which geographical representation is considered in federal governments, and the concern generated by findings of state overrepresentation in the Commonwealth Public Service. It was found that under Whitlam and Fraser, the ministerial staff group was biased towards the two largest states, and their capitals, Sydney and Melbourne. Table 5.1 indicates that there has been some evening of representation under the Hawke government.

New South Wales remains overrepresented, and Victoria slightly so, but Sydney now appears underrepresented, and while Melbourne remains overrepresented it is less so than under Fraser. Queensland and South Australia remain underrepresented, Western Australia is now fairly represented, and Tasmania and the

Table 5.1   Birthplace of Ministerial Staff (of those born in Australia)

	December 1974 (Whitlam) percentage	November 1976 (Fraser) percentage	August 1983 (Hawke) percentage	Percentage of Australian population living there in 1981
New South Wales	45	45	41	35
Sydney	(32)	(28)	(20.5)	(22)
rest of State	(13)	(17)	(20.5)	(13)
Victoria	28	30	28	26
Melbourne	(17)	(28)	(23)	(19)
rest of State	(11)	(2)	(5)	(7)
Queensland	14	6	10	16
South Australia	6	4	5	9
Western Australia	3	6	8	9
Tasmania	3	4	5	3
Australian Capital Territory	1	4	3	1
Northern Territory	—	—	—	1
Total	100	100	100	100

ACT (particularly) are still overrepresented. Under Hawke, 72 per cent of staffers come from the two largest states and the ACT (under Whitlam and Fraser it had been 74 per cent and 79 per cent respectively).

The 1981 census showed that 21.8 per cent of Australia's population were born overseas: 10 per cent of Whitlam staffers, 15 per cent of Fraser staffers, and 15 per cent of Hawke staffers were in that category.

Education

In comparison with the secondary school backgrounds of Whitlam and Fraser staffers, the Hawke group is somewhat closer to being a representative group. Table 5.2 shows there has been a rise in the proportion of those who attended government schools (though they are still underrepresented in terms of the entire population), and a correlative drop in the proportion of those from non–Catholic private schools to something nearer the general norm. Those who had attended independent Roman Catholic schools remain overrepresented.

Table 5.2   Secondary Schools of Ministerial Staff

	December 1974 (Whitlam) percentage	November 1976 (Fraser) percentage	August 1983 (Hawke) percentage	Percentage of children at such schools in 1981
Government schools only	43	45	50	77
Government plus Independent	10	2	12.5	
Government schools at some time	53	47	62.5	
Independent Roman Catholic only	24	27	29	18
Independent Roman Catholic and Government	3	2	4	
Independent Roman Catholic at some time	27	29	33	
Independent Non-Roman Catholic only	23	25	8.5	5
Independent Non-Roman Catholic plus Government	8	—	8.5	
Independent Non-Roman Catholic at some time	30	25	17	

The Hawke sample showed a startling increase in levels of tertiary qualification: 89 per cent of those sampled had at least one degree (cf. 65 per cent under Whitlam and 62 per cent under Fraser), including 10 per cent who held a degree plus other tertiary qualifications, 44 per cent who held more than one degree (cf. 21 per cent under Whitlam and 20 per cent under Fraser), and 8 per cent with Doctorates of Philosophy. The staffers have a much higher average level of education than mainstream politicians. And while the Hawke ministry is, in terms of the Australian experience, unusually highly qualified, it is still significantly less so than its ministerial staff: in 1983, 18 of the 27 ministers held one degree (i.e., 67 per cent) and 11 had more than one degree (41 per cent). About 8 per cent of the general population held tertiary qualifications in 1981.

The staffers' most frequently cited sources of first degrees were the Australian National University (20 per cent) and the University of Melbourne (16 per cent), trailed by the University of Sydney, the University of New South Wales, and the Canberra College of Advanced Education (each with 9 per cent). The University of Queensland and University of Adelaide each accounted for 6 per cent. The remaining 28 per cent were scattered around a dozen other tertiary institutions, some of them overseas. When *all* degrees cited are taken into account, the dominance of the Canberra institutions rises, with the ANU and the CCAE accounting for 29 per cent of all citations. The number of overseas institutions cited rises to second place (16 per cent), with the University of Melbourne now third (14 per cent).

Of all degrees cited, the most frequent were generalist arts degrees (BA and MA), some of which entailed major studies in politics and government. The most frequently cited specialist area of study, however, was economics/commerce, followed by law/legal studies.

Marital Status

While a bare majority of the staffers polled were married or living in a permanent relationship (58 per cent), this proportion is less than that which occurs in the general population, especially given the dominance of staff in their thirties and forties, groups generally most likely to be married, or among the mainstream politicians (90 per cent of whom were married in 1981[20]).

Careers

The staff of the Hawke ministry equated relatively closely to the staffers of previous governments in that about half had a public service background (46 per cent, compared to 52 per cent under Fraser and 49 per cent under Whitlam). On the other hand, most of them had *chosen* to work for the ALP government: there was an apparent decline in the number of seconded departmental officers relative to the Fraser and Whitlam administrations (only 13 per cent of Hawke staffers cited secondment as a significant reason for being in a ministerial office; 48 per cent of Fraser staffers had been seconded departmental officers, and 41–4 per cent under Whitlam). No ministers under Hawke had offices composed solely of seconded departmental officers.

The Hawke staffers had less experience in private industry and practice than those of either Fraser or Whitlam (13 per cent, compared with 27 per cent under Fraser and 16 per cent under Whitlam). On the other hand, they had markedly more experience in educational institutions than those of the previous governments (21 per cent, compared to 10 per cent under Fraser and 14 per cent under Whitlam).

The most striking development, however, is the high number of those who had worked in advisory and party positions prior to the election of the Hawke government. Fully 62 per cent of those sampled were in this category, and within this sub-group 47 per cent had worked for their current minister while in opposition, 27 per cent had worked for more than one ALP minister or shadow minister, 10 per cent had worked in staff positions for State Labor governments, and several individuals had worked for federal non-Labor ministers. These findings indicate that the Hawke government is the first to show the manifestations of the institutionalization of advisers for both ministry and opposition. Opportunities have emerged for relatively long term commitments to party and advisory roles, where staff assist with policy development in opposition and policy implementation in government. As a corollary, the Hawke staffers were less likely to look to a 'real' career elsewhere than Fraser and Whitlam staffers had been.[21] Of those Hawke staffers who had worked for the shadow ministry in opposition, or in other party positions, about 80 per cent saw their positions as of indefinite duration, and more than half expected to remain in their offices for three years or more.

Those who were public servants had more limited expectations, estimating their stay on the ministerial staff at around two years, though about 27 per cent hoped to continue indefinitely.

Although a politically engaged group with a high rate of party membership (see below), a minority had considered career openings in mainstream politics: 25 per cent had considered offering for party pre-selection in the past, but only 8 per cent had gone as far as standing; 17 per cent had been candidates for some type of political office, and 4 per cent had been elected (level not specified); 35 per cent would consider becoming a candidate for office in the future. In other words, 75 per cent had not considered representational politics in the past, and 65 per cent had no plans concerning such careers in the future: in the main their attention was elsewhere.[22]

'Public Service' and 'Political' Types

Forward made a distinction in the earlier surveys of Whitlam and Fraser staffers between 'public service' and 'non-public service' types. These were then correlated with 'political' and 'non-political' typologies — the former being assessed on the basis of party membership, reasons for joining a minister's staff, and engagement in political–policy work in the office. The proportion of staffers who were 'public service' types was about the same under all three governments (52 per cent under Fraser, 49 per cent under Whitlam, 46 per cent under Hawke). There were vast differences in party membership, however: only 13 per cent of Fraser staffers were members of either of the coalition parties, 47 per cent of Whitlam staffers were members of the ALP, but 62 per cent of the Hawke staffers sampled were members of the ALP and a further 10 per cent had been members of the ALP in the past. If, as Forward notes, Fraser staffers saw themselves as political functionaries, resisting 'keen party workers' and the pushing of political barrows the better to serve their ministers' purposes,[23] it is evident that the party political element is pre-eminent with Hawke's ministerial staff. By extension, 75 per cent of Hawke staffers cited 'a commitment to carrying out the party's programme' as among the three most important reasons for joining a minister's staff (and 46 per cent rated it the most important reason).

Table 5.3   Types of Ministerial Staff

	Whitlam percentage	Fraser percentage	Hawke percentage
Type A: Political non-public servants	33	34	44
Type B: Non-political public servants	32	45	27
Type C: Political public servants	18	5	19
Type D: Non-political non-public servants	18	16	10

The categories public service/non-public service and political/non-political were used in the previous surveys to generate four types. Table 5.3 introduces comparison with the Hawke sample and shows the ascendance of the 'political types' in current staff positions.

The proportion of 'non-political types' in the Fraser staff group is high (61 per cent), and the largest single group derives from 'traditional' staffing sources — the 'non-political public servants'. In contrast, 'political types' are the largest group among Whitlam staffers (51 per cent), though not so high as to sustain the myth that it was a wildly partisan company. In fact, the Hawke staffers, though having attracted considerably less attention, are most likely to be 'political types' (63 per cent of the group). And though the overall proportion of 'political public servants' — those with a foot in both camps — is roughly the same for both the Whitlam and Hawke groups, the fact that the Hawke ministry employs fewer public servants overall indicates that the public servants that are there are relatively *more* likely to be political. Perhaps most interesting of all, the Hawke staffers, the largest single group of whom are political outsiders (non-public servants), and the people who have been most formally vetted (see above), most closely approximate the charge levelled against Whitlam staffers of being political appointees with little public service experience. On the other hand, they come after ten years in the evolution of ministerial staff practices in appointments, during which time it has been realized, even under the conservative government, that if the system is to be effective, the political element in private offices must be accentuated.

In summary, current staffers are slightly older than their predecessors: in their thirties and forties rather than their twenties and thirties. They are less experienced in private industry and private practice, and more experienced in academic institutions and in prior advisory positions — often in the Labor opposition pool. Like their predecessors, they are mostly male, predominantly Australian-born (more so than the general population), mostly graduates (indeed the proportion has increased), disproportionately from non-government schools (though less markedly than their predecessors), and about half from inside and half from outside the public service. Against this, there has been an evident decrease in the bureaucratic element, with a marked decline in seconded public servants, and a clear ascendance of 'political types', especially in contrast to the Fraser staffers, but also with respect to the Whitlam group. There is an unusually strong Canberra orientation on such disparate variables as place of residence, educational background, and concentration of working time.

In what ways do the characteristics of ministerial staff serve to differentiate them from mainstream politicians and bureaucrats? As it happens, relatively high socio-economic status, and levels of education considerably higher than the norm, are characteristics shared by parliamentary politicians and by bureaucrats.[24] In the Australian instance, however, the current group of private office staffers has a higher level of tertiary qualifications than parliamentarians generally, or than the ministery (which itself is more highly qualified than the parliamentary norm). Advisers are in general a decade younger than politicians, and about the age when serious bureaucratic careers are getting underway.[25] Most obviously, advisers are differentiated from politicians by their preference for the *private* office rather than the public podium, and from bureaucrats by their admission of political commitment and their relative disinterest in administration.

How can one begin to move into fruitful generalization from this point? It may be argued that given the high salience of intellectual training, and the commitment to policy, this group is part of the intelligentsia; 'intelligentsia' here refers to those who have acquired specialized technical skills or higher education, and whose career advance then depends on successful utilization of the practical intellectual capacities thus generated. This clearly covers both particular skills (such as those of the journalist) and the high qualifications of the minders surveyed, as well as their policy aspirations. It does not suggest that they necessarily see themselves as an intelligentsia — the term serves as a categorization summarizing certain characteristics, not as a term of self-ascription. Nor does it suggest that many of the group are intellectuals: these are people committed to ideas-work, but most of them would scoff at the suggestion that they were intellectuals. In any case, the term 'intellectual' has too often been taken to entail critical detachment from, rather than engagement in, social action to sit easily with this group. It is therefore useful to remark that while 'intelligentsia' encompasses a sense of intellectual work, in its original sense it also implied political engagement rather than the detachment, even alienation, more commonly ascribed to the intellectual.[26] Yet it would be hard to deny the claim that politicians and bureaucrats too might well be described in these terms as members of the intelligentsia — another essay might link the sociology of knowledge with the appropriation by the intelligentsia of modern political institutions.

It is important to recognize that the minders in politics are a particular sub-set of the intelligentsia: and that there are ramifications of the term 'minder' in this context which further differentiate them from ministers and mandarins. The minder, despite a training which entails technical skills and intellectual capacities, is nonetheless removed from the intellectual, who is so often assumed to maintain a critical distance. That is, the contemporary minder is usually a person of learning but also a political operative: to state the obvious, he/she is not detached, but engaged. The fact of engagement also distinguishes the minder from the mandarin, for whom commitment to a political vision has had to be subsumed by the appearance of a 'neutral' technicism deemed appropriate to the bureaucracy. But the fact of being engaged political operatives does not of itself make minders akin to that other subset of the intelligentsia, the mainstream politicians — they have not chosen to pursue their ideas in the public forum, and the term 'minder' should always remind us of the dependent status of this group as the functionaries of mainstream politicians.

So far this book has entered into description in considerable detail of those political operatives I have called minders. It will augment understanding to attempt a more psychologically and sociologically informed analysis of their place in the political arena. This will entail three groups of questions:

— questions about the propensity for work with ideas, and in small groups;
— questions about the nature of policy-making groups, and the role of the minders within them;
— questions about the sociology (of knowlege and of institutions) behind the rise of the minders.

The first of these groups of questions is discussed in this chapter; the other groups are discussed in chapters 6 and 7.

The psychological proclivities for work with ideas — primarily through talk and writing, and through small groups — have not been sufficiently pursued by social scientists. The 'psychological birth' of the politically engaged intellectual is still better approached through a number of psychologically informed intellectual biographies[27] than through bodies of applied research. Davies' careful and illuminating conspectus, after Lasswell, is the only discussion to open up an otherwise attenuated field of theory.[28] Further, I can offer only fragmentary biographical evidence relating to the minders — my interviews have been closely focused upon work within private offices, and upon processes of policy-making. However, some of the fragments I *do* have are too interesting to pass without speculation, since they can be seen to relate closely to the patterns of intellectualization, passion for judgement, poverty of affect, and suspension of action, which Davies brings to the foreground in analyzing those whose penchant is for work behind the scenes rather than in a public arena.[29]

From the biographical sketches that can be assembled from public sources of advisers (such as have been used earlier in this book), there is some evidence of the dominance of first-born or only children amongst them. Occasionally the picture of the bookish, entirely adult-oriented child emerges strikingly — see, for instance, the published account of Wilenski's youth.[30] A first, or only, child who is aware of concentrated adult interest and involvement often comes to feel a strong need to achieve;[31] a child with a precocious interest in adult matters and reading is already at a remove from peer group interests, inclined to be a spectator of, rather than an activist in, the peer group's concerns. But neither is the adult-oriented child at one with the adults who are a constant reference — some of the features of *being* an adult remain unintelligible (the Freudian account, of course, emphasizes the child's exclusion from adult sexual union), and hence intense curiosity is engendered. Such estrangement may render unintelligible matters of emotion in particular — thus Lasswell remarked on the emotional detachment of the theorist.[32]

Despite the speculative nature of this constellation, chance autobiographical remarks from my respondents, as shown below, do testify to just such detachment, intense curiosity (and the correlative concern for knowledge), ambition to achieve but often through others, and the high salience of politics as spectacle rather than the forum for personal action.

Interestingly, where conventional politicians usually refer to particular events or crises as the initial stimulus for their interest in politics,[33] advisers frequently find that stimulus in books, as in this instance:

I remember at a very early stage in my secondary education reading Sydney and Beatrice Webb's *Soviet Communism* and *Decay of Capitalist Civilization* and making my first — unsuccessful — attempt at *Capital* . . . At the same stage I was reading *Grapes of Wrath* which again was a very influential book for me . . . I guess all serve to stir up social conscience . . .

An even more striking instance of this tendency is to be found in Graham Freudenberg's discovery of politics (and a vocation) in a biography of Disraeli (see biographies to chapter 6). Such passages suggest the tendency to apprehend through intellectualization rather than experience.

The powerful push of curiosity is always evident. Here are two instances from different respondents:

in the end, my life is a quest for knowledge. I suppose I am more an inquisitive person than one who wants to change or modify things.

I am interested in research and ideas rather than in the handshaking or compromises of politics.

The second respondent here indicates the resistance to the practices of everyday party politics, which others make even more evident:

It's not that I haven't wanted to be a supporter but, you know, branch membership is not very rewarding and I sort of felt that what I was doing was at an entirely different level . . .

I let my membership lapse many years ago . . . I haven't renewed it more recently because I'm too embarrassed to do so. People in the party would be amazed to know that I wasn't a member. Anyway, I have no interest in branch meetings.

I've been active in the party, but I've never been interested in representational politics, or in the machine things. My work has always been policy oriented and task-oriented . . .

Against this, however, may be set their absorption in the high level politics of the inner circle:

The reason I moved into the arena I think, apart from strong Labor convictions, was an interest in the policy-making side of government. Having been reporting governments, and politics, and elections . . . the chance to have a look at it from the inside was too good to pass up.

The job itself is enormously fascinating. It's incredibly interesting. You are caught up in great events and boredom is utterly unknown . . .

The primary motivation is the fascination of politics as such rather than involvement in the cause — not that I'm suggesting for one moment that the cause isn't important to me, I'm . . . very deeply committed, and it is a tremendous satisfaction . . . to know that one is one of the principal articulators of a particular cause. But I would have to say that the buzz really comes from the involvement in politics as such.

there's the satisfaction of helping to attain the objectives I've mentioned, but as well as that it just is immensely interesting . . . Trying to find a way through a large set of self-interested and competing institutions simply is of absorbing interest.

Here (and the examples could be multiplied), there is ample evidence of 'a world . . . treated as spectacle',[34] or, as in the last case, as an intellectual game or puzzle.

Though these people are fascinated observers driven by curiosity and a penchant for inside knowledge, it would be a mistake to ignore the projects which they pursue in their work. After all, it is the pursuit of such projects which differentiates them from conventional intellectuals. That is, they *are* seeking to realize ideological aims and practical programmes, not simply to see what it is like on the inside:

I spent seven years working on alternative economic policies . . . Of *course* there are specific ideas, as well as certain values, you want to see acted on, put into effect. You wouldn't do this work if there weren't!

I thought . . . [we] should have an explicit concern, a political concern, with the values, philosophy, and politics of the government . . . I think one of the things that enabled me to perform the job was that I have a clear view of how I believe Australia should be governed, and I think that appealed to ＿＿＿. So I was doing it not as a Liberal Party activist, but as an individual person contributing a particular viewpoint. I supported the Liberal Party because they were the closest approximation to, or gave the closest expression to, the values I adhere to. That was my only reason for doing the job. So I don't see myself as doing it as a 'party' person — it is rather that I am trying to realize my own ideas through the Liberal Party. There is an adequate coincidence there.

There are feelings here of 'mission', of ideological convictions that assure 'direct contact with the sacred'.[35] However, approaches like those above do not entail acting independently but acting *through* others, not only through a party, but also through a leader. No matter how important one's project, it must be attached to such larger projects. This line can be pursued by looking more closely at the work chosen by, and expected of, political advisers.

6

The Work of the Minders

The significance of what advisers do depends upon the assertion that their work has importance. For instance, the influence of irregulars in building interstitial organizations that acquire a policy role has already been discussed: for example, Conlon's Research Directorate, but note also Wilenski's part in mapping the outlines of Whitlam's ministerial staff and in making the PM's Office an active unit, or Kemp's elaboration of the PM's Office into a significant policy resource. This chapter looks closely at the work of the minders and its impact on the political system. First, the characteristic roles ascribed to advisers in Britain, America and Australia will be noted. Second, the role perceptions of Australian ministerial advisers, with their assessment of how much time is devoted to different tasks, will be discussed. This is followed by a substantive analysis of what such roles actually encompass which will be the ground for a broader consideration of adviser roles in policy decision-making groups.

A recent comment rates a cabinet minister's principal private secretary as of equal importance to a departmental head, and indicates some of the former's roles. Deborah Snow, in commenting on the difficulties foreign minister Bill Hayden faced in replacing his departmental secretary and his principal private secretary at the same time, remarked:

While the secretary's appointment will be the most important for Mr Hayden in the departmental sphere, an equally crucial appointment in political terms will be the person he chooses to take over as his principal private secretary.
   . . . The principal private secretary's position is a particularly important one as it involves close liaison not only with the senior levels of the department, but [sic] with other ministers' offices and with Mr Hayden's power base within the party . . . it will be a difficult task finding a candidate with the essential qualities of a deep background in

foreign affairs and an intimate knowledge of the workings of the Labor Party . . .[1]

The roles envisaged here are clearly those of a functionary, a facilitator, but one who makes the important links for a minister between bureaucracy, cabinet and party factions. With our interest in the origins of advisers in the intelligentsia, note the significance ascribed here to specialist knowledge and to party political knowledge.

In fact, while there are a number of useful discussions of the roles of political advisers in Britain,[2] America,[3] and Australia,[4] and I have drawn on all of these below, all of them recognize, as does the passage quoted, that the primary role of personal advisers is that of supporting a political master, and that the components of that work will sometimes be personal, oftentimes technical or expert, and nearly always political.

Perhaps the most evident form of support is simply that of efficient administration of the private office: the management of the flow of paper, appointments, travel and callers, and the organization of the tasks of personnel, with the least possible hindrance to the minister. Among the more directly personally supportive roles of advisers, Alexander George identifies providing for a leader's cognitive needs (for information which will assure contact with reality), emotional support (in coping with the stress of difficult decisions), understanding (through the shared solicitation and consideration of views), and political legitimacy (through the shared responsibility of the group).[5] A private staff member can serve a leader as a sounding-board and confidante, a comrade on the leader's side in battles with political peers and bureaucrats, perhaps a participant in inside jokes that relieve the pressure of the daily confrontations which elsewhere the politician must represent as serious. (My observation has been that a rapport based on shared jokes frequently characterizes the more successful ministerial private offices.) In other respects, the adviser can provide personal support by attending meetings on the minister's behalf (though most ministers do not encourage staff directly to stand in for them), going out into the field for the minister (an aide to a minister for labour might, for instance, move around the unions), participating in discussions and speaking for the minister, responding to inquiries, assisting with parliamentary duties and legislative tactics, acting as extra eyes and ears and points of contact for the minister, even as a tester floating ideas outside the office to assess reactions without these being directly connected with the minister and acting as a buffer. The tasks of loyal aide, however, will frequently be cast more directly in terms of technical or political roles.

The staff at the upper levels of the private offices of political executives have been shown to be relatively highly educated. Though duly certified by our institutions of higher education, they are more frequently generalists than technicians or experts, and as already stated, would be unlikely to describe themselves as working intellectuals. Nonetheless, their knowledge and, more importantly, their ability to tap sources of knowledge, have been important factors in their arrival in the inner circle. To this extent they are expected to provide a technical service. If expert, they will be expected to contribute their expertise directly to relevant policy discussion. More usually, as generalists they will be expected to bring a critical intelligence to bear in sifting through the papers, submissions and briefings that come to their minister. They will be expected to be informed devillers, with the skill to chase ideas through 'ideas networks' (research institutions, libraries, archives, other experts). To this end, they will be expected to have, or to have the ability to acquire, a range of contacts in institutions relevant to their minister's policy area. Having marshalled information, they may be expected to be able to abstract themselves in order to think through debates and issues, and then to provide relevant commentary. As a concomitant, they will be expected to have skills of articulation and communication: the ability to write relevant research succinctly, to prepare coherent briefing papers, to draft speeches. In short, it is through a range of technical skills — an outcome of their education — that they will be expected to contribute to policy formulation, not through being the originators of policy ideas. And usually, the exercise of such skills will be mediated by attention to political imperatives.

With respect to manifestly political work or advice, there are several levels of 'politics' to which an adviser may be expected to attend: the politics of the national electorate, the politics of inter-party conflict, the internal politics of the party in power, and the politics of the bureaucracy. At the first level, some advisers have proved adept at assessing the changing ground of electorate opinion, of what the public will 'wear' and what polls mean, and these have become significant campaign strategists. (Both 'intellectuals', like David Kemp, and 'machine-men' like Bob Hogg, have been credited with such roles.) A staff member may also work as point of contact for the electorate: usually as the person to whom pressure groups or aggrieved parties will be directed in the first instance. With respect to the party conflict, advisers can be a source of intelligence by being freer to move about the journalistic network, among opposition staffers, and in the dining rooms and bars of parliament (and of Canberra), than are mainstream politicians. In terms of the party served by a personal staff member's minister, that staffer can be expected to understand the party platform and how it has evolved. He or she will also be expected to know, or to acquire knowledge, of the factional workings of the party, and to develop contacts in and maintain liaison with the key elements of the party organization in the minister's interests. Liaison with other ministerial offices will also be important. It is unlikely that advisers generally will be able to maintain a watch on the internal politics of the bureaucracy, since as a group they are disliked by the public service — though some of the 'political public servants' (see above) choosing to work on ministerial staffs may retain that capacity. On the whole advisers will probably serve their ministers more successfully by closely monitoring the bureaucracy's execution of policy decisions.

A range of roles is canvassed here and most ministerial staff will not work across the range: some will concentrate on administration, others on research and writing, some will specialize in personal support and some in party, bureaucratic, or public liaison. A clearer idea of their own sense of their work and the importance they attach to it was gained by asking them about it.

As part of the survey referred to in chapter 5, the ministerial staff of the Hawke government were asked a range of questions about work in the private offices. They were asked to indicate 'What in practice are your main roles?', and given nine roles[6] of which they were to rank the three most important. Some chose to rank more than three, and 13 per cent of the sample indicated important roles but refused to differentiate between them. The following figures are based only on those who answered the question as asked, and ranked the roles. The highest priority among all respondents was given to 'advising the minister on policy': fully 76 per cent of respondents cited this as amongst their three main roles, and 36 per cent ranked it their most important role. Next in order of importance was 'liaison with the public service', for 57 per cent of the sample one of their important roles, and for 24 per cent the most important role. Following these two outstanding priorities, other functions fell into rough groupings of decreasing importance. First can be grouped 'general trouble shooting' (48 per cent placed this in the top three, but only 9 per cent gave it first priority) and 'general office administration' (for 43 per cent an important priority, and for 14 per cent their first priority). The next group consists of 'personally assisting the minister' (26 per cent rated this important, 9 per cent gave it first priority,) 'dealing with the press' (important for 21 per cent, first priority for 5 per cent),[7] and 'speech writing' (important for 19 per cent, first priority for 2 per cent). Then come two functions a minority rated as among their three most important, but which no one cited as a first priority: 'political party work' (for 7 per cent an important role), and 'handling electorate matters' (only 2 per cent rated this among their three most important roles).

These findings were at variance with an earlier survey of Whitlam staffers,[8] where it was found that 54 per cent rated 'liaison with the public service' amongst their most important roles, and this was followed by 'general office administration' (41 per cent), 'advising the minister on policy' (39 per cent), 'general trouble shooting' (37 per cent), and 'personally assisting the minister' (35 per cent). Then were grouped 'dealing with the press' (23 per cent) and 'speech writing' (18 per cent); followed by 'political party work' (10 per cent), and 'handling electorate matters' (6 per cent). While public service liaison and general office administration are rated as equally important by Hawke and by Whitlam staffers, the significant accentuation of the policy advising role by Hawke staffers, and their increased attention to general trouble shooting as opposed to such functional roles as personally assisting the minister, confirm the impression that this group is more policy-orientated and politically engaged than their predecessors (though it is notable that they rate the hack work of party and electorate very low).

Staffers were asked to estimate the proportion of their time allocated to various tasks in percentage terms. Respondents' answers were consolidated, and averages of all estimates calculated. Answers indicated that in combination they spent almost half their time working with their ministers (20 per cent, about the same as the Whitlam sample) or with other staff attached to their office (27 per cent, a slightly higher level of time allocation than the Whitlam sample). They spent a slightly higher proportion of time working alone than did the Whitlam sample (20 per cent compared to 15 per cent), and it is notable that this rated as highly as any single item except working with others in the office. Dealing with public service and other government employees was rated relatively highly in terms of time consumed (16 per cent, compared with 14 per cent for the Whitlam sample). Then followed contact with the public (9 per cent of time), dealing with other ministers and MPs (7 per cent), and dealing with the press (5 per cent). It appeared that time demands on the Hawke staffers were relatively similar to those experienced by the Whitlam group: in some respects the nature of the work has not altered substantially. On the other hand there has been a growing concentration on work in Canberra: the Hawke sample indicated that 81 per cent of their collective working time was spent in and around parliament house in Canberra compared with 65 per cent of the time of the Whitlam staffers. The Canberra orientation is augmented by residence figures: 77 per cent cite Canberra as their place of principal residence, 6 per cent live in their minister's electorate, 8 per cent live elsewhere. The corollary is a substantial diminution of time spent in State and regional offices of the minister (6 per cent, cf. 13 per cent for Whitlam staffers); in the minister's department (3 per cent, cf. 10 per cent for Whitlam staffers); in the minister's electorate (3 per cent, cf. 5 per cent for Whitlam staffers), and elsewhere, mostly travelling (6 per cent, cf. 9 per cent for Whitlam staffers). It is pertinent to note that the increase in time in Canberra is not related to an increase in time spent in departments — perhaps another indication of a concentration on the politics of policy rather than on bureaucratic considerations by contemporary ministerial staff.

The Hawke staffers were more insular with respect to broad dealings in the staff pool of the entire ministry than were either Fraser or Whitlam staffers: only 4 per cent reported extensive working contact with the staff of other ministers (cf. 39 per cent under Fraser, and 24 per cent under Whitlam), though 44 per cent reported fairly wide contact (cf. 33 per cent under Fraser and 41 per cent under Whitlam); 50 per cent spoke of their contact with other ministerial staff as limited (cf. 28 per cent under Fraser, and 32 per cent under Whitlam), and 2 per cent described such contact as rare (cf. 4 per cent under Whitlam). The differences in these figures suggest that staff of earlier governments may have been more successful than staff of the Hawke government in establishing '. . . an informal infrastructure that would serve the interests of the ministry as a whole as well as the interests of particular ministers'.[9] Perhaps collective work will flower when staffers have had more experience,[10] but there are indications of a tendency for current staff to focus inwards on the private office.

Hawke staffers, like Whitlam staffers, tended to report a higher degree of contact with their permanent heads than did the Fraser group: 29 per cent of the sample said their work brought them into contact with the permanent head very often (cf. 42 per cent under Fraser and 39 per cent under Whitlam), 48 per cent said such contact occurred often (cf. 15 per cent under Fraser and 35 per cent under Whitlam), 22 per cent said it was occasional (cf. 35 per cent under Fraser and 24 per cent under Whitlam), and none said it was non-existent (cf. 9 per cent under Fraser and 1 per cent under Whitlam). Their contact with second division officers was of a similar nature to that reported by both Fraser and Whitlam staffers: 73 per cent spoke of its occurring very often (cf. 69 per cent under Fraser, 66 per cent under Whitlam), 21 per cent stated often (cf. 18 per cent under Fraser, 23 per cent under Whitlam), 4 per cent said it was occasional (cf. 11 per cent under Fraser and 9 per cent under Whitlam), and 2 per cent said never (cf. 2 per cent under Fraser and 3 per cent under Whitlam). The Hawke staffers, however, were less likely to work with third division officers than their counterparts in the earlier Labor government, though still more so than the Fraser staffers. Of the Hawke group, 13 per cent cited high contact (cf. 24 per cent under Fraser, 42 per cent under Whitlam), 35 per cent medium contact (cf. 18 per cent under Fraser, 33 per cent under Whitlam), 50 per cent occasional contact (cf. 38 per cent under Fraser, 23 per cent under Whitlam), and 2 per cent no contact (cf. 20 per cent under Fraser, 3 per cent under Whitlam). Forward notes that the proclivity for dealing 'down the line' by Whitlam staffers was taken as an indication of their interventionist and 'confrontational' style, and remarks on better relations between ministers' offices and the public service under Fraser.[11] Though more likely to deal with the upper divisions than with officers down the line, Hawke staffers report their relations with the public service in slightly less glowing terms than the Fraser group, but in generally more positive terms than the Whitlam group: 23 per cent described their working relationship with the public service as excellent (cf. 52 per cent under Fraser, 31 per cent under Whitlam), 42 per cent as very good (cf. 13 per cent under Fraser[12]), 23 per cent as good (cf. 24 per cent under Fraser, 55 per cent under Whitlam), 10 per cent as middling (cf. 11 per cent under Fraser, 13 per cent under Whitlam) and 2 per cent as poor (cf. 1 per cent under Whitlam). Perhaps they are more pragmatic in dealings with the public service than Whitlam staffers, though less likely to be under the departmental thumb than Fraser staffers.

Despite the hiving off of public relations activities to a separate media group under the Hawke government, ministerial staff maintain fairly general contact with journalists: 25 per cent spoke of high levels of contact with journalists (cf. 41 per cent under Fraser), 37 per cent said contact was medium (cf. 4 per cent under Fraser), 37 per cent said low (cf. 33 per cent under Fraser), and none mentioned having no contact (cf. 22 per cent under Fraser). No comparable figures exist for the Whitlam group, although on average they spent more of their time in contact with the press than did Hawke staffers (10 per cent against 5 per cent).

As a final measure, the Hawke staffers were asked to assess the importance of the contribution made by ministerial staff to the policy-making process: 46 per cent rated it as 'very important', 40 per cent 'important', 5 per cent as of 'limited importance', 4 per cent claimed it varied, none designated it 'unimportant'. Interestingly, when the group of those designated 'political types' is considered separately, their ratings are the same as those of the sample as a whole: a high estimate of the importance of policy work is general to the group.

A clearer sense of role content will be established by allowing advisers to speak to the specifics of what they do. The material in this section was obtained by interviewing advisers of the

Whitlam, Fraser and Hawke governments between 1977 and 1983.[13] I have chosen to quote extensively, giving detail in their own words. But because of the differing circumstances under which interviews were obtained over this long period, I have elected to preserve confidentiality by making no attributions except where this is essential to the argument.[14] Where possible, I have also referred to public sources.

Preparing for Power

In examining the policy influence of the minders, it is important first to note the ramifications of work done in the periods where their political masters are not in power. Indeed, it might be argued that the major energies devoted to policy *development* by political parties are expended in opposition, for when they are in government they are concerned with implementing and managing. Advisers therefore may be especially significant in this opposition stage as they provide parties with the programme content with which they attempt to provoke the interest and support of the electorate. The period leading up to the accession to power of the Labor government in 1972 provides a particularly clear instance of this: the proliferation of policy under Whitlam 1967–72 made the ALP appear to have 'answers' at a time when the L-CP government appeared divided and unsure of its direction.[15] Whitlam was given much credit for the generation of policy, but as he said himself: '. . . I . . . try and work out means of achieving what I think are my Party's objectives — how to marshal the examples in other countries, how to marshal the advisers in this country . . .'[16]

Thus, Whitlam was an important originator of initiatives, but detail was very much the province of his advisers.

In the development of policy, Whitlam relied very greatly on outside advice. Whitlam developed the original themes, the three great areas: schools, health and cities . . .

In the development of policies the input of the staff prior to 1972 was enormous, particularly in the case of Race Mathews . . . The specifics of the health insurance programme . . . came from the Deeble and Scotton proposal, but the details of it were worked up very much by Mathews . . . Mathews also contributed greatly to the specifics of the urban programme. But the drive came from Whitlam.

(*Graham Freudenberg, interview, 20 July 1977*.)

I have spoken to many experts consulted on policy detail in that period who affirm Mathews' significance as contact and link-man: 'You have to be aware of the importance of men like Race Mathews, who did the groundwork and built up the contacts needed to facilitate Whitlam's ideas'. (*Pat Troy, Urban Research Unit, ANU, interview, 27 May 1977.*)

Mathews himself gives extended and instructive illumination of key instances:

One of Gough [Whitlam's] primary interests was in the development of hospitals — he saw all health services as being potentially and preferably hospital based. Then we had the related preoccupation . . . of people like (Labor MP) Moss Cass with salaried medical services, not necessarily hospital based, which ultimately grew into the community health centre concept . . . There was a yawning gulf between those concepts and what ordinary people identified as the health-care problem, which was the health insurance system. Something had to be done to bring those things together.

Moss Cass had originally gotten to know Deeble and Scotton, academic economists who had taken on health insurance and related matters as a subject for academic study. They had set about devising an alternative model largely for academic comparative purposes. (My predecessor) John Menadue had followed up Cass's contact with them, and Whitlam had met them . . . but later the contact had gone cold.

I came on to the scene [in 1967] completely innocent as far as health care was concerned. Early on, Whitlam was offered a speaking engagement at one of the major teaching hospitals, and decided that it was to be a set piece on health care. And so I looked at the material that had previously been developed around hospitals . . . and I felt that it just wasn't adequate for the purpose. So I went and saw Deeble and Scotton — to me they were just names on our file — and I went and introduced myself and talked to them.

It was from that point that Medibank . . . as we knew it in, say, '75–'76, began to germinate. It was a process of taking proposals which had been developed in a political vacuum, for academic purposes, but which were intensely practical in economic health care terms, and giving them an appropriate political orientation . . . Medibank is a good example of the power in an essentially academic idea passed into the lime-light of political attention . . . My role was as a catalyst. You need three things to make the system work. One is a leader who is basically policy-orientated, and . . . who has got a fascination with ideas. Secondly, you need people who have got ideas, and have a capacity for hard work and documentation. And thirdly, there has to be somebody who brings those two things together — who has got the confidence of the leader on the one hand and who, as it were, knows where the bodies are buried on the other . . .

Take another case, the Schools Commission. I guess the notion of the Schools Commission and . . . [of its] role was Gough . . . following precedent and using the notion of the Universities Commission which he's always regarded as one of Menzies' most significant achievements. Following his initiative, David Bennett and I wrote a paper . . . as a background for delegates to the 1966 ALP Conference, in which we raised most of the areas of concern and some of the administrative structures which later passed into the Schools commission. That '66 paper . . . became the basis of a lot of stuff I worked into speeches between '66 and '69.

A contributing factor in these developments was a trip to England by Whitlam and Freudenberg in 1968. I suggested to them that they might take the opportunity while they were there to talk to people associated with the Plowden Committee on education and they came back loaded with material . . . that served to buttress the notion of needs that David Bennett and I had put forward in '66 — that ultimately became the Disadvantaged Schools' Programme . . .

By 1969 the notion of the Schools Commission was just about fully fledged . . . It got passed into Party policy at the 1969 conference, and . . . carried through until 1972 when Peter Karmel and the interim committee were given the job of refining it . . .

The third thing . . . that ultimately became DURD [the Department of Urban and Regional Development] . . . came out of Gough's great interest in urban services because of the deficiencies experienced in his own electorate. He, and I think Menadue even more, had been interested in the Johnson administration's efforts at urban renewal — the cities programme in the US. Menadue had built a relationship between Gough and . . . the principals of a Sydney firm of architects and planners, and he had done a speech on 'Cities in a Federation' some time before I joined him.

I put together a relationship with the people at the Urban Research Unit at ANU, and in the School of Architecture at Melbourne and at the University of Queensland . . . and later with Hugh Stretton at Adelaide . . . That network was instrumental in putting together the bible of the whole operation . . . the guts of the urban, the cities programme. We worked hard on that until 1969 and then we handed it over as a package to Tom Uren, who was enormously dedicated to the whole thing thereafter . . .

In the same way we handed over Medibank to Bill Hayden in 1969 . . . So there are three particular fields.

(*Race Mathews, interview, 3 January 1982.*)

Whitlam's key staffers did not serve as experts or policy originators but, in Mathews' terms, as catalysts. Nevertheless,
Mathews' case shows the impact of what they did, and they were
in no doubt of its importance. Mathews himself, who left
Whitlam's staff to run for federal parliament in his own right in
1972, has said:

Those five years were probably the most useful I'll ever spend, certainly
the most interesting. I just made an appalling mistake when I decided to
go into federal parliament . . .

I should have stayed on the staff . . . as private secretary to the prime
minister . . . I would have been infinitely more useful as private secretary
than I could ever have been as a backbencher . . . even if I had moved
into the ministry, if the thing had gone on, it still wouldn't have had the
same order of importance.   (*Interview, 3 January 1982.*)

Perhaps Mathews underestimates the limitations faced by the
advisers when their masters come to power, as discussed below.
He speaks, however, to a pattern which was to be repeated again
and again in ensuing years, as oppositions of both the left and
right enlisted personal advisers as catalysts, experts and ideologists
in the process of self-examination and policy clarification seen as
central to the return to government.[17] Their contribution was not
limited to the long run up to election: election campaigns in
particular confirmed advisers as integral members of the inner
circle. To cite only two of the most recent instances: David Kemp
and Tony Eggleton were architects of Fraser's election successes
(and Kemp, notably, was absent during the near disaster of 1980
and the defeat of 1983); Bob Hogg as strategist and Peter Barron
as media adviser and handler constantly weave through accounts
of Hawke's election campaigns in 1983 and 1984.[18] The centrality
of the adviser at this juncture is shown in this passage:

X and I had worked on the policies in [this area] during all of the period
of opposition. But (for reasons entirely to do with the internal politics
of the party leadership) X was transferred in a shuffle of the shadow
ministry shortly before the election campaign, and Y took over.

In fact, the election campaign itself didn't go too badly. I actually
drafted the _____ policy proposal that came out during the campaign, and
Y based his electioneering on that. He espoused the policies we'd worked
on. I accompanied him everywhere, writing his speeches, passing him
notes to help answer questions in television studios, literally putting the
words into his mouth.   (*Labor staffer, 1983.*)

To this point the partisan adviser is in a privileged position as primary source of, or conduit to, relevant knowledges. When a party comes to government, new constraints come into play, as the respondent quoted above remarked:

After the election, nothing seemed to be said for a while . . . Then he told me he had made the decision to have a (departmental) person as his principal private secretary, that they in fact were going to nominate his PPS. I was absolutely staggered! I had worked for years for that position. He said at first it wouldn't matter because the PPS would only be a paper shuffler, but that is bullshit because the chief paper shuffler inevitably becomes the chief policy adviser in the office because of his access to, and control of, information . . . I think Y did it because he had taken over the portfolio so late and he felt very insecure. He couldn't get on top of the area, and so he decided the only way he could cope was to make sure [the department] looked after him.

Others spoke of the way public servants played up to and capitalized upon the insecurity of new ministers:

I was displaced by a Public Service *fait accompli*. On the morning that the ministry was sworn in, I went down to (my minister's) office. I found the departmental secretary was already there, and he had brought over a senior private secretary, a private secretary, and a stenographer. Perhaps it was an interim measure — the (departmental secretary) had (Party) connections in the past, and so (my minister) trusted him. Still the departmental people were entrenched initially. And even when the minister eventually replaced them with his own appointments, I never got back to the position I'd had previously.   (*Labor staffer, 1983.*)

Paradoxically, then, long-term staffers may experience the transition to power in terms of losing their place in the sun: '. . . the old staff, the family, in government was only a subsidiary. We were crowded out by the official public service.' (*Graham Freudenberg, interview, 20 July 1977.*) However, given the significant augmentation of staffing resources when a party assumes power, it is appropriate to remark that most minders serve as advisers to government, and it is this work experience which will now be discussed.

Negotiating a Role in Power
The passages above illustrate the quirks of personal relationships upon which the adviser role often depends. Reflecting on the

importance of personal staff in Whitlam's development of policy, Freudenberg remarked:

> at the time that Race was appointed it could not have been clearly envisaged how significant in policy development his role would be. It was significant because he made it so and Whitlam allowed him to make it so. Similarly with my role, but . . . that whole operation depended on a very close network of personal relationships.
>
> (*Interview, 8 January 1982.*)

The adviser who is expert in a particular area, whose political patron and ally is moved elsewhere, is vulnerable particularly when the new master is more concerned that his department should look after him than with alternative policy development. The parallel with court politics is unmistakable: '. . . in *all* of the offices in which I have served, the various roles have been defined much more by personal factors than by structures and official gradings and titles'. (*Graham Freudenberg, interview, 8 January 1982.*)

The absence of job descriptions and the centrality of personal relationships mean that, in the first instance, adviser roles are open to negotiation, and to the adviser's own decisions (drawing on established skills and preferences).

> people carve out roles for themselves . . . Nobody ever really told me what I was supposed to do . . . you just dealt with the situation and it evolved around you. You have your own experience, your own knowledge, and this enables you to do certain things, and you do those things . . .   (*Liberal staffer, 1982.*)

The process of role determination might be directed not only by particular experience or knowledge, but also by a clearly articulated philosophy on the part of the adviser:

> I saw the ministerial office's work as an extension of the minister's role in its directive or controlling aspect . . . The ministerial officer should help the minister to perform *his* tasks more effectively in relation to the public service, the party, and parliament.
>
> . . . [Hence] we were concerned with policy and with the politics of policy, with the object of integrating the philosophy, politics, and policy of the government.   (*Liberal staffer, 1982.*)

Orchestrating the Private Office

The roles were also dictated by the contingent demands of the private office:

there were a number of individuals, each with their own tasks. I played a co-ordinating role in relation to those tasks in the sense that I had an idea of who was working on what, I had an idea of who was going in to see the prime minister.

Before anyone went in to the prime minister, normally they'd pop into my office to ask if anyone was with him and to tell me what they wanted to see him about. I could then say whether that had already been dealt with, or if someone was working on it . . .

I was able to do a fair amount of the co-ordination within the office itself, and also I was aware of the papers that were coming through the public service . . . so if people wanted to discuss this, that, or the other, I was able to tell them what was coming up.

Sometimes ministers wouldn't want to see the prime minister. They might just come along and say 'Well, what do you think his reaction would be to so and so?', and you'd do your best to give a reaction . . .

I watched the flow of paper that came through from various government departments for the prime minister, and I sometimes made some comment on it to him or drew his attention to other things that were happening.

Then there was the normal role of making sure that everything worked and that everyone was actually doing the things they were supposed to be doing . . . I had to make sure it was clear who was writing what, when it would be ready, what would then be done . . . there was all that sort of housekeeping work to be done . . .

Now, I don't think there was any sort of hierarchical system in the office. Each individual had his or her own relationship with the prime minister . . . and mine I think was more a co-ordinating or facilitating role than in any sense a hierarchical one.

And then there was a lot of travelling about with the Prime Minister. And there were, I suppose, the most exciting times — when policy or political issues were more exciting — when you might talk with Whitlam about some current issue or events, or due to some other set of circumstances have an input.   (*Labor prime ministerial PPS, 1970s.*)

The orchestration of the private office can be seen here to be work of signal importance. If ministers are to cope[19] it will only be by virtue of having a support system responsive to the minister's political imperatives and capable of leaving him/her free to act on them unencumbered by the 'housekeeping'.

A minister's primary concern is to stay in power, and to ensure this he must pay attention to party factions, to the demands of the party generally, to his constituency, to the media, and so on. So the amount of time he devotes to his portfolio is probably less than 50 per cent. Now most public service heads would find that unbelievable. If the system is going to work somebody has to look after administration and keep the paper moving, and that is this office's function.   (*Labor staffer, 1983.*)

The housekeeping role largely involves mechanical application, but even this entails a degree of judgement that may have political effects.

I was very much the man who made things happen when they were meant to happen in the immediate vicinity of the PM . . . I was the guy who made sure that information came up to him when it had to come. I had a large part to play in getting his invitations, his programme, properly handled . . . It was an enormous task trying to vet and assess the flood of invitations to do things, and then when they are accepted there is briefing material to be arranged and so on. Making all that work was my job.

. . . the political letters used to end up on my desk . . . all the difficult letters. I used to get to answer those . . . It was just, perhaps, through an ability to handle them fairly quickly because most of them fell into a pattern you could recognise just through experience . . .

I was also the person who decided whether he could be interrupted. If people came bursting in saying something was urgent . . . it was me who decided whether it was really urgent or not . . . Once again, through experience, I seemed to develop pretty well a skill of knowing what he'd agree was urgent and what he wouldn't. It was really me reflecting his priorities . . . I reckon I helped him make effective use of his time.   (*Liberal prime ministerial aide, 1970s, interviewed 1982.*)

There were other demands on the office — and not just by letter — which the staff might be called on to mediate:

There would be requests to meet delegations. When he was meeting delegations we would prepare detailed briefing notes for the minister suggesting areas of questioning and probing. He would be fully briefed on the industry background as well as the economic background of any

delegation, as well as where it (or its demands) might fit into the decision-making process. On that basis we would suggest lines of discussion.
(*Labor staffer, 1983.*)

The subtext of much of the discussion of office management was that of organising time: 'One of our multiple functions, an important one, is the efficient management of time — ensuring that the minister's time is not wasted, and that his attention is focused on essentials and not on inessentials'. (*Labor staffer, 1983.*) Some staffers judged their success on this criterion, and developed technical expertise to facilitate it:

He said that I was the best ministerial staffer he had ever had, because he found the average time he could use at his discretion increased by about 60 per cent. He had time to think because of the way I organized his office. (*National Party staffer, 1980s, interviewed 1983.*)

This respondent had in fact designed a computer programme and supervised a computer installation with direct links to his minister's department and electorate office to improve the information flow and responsiveness of the private office. Having worked on the initial stages of this under a coalition minister, he was subsequently (and unusually) employed by a Labor minister, under whom he continued to develop his system: 'Ministerial offices still operated as they had in the Menzies era when I started, but there have been incredible changes in processing information and in technology since then . . . This will help to lift them into the twentieth century'.

Proximity and Access to Decisions-makers

As these passages indicate, the importance of office management and administration should not be underrated — though it has been noted in an earlier section that less than half of ministerial staffers give it a high priority. If the primary motive is to augment the minister's effectiveness, a subsidiary effect can be to give the staffer a degree of control. Picking up a theme adverted to in much of the above, one adviser remarks: 'I make judgements about what people or papers should get to him — but these judgements reflect what I know to be the minister's priorities'. (*Labor staffer,*

1983.) The staffer can be assumed to know these priorities because of a close, daily working relationship with her/his principal that is not enjoyed by others, and this acts as an alert to look for the significance of contiguity and control of access in assessing the work of the minders. Usually they were aware of their advantage:

If you get your relationship with the leader right, your access to him for practical purposes is near total. Nobody else has that sort of access. They're all constrained in some sense to make appointments, or they become totally reliant on the telephone . . . and even that will normally involve an intermediary.   (*Labor staffer, 1970s, interviewed 1982*.)

However, this was frequently cast in pragmatic terms:

that sort of buffering role is inevitably . . . Often there would be a degree of filtering of people making approaches from outside the public service. The minister is very busy, and often these people could be dealt with by an administrator. Then again, sometimes I might ask what they wanted, and make a decision about whether the minister was already well enough informed about that matter . . . or even whether he was interested. Sometimes there was just no point in them seeing him, since he had already been presented with the same argument a number of times. On other occasions I might act as a sounding board for others wanting to know what the minister was thinking.   (*Liberal staffer, 1982*.)

Still, it could not be denied that the fact of enjoying this position gave the staffer influence: '. . . you spend hours and hours in his office late at night discussing and turning the issue over with him'. (*Labor staffer, 1977*.)

where public servants had been used to their word being the last word in a minister's or a prime minister's ear prior to his making a decision, that was now altered. They found that other people were looking at the advice they gave, and the last word came from the staff rather than . . . from them. Of course it is very important to have the last word, because that last word isn't open to rebuttal . . . That's always the danger of privileged positions of access in our sort of system where issues are not fully publicly debated before decisions are taken.
    (*Labor staffer, 1970s, interviewed 1982*.)

Dealing with the Public Service

By and large, advisers did not see themselves as competing with the public service for the 'last word'. They could capitalize on their relative advantage to ensure good relations with the public service: 'I get on well with senior public servants because I sit in the office next to the PM and know what he thinks, and they *want* to know. (*Labor prime ministerial PPS.*) But they were well aware, too, of their relative limitations: 'There are only a handful of us here and there are thousands in the department — how could we possibly compete given that paucity of numbers?' (*Labor staffer, 1983.*) Rather than acting as generators of alternative ideas, staffers played a role in assisting ministerial evaluation of the departmental submissions:

When the department makes its pitch, I am usually there with one of the private secretaries. Afterwards we evaluate the advice, or even while it's being given we can question the departmental officers. Then we can give an opinion, or help if the minister has any questions. It's opinion rather than advice. We are part of the policy consultation process *before* the decision, but . . . the decision is always his.   (*Labor staffer, 1983.*)

We look initially at departmental briefs, submissions, and correspondence, and determine their adequacy . . . in terms of the party platform, our minister's preferences, and their consistency with decisions elsewhere in the ministry.   (*Labor staffer, 1983.*)

In this office, nothing is seen by the minister until it is seen and commented upon by one of the private secretaries. The purpose of these comments should be to assist, or short-circuit, or simplify his consideration without pre-empting his decision. We make some assessment about whether materials coming through are right, or good enough. If necessary you might jot down on paper the steps that would have to be taken to reach a decision . . . There is an assumption that we know his likely reactions and can anticipate what sort of comments would be helpful. That sort of vetting is essential in a big portfolio, and it spreads the decision-making burden.   (*Labor staffer, 1983.*)

Sometimes, in the course of such vetting, the advisers will intervene with the department to change the nature of its product:

If a brief ignores something of major importance or contains something we've already rejected, there are three things you can do: one, show it to the minister as is; two, send it to the minister with a covering note; or, three, ring the department and point out the problem and ask if they want to change it. Usually they will, and in the process they save face, you end up with a better product, and you've had an impact.

(*Labor staffer, 1983.*)

Sometimes I would ring the department and say 'Look, I've got your paper, and if you want me to put it to the PM I will, but I think a, b, c, d, e, f, and g, what do you reckon?' And they would normally say, 'Well . . . we hadn't taken that into account. Send it back to us and we'll have a look at those things and re-do them'. The PM wouldn't even be aware of that. That would be something that I would be doing . . . extrapolating from what I knew his views were, and my own knowledge of the bureaucracy . . . I wasn't out to get credit for it — that was that.

(Labour prime ministerial PPS, 1970s.)

In such interrelations between the private offices and the department, some individuals assume a special role because of particular gifts or knowledge:

C is a fixer . . . he knows everybody in the Commonwealth Public Service of any significance. He knows precisely what their functions are, and who to talk to about particular problems, and how to get them to move — and that was basically what he was doing for [the PM].

(Labor staffer, 1970s, interviewed 1982.)

None of the activities canvassed above involve a particular policy input from the staff end, but all affect the product of the public service. When advisers *did* have specific policy options in mind, they sought to have them elaborated by the public service rather than pushing them as alternatives.

If different policy lines are to be achieved the emphasis must be on the right questions being asked. As a means of influence, this shouldn't be underestimated. Departments *can* be swung to looking at issues in a different way, for instance by questioning the adequacy of their brief. If they can't sustain their argument, the minister won't be able to sustain it in cabinet. In all this, gentle prodding and questioning is important.

(Labor staffer, 1983.)

A great deal of the work done by the Prime Minister's Office was that decided on by the office. It would give priority to the issues it believed to be important, and then work out positions on those issues, and present the arguments on those issues to the prime minister . . . It might sometimes lead to advice at odds with the trends of departmental advice, but on the whole we tried to get the public service departments to do the work for us. We would try to stimulate them to work along certain lines . . . we would call for inputs from departments on certain matters.

An advantage that this Prime Minister's Office has had that was not shared by the Labor Government's Priorities Review Staff . . . is that the Prime Minister's Office is strategically placed to make the best use of the expertise available in the public service.

(Liberal prime ministerial adviser, 1981.)

Our job is to keep asking questions — there's no way we have the resources to duplicate or to put up fully orchestrated alternatives to what the department provides. We're in the business of poking sticks into the ants' nest.   *(Labor prime ministerial adviser, 1983.)*

In recent years, it has only been in extreme circumstances that advisers have taken more antagonistic or interventionist roles with respect to the public service: but then the role taken may be crucial, as these instances attest.

They can be incredibly lax. Once we had a case of the department defending a submission from our questioning on the grounds that it was in accordance with 'policy' — but it was the previous government's policy!   *(Labor staffer, 1983.)*

There are no first-rate people in this department. It is one that people move through on the way to somewhere else. There are some high-flyers, but they are often young and brash . . . We have to serve as a check on their incompetence, which means carefully vetting what they do. For instance, recently we had a briefing note on a politically sensitive matter where all the statistical figures cited were wrong, as a check with ABS figures showed. So we simply have to do the work.

(Labor staffer, 1983.)

I worked with the minister in opposition, and we have a long and close personal relationship. I understand his interests.

This portfolio is different from the one he had a shadow minister — neither of us have any background [in this area]. This department has also taken on new areas because of decisions made when the ALP came to power. Nobody is quite sure what some of the minister's responsibilities entail. We spent a good deal of time working on this, bartering with the PM . . .

Since then we've run into massive problems in the policy area . . . This department was fundamentally a service department with a limited research and policy capacity. It had been one of those suffering cut-backs under the coalition . . . in terms of policy needs it was right down the bottom of the pecking order. It had been stacked by the Liberals with cretins.

We have found it incapable of delivering competent or sensitive material, or accurate data consistent with the minister's desires. We are constantly having to redraft and rewrite and send stuff back and bounce people. We even had to rewrite all of the budget press release material relating to this portfolio. Yesterday we simply shredded the notes provided for the minister for question time.

Because of this incapacity we are going to request a ministerial advisory unit of about ten within the department to assist in the policy function.

. . . Don't get me wrong, we made a great attempt at first not to be abrasive, and to consult, but time is limited and eventually you just can't afford that patience and good will. It didn't get the result we wanted, and in the end everything fell back on this office and on outside consultants . . . We have to serve the minister, and if we need to consult widely to get the best advice, we'll do that.

The nudging and pushing role in the initiation of policy advice is coming from here, and not from the department, and perhaps that's unique to this office — it creates a very high work load. We have to keep files here because the department locks up at 4.51 and goes home!

We even have to take a part in the mechanical aspects . . . at the moment *we* are vetting the selection and appointment of ___ appointees in the department. That must be very rare, but the minister simply doesn't trust them to act in the ___ area.

In this job, ideally you should be free to think about issues and priorities, to weigh options being presented in the light of the minister's needs, and advise on their political implications. It's a wicket-keeper role if you like. But here we bloody well have to bat and bowl as well!

(*Labor staffer.*)

Party and Electorate

Dealings with the public service involved not only debate over whether policy options sufficiently recognized government intentions, but regard for whether the bureaucracy and the minister were attentive enough to party and electorate.

We elicit feedback from the party, looking for their concerns and criticisms. It is useful that two of us (as chief advisers) are from the major States and have good party connections in those States. It is my view that we should talk to the party before putting things in place.

(*Labor staffer, 1983.*)

We were concerned with politics in that politics included relations within the party organization. We were concerned with the management of relations between the PM and . . . other institutions, and that included more or less private groups outside those institutions — pressure groups and interest groups. . . . [Then] there is the politics of simply governing in a way acceptable to the people . . . that is determined by anticipated reactions, by a conception of what the Australian people want.

(Liberal prime ministerial adviser, 1982.)

The job of the private office is to point out to the minister, if he doesn't happen to notice it himself, that if you follow *that* option, you might upset *this* important section of the community — which might be one your party depends on. *(Liberal staffer, 1982)*

Articulating Policy

Such concerns extended to consideration of what should be said and how, and advisers could contribute to outcomes by being the articulators of ideas and decisions. An earlier instance was given of a Labor adviser who drafted the key policy document in a specific area during a campaign, and travelled with the relevant minister 'putting . . . words into his mouth'. An adviser from elsewhere gives particular focus to this:

I began by helping my candidate to put his own thoughts into words, but after a few months it became impossible to tell which ideas were his and which were mine. An extraordinary interdependence developed . . . Eventually he came to view me as a reliable extension of his own personality. By the end of the campaign, I had been given the authority to issue statements in his name . . . even if he had never seen the material . . .[20]

Whitlam's speech writers, though insisting that the operative ideas were his, attested to a related symbiosis:

[He] depended on a very close, on-going relationship with the people who were writing speeches for him . . . Because you're living with the bloke from day to day, you know what he wants to say . . . you don't really have to sit down with him for an hour . . . you know what he's going to talk about, and you do it . . . you write it.

(Graham Freudenberg, interviewed 20 July, 1977.)

In such circumstances, Graham Freudenberg became recognized as, and expressed his own gratification in being, 'one of the chief articulators of the cause'. In the Fraser period, David Kemp and Owen Harries in particular were seen as specially significant in giving form and substance first to philosophy, then to policy.[21]

In the area of communication, press officers were as important as speech writers:

[We were concerned with] . . . handling media inquiries, briefing journalists, advising the prime minister on how the media was receiving government positions, suggesting courses of action to him, warning him of events as they were developing, letting him know what was happening in the building. The press gallery was a channel of communication for him between opposition and government . . . an important method of learning what the opposition was up to was via the press, (and vice versa) . . . We'd also run back and forwards between ministers' offices, so one heard things. You're in a position to judge the temper of the times, events that are running, like a meteorological office or weather bureau. You told the prime minister what was going on, you told the prime minister what you thought — how best you thought events might be handled.   (*Liberal prime ministerial press officer.*)

Here, again, what was communicated was mediated by the staffer, a professional with his finger on the pulse.[22]

Direct Influence on Government

The influence of advisers on government decision-making may be primarily indirect, though nonetheless significant for all that. Yet most staffers felt there were also finally some means of direct input.

I suppose the extreme case would be where you could actually design a policy and see it adopted.
And this was done?
Oh yes, although it's not possible to go into details here at the moment . . .   (*Liberal staffer, 1982.*)

In large measure our currency are ideas . . . A lot of the time they don't go anywhere, but we've had some successes. Some initiatives have been generated by a spark from this office. Then they're developed by the department and eventually taken through cabinet to end up as government policy.   (*Labor staffer, 1983.*)

[In Whitlam's time] there were certainly issues that would have been resolved differently without the ministerial staff . . . there were certainly foreign policy issues that would have turned out differently . . . both foreign policy and foreign aid issues. There wouldn't have been an Australian Development Assistance Agency . . . There would have been a somewhat different line in relation to our continuing involvement in South East Asia and our relations with the United States. [On the domestic front] there was the whole issue of child-care . . . the idea of having a women's adviser was mine — I chose Elizabeth Reid and was her ally in the PM's office to get a lot of our women's programmes going. You've probably heard of that tax on so-called unearned incomes referred to as the Spigelman tax . . . For better or for worse it's identified with Jim [Spigelman] . . . On economic issues . . . Nugget Coombs had a very influential position . . . in the family of advisers.

. . . I think that there were many things that in the end were different . . . but when I say that they would have been different without the intervention of ministerial staff I don't mean by that that the ministerial staff came in pushing a particular line, over-turning what the PM's decision might otherwise have been . . . Rather, what they did do was they came in with an additional set of facts and options . . . and thus provided him with the opportunity to move down those lines.

(Labor staffer 1970s, interviewed 1982.)

The technique was very much to do with extending options, as the same respondent elaborated:

my role was not so much to put forward a detailed and coherent policy proposal, but rather to sort out in my own mind what a new option that Whitlam needed to look at might be, and then to get the person or the organization who would present that option access to the prime minister. You didn't have to feel that you were every day discussing matters of high policy, because there are many ways of influencing policy and one of those is to ensure that options that might not otherwise be considered get up and get access to high-level decision-makers.

Others paid attention to the policy agenda:

influence can come about by defining governing concepts, or by defining certain areas, or by directing attention to particular values, or items on the agenda. All this determines the sort of advice coming forward. You might choose to place emphasis on a specific paper, or on a counter argument, when it comes through . . .   *(Liberal staffer, 1982.)*

On some occasions, ministerial staff play a large role in a particular area simply by stepping into a vacuum.

the ⎯⎯ treaty was very much mine. It wasn't my idea, it . . . had been
floating around for a long time. Whitlam had expressed a positive interest
in bringing it to fruition and I did provide some initiative . . . to get the
things off the ground, to push the department.

(*Labor staffer 1970s, interviewed 1982.*)

This minister likes to *start* a lot of things. He initiates lots of ideas, then
the staff may pick up some of them and run with them — this then becomes
their primary responsibility. One instance was an 'industrial democracy
project'. Our department had some people interested in this area, but
they were too theoretical, too impossibly airy-fairy. So my role became
to represent the minister in this, making it clear that he was behind it
— as he was — and mediating the airy-fairy stuff by making practical
suggestions. I was concerned to intervene, pushing pragmatic con-
siderations.   (*Labor staffer, 1983.*)

In some cases a vacuum may be created by a minister's lacking
interest in part of the area for which he is responsible, and being
happy for a staffer to 'administer' that for him: it is no coincidence
for instance that the 'Spigelman tax' originating from Whitlam's
office (see above) should fall in the area of economics, for that was
where Whitlam had little interest himself.

But a more generalized need for most ministers is for expert
knowledge, *and* for that expertise to be informed by philosophies
and assumptions congenial to the minister's politics. Certainly
most departments have such extensive resources as to be able to
claim a virtual monopoly of expert knowledge and technical
capacity in policy areas — and most staffers, as noted above,
rightly concede their inability to compete on this level. Yet a
continual theme of this discussion has been that knowledge and
the deployment of technical capacity are not value-neutral, and
that the political executive will frequently experience the values
of their departments as inimical to their own. Thus, for instance,
an economic adviser to a Labor government remarked:

the fault with Treasury is not to do with its competence or expertise, but
that the people within it work on certain unprovable assumptions about
the real world, and are very doctrinaire about them. If you operate on
different assumptions, you can simply never see eye to eye.

It is this situation which may give a handful of 'Davids' on the
ministerial team the upper hand in playing the politics of expertise

against the 'Goliaths' of the bureaucracy. Instances of this are relatively easy to identify.

During the late 1970s and early 1980s, Professor Owen Harries, as adviser to Andrew Peacock as foreign minister and then to Malcolm Fraser as prime minister, was able to translate his international relations expertise into considerable influence over foreign policy and then over the direction of government generally. He was able to do this not because he was a more accomplished expert than those within the departments of Foreign Affairs and Prime Minister and Cabinet, but because he enjoyed personal relationships with both men, had strong philosophical commitments which accorded with their own, and was able to translate insights derived from that philosophy into a comprehensive policy framework.[23] To take another instance from State politics, David Hill, once a university economics tutor, then staffer to premier Neville Wran, proved adept at discovering the state of New South Wales' finances despite the resistance of Treasury and statutory authorities. Then, as a colleague remarked:

David Hill . . . was the founder of the ministerial advisory unit . . . One would say that he was the architect of the whole financial strategy, both in its pure economic aspects and its political aspects, of the Wran government for the whole of the five years prior to the last elections.

(An adviser to the premier, NSW, January 1982.)

Hill left Wran's personal staff to become executive director of the NSW State Rail Authority.

Perhaps the most striking and most publicly aired instances of such influence have surfaced in analysis of the making of federal budgets. In an earlier reference to the potential for advisers directly to influence central policy-making (see chapter 3), mention was made of the making of the 1974 budget. This was clearly a case where elements of the ALP cabinet and caucus did not see eye to eye with Treasury on philosophy or on basic assumptions,[24] and one in which Treasury finally felt that it had lost out to ministerial advisers.[25] Far from regaining its influence under the subsequent Fraser-led coalition government, Treasury had to work in concert with academic economists, Professor John Hewson and Professor John Rose in the offices of the treasurer and the prime minister, and these were credited with as much influence on economic policy as the treasury secretary, John Stone.[26] Their influence was later augmented by the addition of Professor Cliff Walsh to Fraser's staff. Commentators noted an increasing tendency on the part of prime minister Fraser and treasurer John Howard to short-circuit lengthy bureaucratic deliberation by turning to the assessments and opinions of these advisers. The extent of their influence was most extensively canvassed in discussions of the 1982 budget — from the strategy of which the Treasury, as in 1974, was careful to distance itself. In brief, the Treasury's counsel of restraint was diluted in favour of a significant expansion of the deficit, on the advice of Cliff Walsh and John Hewson with PM and C economist Ed Visbord. The events were described as 'a secret power struggle . . . [in which] a troika of advisers to prime minister Malcolm Fraser and treasurer John Howard . . . emerged as the nation's most influential economic think-tank'.[27] Treasury officials defended against, and distanced themselves from, the document by referring to it as 'Cliff Walsh's budget'.[28] Treasury secretary John Stone later launched a vitriolic attack against these 'meretricious players of the advisory stage',[29] one which, in concentrating on warning of the pits governments 'dig for themselves when short-term political expediency comes to hold sway over longer-term economic principle', did nothing to dispel the implication that Treasury advice had been disregarded and that private office advisers were indeed the architects of the budget. Cliff Walsh himself addressed these issues in the following year in speaking of Treasury's antagonism to the advisers, describing Stone's outburst as a reaction to his department's loss of some power and influence, and asserting that while bureaucrats will remain the repository of information 'advisory staff will very much have the role of educating the bureaucrats . . . to the direction that the government wants to go in'.[30]

Ironically, John Stone was able to play on the complexity of the economic problems left by the L-NP coalition (including the then unrevealed blowout of the budget deficit) to assert his indispensibility to the incoming ALP administration in 1983, although many had expected that he would be replaced immediately. At first there was little evidence of conflict with the incoming government, even though prime minister Bob Hawke and treasurer Paul Keating appointed their own counterparts to Walsh and Hewson in economic advisors Ross Garnaut and Barry Hughes.

The accord stayed in place through the 1983 budget (though a former colleague of Ross Garnaut's, who had worked as an adviser to the New Guinea government at the same time as him, argued that Garnaut's influence was evident in many of Hawke's economic pronouncements). By mid-1984, however, there were reports that Stone was being frozen out by Keating.[31] At last, only six days before the 1984 budget, Stone resigned in what was widely interpreted as an expression of disenchantment with Labor's economic policies.[32] The impression was confirmed in several later lectures in which Stone took the opportunity of castigating recent governments of both persuasions for their economic failure and wrong-headed approach to policy — a tack which substantiated the diminution of traditional departmental influence.[33]

In the light of these examples, it can be seen why personal advisers frequently feel that:

Being a senior adviser to a minister, one can have considerably more influence than, say, an opposition member, more even than a government member, perhaps even more than other cabinet ministers on the particular issues you're charged with. (*Labor staffer, 1983*.)

Most, however, remain sensibly aware that they cannot play an independent role, and that they are the creatures of their ministers.

Our policy role is not independent of the department but complementary to it. We're not always trying to second guess them. In fact about 90 per cent of issues could be left to them. But there are 10 per cent of issues that are of vital political importance . . . on these sorts of issues, it's the minister who sets the parameters. (*Labor staffer, 1983*.)

Limitations
Finally, it is worth pausing to note the limitations advisers felt to be inherent in their work. It was remarked earlier that advisers may experience the transition to power as a loss of their place in the sun, and some respondents elaborated on this: 'I went with the portfolio . . . I wrote the policy, and now I have to watch it being administered by incompetents.' (*Labor staffer, 1983*.) 'I worked for seven years to develop genuinely alternative policies, only to see it all slip away once we got into government'. (*Labor*

staffer, 1983.) Another constraint noted was that efficacy in the role may depend less on prior knowledge and skills than on institutional acculturation:

In the end I realised that you don't bring much in. The knowledge that is important is developed within the system . . . I was often sitting in meetings with senior public servants thinking 'I wish I knew what is in your head'.   (*Labor staffer, 1974, 1983, interviewed 1983.*)

It was felt that engaging in deliberations near their endpoint frequently limited opportunities:

Our chief constraint is that things get to the office at a fairly late stage. A lot of the little steps have been taken, and things are already lined up. They have an established momentum which is very hard to go against.
                                                              (*Labor staffer, 1983.*)

In any case, the pressure of events often militated against calm reflection, or a systematic approach to work:

we don't do any solid background work any more. What we do do is hurried and doesn't have the depth I'd like . . . But when do you have time to sit down, have a drink, thrash things out? That's how you did it before getting into government. The minister expects us to come up with alternative advice, but we're not in a position to . . . We don't have time to develop independent access to information so the data from the department goes unquestioned. I still get journals and papers but I don't have time to read them — they used to be a main source of ammunition against the previous government, but now I don't have time to find that ammunition as a check against the department.   (*Labor staffer, 1983.*)

[You had] . . . a bunch of people flat out doing things, writing speeches, coping with the media, drafting press releases, organizing overseas trips, running messages, and finding out things — and all of them putting forward policy suggestions to the limit of their ability . . . the continual attempts to . . . get a system going never actually worked . . . they got caught up in administrative details. The people had the pressure on them to perform specific tasks.   (*Liberal staffer, 1982.*)

the minister's office is the cement between the whole lot of elements . . . the party, the government, the [party] philosophy, the ministry, the bureaucracy, and the wishes of the country . . . The minister's staff can't do any one job as well as any one of these elements, but the office *has* to be the interface between all of them.   (*Labor staffer, 1983.*)

Most staffers were sensibly aware of the limits entailed in working through another, that is, in being minders:

We don't make our suggestions just on the basis of the minister's ideas — I've been in the policy area for ten years, and of course you draw on your experience. But I'm only an agent of the minister and I draw my legitimacy from him — it would be fatuous to take a higher profile.
(*Labor staffer, 1983.*)

Finally, the initiative belongs in the politician's court, no matter how distinguished the adviser. H. C. Coombs, a figure of national stature, and identified by a staffer above as one of the most significant influences in Whitlam's 'official family', has said:

[Whitlam] always made it clear that I could talk to him, or write to him about things, but it would be silly to pretend that there weren't quite substantial periods of time when he wasn't taking any notice of the advice that I was giving.   (*H. C. Coombs, interview, Canberra, 25 July 1977.*)

In the end, this may be the most debilitating constraint of all — to be the minder rather than the mandarin or the minister:

You're always drafting letters for someone else to sign, thinking about their reactions to a problem or a situation before you think about your own . . . always putting yourself into the background and promoting them. Eventually you think, 'Oh bugger it, it's time I was promoting myself instead of somebody else' . . . You'd spend a fair bit of time sitting outside the doors where meetings were going on inside . . . So there you are, in your support role . . . you are just a bit . . . excluded from some of the discussions, and you feel that you want to be in there . . . doing you own things and signing your own name to all that you write . . .   (*Liberal staffer, 1983.*)

Policy Deliberations as a Group Enterprise

Looking back across the work experience detailed above, it is evident that despite the fact that advisers can finally identify cases of (and hence opportunities for) direct influence, most of their work is far more indeterminate in its effects than that. It is apposite to conclude this chapter by remarking that the attempt to locate a benchmark by seeking to trace the influence of individuals is a somewhat artificial quest. Certainly a case can be made in such terms in a few instances, but the complexity of the policy process must be conceded and it should be noted that the adviser is, for the most part, a bit-player in a group enterprise.

Consider the question of how something becomes an issue on which governments must make a policy decision, and the process by which decisions are made and implemented.

A great deal of the work of any government is routine work generated by the structure of the system all parties accept: it is the work of management where there seems little room to move. Even in matters where political choice seems most pertinent, such as in the framing of budgets, there may be severe constraints. A government which contemplated far reaching redistributive measures, for instance, might find that the very mention of such policies precipitated the redirection of investment away from the country — severely affecting the economy and the government's ability to pursue its objectives — as investors sought tax havens elsewhere. Conversely, a government seeking to foster 'free enterprise' by reducing the scope of government activity might find itself unpopular because the level of accepted demands on the state — not only on welfare issues, but also on impeccably conservative matters like defence — make it politically impossible to cut back the public sector or the level of state intervention. At best, policy-makers play in a limited field where even the grandiose claims of a platform, let alone the work of individuals, may have a limited bite.

How are issues where government choice does seem necessary and feasible identified? In broad terms, they may be suggested by party philosophy, articulated in party platforms. They may be raised by the bureaucracy as matters of administrative necessity. They may be thrust on decision-makers by pressure group demand. They may originate from a party or even a parliamentary policy committee. They may be created by governments wishing to sell some 'goody' to a restive electorate. They may arise from campaign promises. They may be a sop to a disruptive faction within the party. In many cases, there may be competing demands about a particular issue from a variety of such sources.

Given that an issue, with its train of attendant demands, reaches the policy agenda, how is a decision reached?

For the moment, it suffices to identify participants. Wherever the policy demand originates, the matter will first be taken up by the relevant minister who will ask his/her department to put forward options. The minister's personal staff may facilitate this work by consulting with, even directing, aspects of department work. They may seek to raise alternative options by canvassing extra-departmental advice. They may have the last word, or raise the last questions, when the minister considers the department's briefing or submission. Throughout, the minister, or his/her department, or an adviser, may choose to champion particular options. Whatever decision is thus reached will be taken forward to cabinet in the minister's name. There it will be debated anew and may have to jockey with competing demands for limited resources. At the least, it will be subject to analysis by those with differing views of the political imperatives facing the government. The decision might be rejected, amended, or transformed in cabinet. It might then be subject to pressure or criticism in the party room. When all this is done, it will be the subject of legislative drafting, in which process it might be subtly altered again to accord with such abstract notions as established practice. Legislative measures may be altered further as the result of parliamentary debate, senate opposition, or public reaction to what is proposed. At the last stage, when legislation has been passed, it will go back to the public service for implementation which may or may not fully honour the intentions motivating the legislation — if these are any longer clear.

The complexity of this train of events indicates how difficult it is to equate intentions with outcomes, or to trace the contribution of particular individuals to the process, whether minister, party member, public servant, personal adviser, pressure group spokesperson, or whatever.[34] The contribution of individuals is particularly difficult to trace because deliberations are largely filtered through a group process. The modern political executive is best seen not as an individual in a particular role, but as the core of a small work group.[35] Each minister has his/her retinue, and the operation of the private office can thus be thought of in terms of group dynamics as much as in terms of the performance of the minister. Indeed, the operations of the ministry at large might be thought of in terms of the interaction of these minister-centred work groups, as much as in relation to interaction between individuals in cabinet.

What does this mean in practical terms? Consider again the process of formulating recommendations in response to events demanding a policy decision. Formally, the task falls to a particular minister. Suppose the minister has in turn asked for a response from his/her department. He/she has forwarded a series of questions to them, some of these have been suggested by an adviser. Meanwhile, the adviser — who has been asked to act as the minister's devil on this issue — has started canvassing opinion on options from his/her contacts in the party and from academics expert in the area. Before any departmental brief arrives, the adviser is telephoned by a departmental officer, who asks his/her opinion on whether the minister will accept several options. Of these the adviser reminds the departmental officer that 'a' is at odds with party policy, and that 'b' conflicts with the minister's own constituency interests — the departmental officer agrees to review them and to elaborate others. When the departmental submission arrives, the adviser reads it and adds some commentary, pointing out matters of party interest, and areas where (on the advice of his/her contacts) other options might be pursued. Worried about options which have still been overlooked, the adviser discusses the matter with a colleague, and they arrange a meeting for the minister with spokespersons for the group potentially most affected by the policy. The minister then calls in his/her departmental officers, and with the advisers present, discusses the submission with them. The departmental officers argue — persuasively in the minister's view — that some of the suggestions raised by the minister's staff would be difficult to implement, but accept the virtue of other suggestions. Afterwards the minister's advisers make some comments on the departmental officers' presentation. That night, the minister calls a trusted colleague in his/her home State, then chats to a minister in a related field, before going back to the office to discuss the issue with his/her senior private secretary (not the adviser who had 'devilled' on this issue). Out of this a decision emerges which will be taken to cabinet. The process it will go through thereafter has been touched on above.

This hypothesized scenario is perhaps oversimplified — it will be extended in a moment — but even at this level it can be seen that the eventual decision, though influenced by all participants, could not with confidence be said to be crucially dependent on any one of them. The minister charged with carriage of the decision (perhaps at the same time as being tied up with a knotty party battle), as usual has not had time to become acquainted with all relevant discussion. He/she has relied on the staff. The adviser briefed to act is probably not expert in the area but will have general notions of the minister's interests, and perhaps holds strong personal opinions. The bulk of detailed work is done by the department which has a record of what has worked in the past and what it thinks feasible to implement now. The party, expert, and interest group opinions mobilized by the adviser may modify the minister's view of the departmental submission. Further transformation is suggested here by the comments of the State activist (whom the minister takes to be in touch with the 'grass roots') and the other minister, who is likely to draw attention to parallel work in his/her own department. But things only become sufficiently clear for decision after discussion with the senior private secretary, whose knack of being an effective sounding board depends on a close personal relationship with the minister.

The scenario suggested here may oversimplify by accepting that the group's ostensible object — a particular decision as solution to a specific problem or demand — directs its agenda. In fact there are always other pressures on the ministerial policy group — it is embattled from without (its contest with the opposition) and from within (rivals in the party seeking the minister's job) — and these may impel a tacit agenda dictated by survival. The tacit agenda, therefore, may have to do with maintaining the group (which is particularly important for the adviser who depends solely on the group, and on patronage within it). The usual tactics are those of avoiding fragmentation by suppressing internal dissidence, accentuating the leader, and stereotyping 'bad' opponents — all factors which inhibit objective appraisal of alternatives to do with a specific matter, and induce what Janis has called 'groupthink':

a mode of thinking that people engage in when they are deeply involved in a cohesive in-group, when the members' strivings for unanimity override their motivation to realistically appraise alternative courses of action . . . Groupthink refers to a deterioration of mental efficiency, reality testing, and moral judgement that results from in-group pressures.[36]

To establish the existence of such a process in a scenario like that sketched above, one would need to trace the detail, seeking evidence for the hypothesis that concurrence-seeking had replaced reality-based estimates of the efficacy and morality of policy options being considered.[37] For instance, one might find traces in the ministerial group's giving public servants a *particularly* hard time, since they have another institutional base and can afford to differ, or in an adviser taking strenuous steps to 'protect the group from adverse information that might shatter their shared complacency about the effectiveness and morality of their decisions'. Advisers, who by necessity are so much the minister's creature, can be assumed to be particularly prone to adopt this role: the role in Janis's terms of 'mindguard'.

The scenario can be read in other ways to suggest other levels of analysis and tacit agendas. Consider again the characteristics of the key participants, politicians, bureaucrats, and advisers. In institutional terms, the politicians and the bureaucrats are central, and their general characteristics well known:

The bureaucrats are slightly older and have sat around similar tables for many more years than the politicians, almost all of whom have had careers outside national government . . . The bureaucrats have risen to the top through a rather closed world where long apprenticeship, prudent judgement, technical expertise, and ability to get things done inside a complex organization are greatly valued. The politician lives in a world where 'selectorates' are more diverse, competition makes the job riskier, and the ability to appeal to outside interests and to articulate broader ideals is the key to success. The bureaucrats are steady endurance runners, whereas the politicians are flashier sprinters, and the two groups have followed different training routines . . . the bureaucrats are likely to be better informed when the conversation turns to technical matters, although the politicians may be quite eloquent on matters of principle.[38]

In contemporary politics, both politicians and bureaucrats are likely to be relatively highly educated but the bureaucrat is likely to have had more formal education.[39] Each will be subject to different institutional imperatives. The bureaucrat probably thinks in the long term and feels the pressure of precedent and continuity, his/her department's accepted practices and shared assumptions outweigh innovation in the bureaucrat's view of what is 'responsible'. The bureaucrat may also be concerned with consolidating an empire (and his/her place within it) that has a longer span than the government of the moment. The politician, in contrast, is a partisan and an advocate, seeking not the technically appropriate solution so much as the one which will 'sell'. The particular policy may be of less importance than the way in which it will serve as ammunition in the politician's fight to preserve his/her place (or gain promotion) in the ministry, to foster the influence of his/her faction, and to keep his/her party in power. In short, though the group comes together to consider a specific policy matter, again it might be argued that the ostensible agenda is complicated by the tacit agendas which influence the participants. Each participant will have some awareness of the other's tacit agenda, but on occasion the bureaucrat may refuse to concede that the politician's tacit agenda accords with 'responsible' policy, while the politician may interpret the bureaucrat's tacit agenda as resistance to his political will. (Both of the battles over budget-making described earlier might be so interpreted.)

How does the adviser stand in this context? The adviser will also be highly educated — at least as much as the bureaucrat, probably more so than the politician. In general, the staffer will be a decade younger than either the politician or bureaucrat.[40] Given the adviser's training he/she will be likely to share with the bureaucrat some appreciation for appropriate technical solutions: as a fellow member of the intelligentsia the adviser will share a common language with the bureaucrat. But as a politically committed activist the adviser will share the politician's commitment to broad principle and ideology. The adviser, too, is a partisan and an advocate. He/she has a high view of the importance of policy, and his/her own potential influence on deliberations. The adviser's own ambitions will be tied up with a particular view of the country and its government, but if he/she has a tacit agenda it must inevitably consist of being alert for what best serves the minister's interests, and this will always override the policy aims. In ways that may significantly affect his/her performance in the group, the adviser may be the most ambivalent member of the inner circle, as can be seen by a review of how the adviser came to be appointed.

After all, the adviser is a politician *manqué*, consumed with a vision of how things should be, but for some reason the adviser has given up the struggle to take up the cause in the public arena in his/her own right. The adviser is, therefore, as was suggested at the end of the last chapter, a person with a project, ever alert for projects which intersect with his/her own.[41] The adviser can only achieve by attaching his/her spoke to a bigger wheel: the politician offers this opportunity. In taking the opportunity the adviser is constrained to join a team, yet the politically engaged intellectual is ambivalent about group life, as attested by the protestations noted in chapter 5 ('I am . . . an individual person contributing a particular viewpoint'; the leader's/the party's views coincide with *mine*), and the tendency for private office staff in general to spend significant amounts of time working alone. Indeed, there is evidence in my study of all three of the private offices of Whitlam, Fraser, and Hawke, that strenuous efforts to organize general group sessions as *routine* tend to fail in the face of the penchant of the minders to work alone except in so far as they each work *to* the leader. (One of Whitlam's principal private secretaries spoke of trying to organize 'a group of prima donnas working for a prima donna'.) This is a tendency that cuts across differences in leadership practice. In fact, one's strongest impression is that the minders, whatever type of leader or of ensemble they are attached to, constantly seek the recognition and response of a 'pairing' relationship[42] with the leader-as-equal (indeed, they may *take* the lead through ideas). The most gifted of the minders — I would put Peter Wilenski and David Kemp in this class — might articulate projects which would not otherwise have received definition by their nominal leaders. And Wilenski's protean career exemplifies the capacity of the engaged intellectual to achieve independence of particular leaders.

Yet in the end the significance of this ubiquitous 'pairing' is that it forces the minders to affirm the importance of the group, since it is via the group that the leader (through whom their ideas and values are expressed) is sustained. If there is a tendency to subvert routine organization, this is defused by crisis which reminds the group of the collective aim and restores the rudiments of group life. As one Whitlam aide put it: 'there's never a time when he's not under challenge . . . and that pushes you back together. You're always bound up in the machinations of who is going to be leader, and a strategy to keep him there.' The minders thus experience political imperatives that their fellow members of the intelligentsia in the bureaucracy do not, and hence they will play a distinct role in the coalition around the leader. At the same time, their sense of political imperatives will differ from that of the mainstream politicians who will also be involved in the inner circle, for where the mainstream politicians can stand on their own platforms, and move on to coalitions with new leaders without leaving the political circus, the minders can be assured of a role only while a patron survives. So in this, too, the minders' role will be distinct. Whether brought in as technicians, or experts, or generalists and ideologists, the primacy of supporting the leader will encourage the advisers to be the leader's scouts in policy-making circles, and hence may devalue their independent intellectual contributions by making them agents for enforcing consensus, which brings us again to Janis's idea of 'groupthink'. Thus did 'the best and the brightest'[43] conspire in prolonging 'America's longest war'[44]: critical intelligence *was* suppressed in the interests of maintaining group unity in the service of the leader. Nonetheless, there can be a positive role for minders in the groups where major political and bureaucratic institutions intersect. They can be the mediators — able to stand back from 'combat politics' to remind the politicians of the importance of ideas and values, and trained to scan the discourse of bureaucrats (intellectuals share a common language) in terms of the *political* will of their patrons. Success may depend on the strength of their own sense of mission, the extent to which their idealized project avoids submersion in the leader's programme.

There is much yet to be said about the group dynamics of inner circles in Australian government. The speculative sketches above provoke more questions than answers: they are certainly only a beginning to the task. However, these are questions that can only be approached through detailed study of particular instances of policy-making based on honest first-hand accounts by the participants. Elsewhere it has proved possible to map the course of policy evolution through tapping participants, as George Herring's fine study of decisions and decision-makers in relation to the Vietnam war attests.[45] Yet the secrecy of decision-making in Australia imposes a considerable burden on researchers who wish to obtain detailed information from bureaucrats, politicians, and advisers. Without that information, it is not possible to expand the rather general picture offered here, or to bring into play the battery of theoretical tools[46] which would give a more precise understanding of group dynamics at the top of government. For the purposes of this book, and for the moment, it is sufficient that on the evidence above the personal adviser plays a significant part in the inner circle and demands as much attention as the other participants.

Illustrative Biographies

It was emphasized in earlier biographies and in chapter 6 that individual staffers will not work across the full range, and that the dynamics of the private office are best understood in terms of the group life of the inner circle, including all participants. Individual biographies therefore have their limitations. Nonetheless, lacking the materials for a detailed case study of a particular ministerial group (for reasons suggested in chapter 1), it may help here to illuminate the argument by reference to the reciprocal relationship between one adviser, working in a particular field, and his principal. That is, this is an attempt at a brief essay on the intersecting biographies of a politician and a minder.[1] I shall take as my object the *pas de deux* between Gough Whitlam and his speech writer, confidante and special adviser, Graham Freudenberg.

The Whitlam/Freudenberg collaboration

Gough Whitlam, ALP leader 1967–77, and prime minister 1972–75, was one of the most forceful, in some respects the most successful, and certainly the most controversial of Australian Labor leaders.[2] Born in 1911 in Melbourne into the family of a career civil servant (his father was to become Commonwealth crown solicitor), carefully nurtured by a mother intensely interested in his welfare, seven years older than his nearest sibling, he was encouraged to develop a supreme self-confidence and belief in his uniqueness and potential. In consequence, however, he was also the archetypal adult civilized child — slightly aloof from his peers, not fully understanding their interests, uneasy in personal relationships. He was educated mainly at private schools, and at St Paul's College, University of Sydney, where he took arts and law degrees. Throughout, his drive and intellectual facility were evident. It was said that his father's concern for civic responsibility and social justice oriented him towards Labor politics. There was never any doubt that he aimed for centre stage.

After war service, and a brief career as a barrister, Whitlam joined the ALP, and ran for both shire council and State office before gaining pre-selection for the safe federal Labor seat of Werriwa which he won at a by-election in 1952. In parliament, he stood somewhat apart from his fellows, but through ability and sheer hard work won the attention and support of powerful patrons who facilitated his rise in the party. In 1960, at the age of forty-three, he was elected the youngest ever deputy leader of the parliamentary Labor Party and soon signalled that he planned to take the top job from ageing leader, Arthur Calwell. His vaulting ambition in fact created impediments, and may have induced Calwell to hang on as leader, but in 1967 he achieved his ambition.

The Labor Party had been in opposition for nearly two decades when Whitlam took over. He proved a brilliant opposition leader — articulate, energetic, intelligent and well-prepared, he confronted the factional battles that plagued the party, steamrollered opposition, and inspired wholesale policy reform. In parliament, he quizzed, hectored, and simply outperformed the flagging leaders of the conservative coalition.

Underlying his success were these characteristics: he was a man of forceful intellect who lacked any trace of self-doubt, demonstrated a strong urge to be in control, was intolerant of constraint, and found great zest in exhibitionistic display. These characteristics encouraged in him a confrontational style of politics in which Whitlam, always convinced of the 'right' course, repeatedly gambled for all or nothing and consistently won against opponents more consciously divided than he. He once described this himself in a now famous sentence: 'When you're faced with an impasse, you've got to crash through or crash'. What brought an added edge to his performance and made him a man of charismatic appeal, was that allied with great ability and his own complete confidence in that ability was a patent enjoyment of his role, a zest in the exercise of power, which was unusual on the Australian scene. When riding high, he induced a level of optimism and high expectations rare in the Australian electorate.

Such was the style that brought him to power in 1972, the first Labor prime minister in twenty-three years. The electorate was to learn that the qualities so effective and inspiring in an opposition leader, so crucial to the reform of the ALP, could have serious drawbacks in a prime minister. Whitlam's mode of operation, his impatience with consolidation, intolerance of the constraints imposed by negotiation with others (indeed, lack of empathy with others), and real inability to discern when the tide was running against him, finally led to an impasse in 1975 where the option of 'crashing through' was simply denied him, and he was defeated.

Perhaps Whitlam's most valuable capacity was to inspire others who saw in his grand vision a blueprint through which they could put their own smaller projects into effect. This was enhanced by Whitlam's lack of interest in the consolidation of initiatives: he was prepared to leave practical details and their development to others, whilst he was always rushing on to the next great imperative. As an outcome, one of the features of Whitlam's career was the frequency with which he paired up with important allies to achieve significant ends. Hence, his early election to the deputy party leadership owed much to the work of an older party ally, Lance Barnard; his reform of the party depended heavily on the groundwork of the then party federal secretary, Cyril Wyndham, and the activity of wily political operators like Clyde Cameron; his generation of policy owed virtually all to outside advisers (programme professionals) who could only have been utilized effectively through the legwork of loyal personal staff like Race Mathews (see this chapter); his reform of the public service was both planned and implemented by his first prime ministerial principal private secretary, Peter Wilenski; even his domination of the sphere he regarded as his own, the House of Representatives, owed much to the astute manager of government business in the House, Fred Daly. And one of the most significant of these 'pairing' relationships,[3] since it was integral to his success as a performer, was with his long-time speech writer, Graham Freudenberg.

Graham Freudenberg was born into a politically conservative

middle-class family in Brisbane in 1934. He was educated at Brisbane Church of England Grammar School, and appears to have been (like others in this sample) a somewhat marginal and bookish child. He, too, was one of those who found inspiration (and direction toward a life course) in reading:

> on the 11th of April 1943 . . . I got chickenpox . . . so I had to stay home from school. And among my father's books . . . there was that little paperback edition of Andre Maurois' *Disraeli*. So I read it, and from that moment on I knew what I wanted to be — a journalist, as he was . . . and a politician, and that of course meant prime minister. . . . I can set the exact date because I used to keep a diary and I recorded the fact the I'd read this book . . . I was nine.
> *(Interview with this author, 8 January 1982.)*

Freudenberg did embark upon a journalistic career upon leaving Brisbane Grammar. However, Brisbane, the somnolent capital of one of Australia's least developed states,[4] was an unlikely setting for an aspiring Disraeli, and Freudenberg left to pursue his career elsewhere. In the mid-1950s, like many another conservative young Australian, he took the journey to England, and happened to be in London during the Suez crisis:

> that had the same radicalizing effect on many of my generation, particularly being in England and . . . being involved in the matter . . . as Spain had had on a previous generation and Vietnam was to have on a later one. So when I came back to Australia . . . I joined the Labor Party. That is, in 1957.
> *(Interview, 1982.)*

In 1961, though then a relatively undistinguished journalist working in Melbourne, he was appointed press secretary to Labor leader Arthur Calwell. It was a step in accordance with earlier aspirations:

> I was twenty-six at the time and would certainly have been thinking in general terms of a political career . . . when I applied for and got the job as Arthur's press secretary, I would have seen it as a stepping stone to a political career.
> *(Interview, 1982.)*

However, he made two rapid discoveries, first that such jobs are not '. . . a particularly advantageous route to parliamentary politics', and second and more importantly, that he was not suited to mainstream politics:

> I wasn't cut out for public life . . . the sorts of things a member has to do I couldn't do at all, the sorts of things one had to do to get preselection . . . So I quite quickly decided that this sort of role, the backward role if you like, the advisory role, particularly with the element I injected into it myself, namely the speech-writing element, was just what I was suited for.   (*Interview, 1982.*)

The terms of this discovery have some parallels with House's decision to become a backroom operative (see biography to chapter 2). And Freudenberg's interest, too, was more in the fascination and spectacle of politics than in the cause: '. . . not that I'm suggesting for one moment that the cause isn't very important to me . . . it is . . . I'm very deeply committed . . . but the primary motive is the fascination of politics as such.' (*Interview, 1982.*) He had no interest in branch level activism, and later let his party membership lapse.

Freudenberg worked for Calwell until 1966. But he had early fallen under Whitlam's spell: 'There's no time since I've known him, going back to 1961, that I haven't regarded him as automatic leader of the Labor Party'. (*Interview with this author, 20 July 1977.*) Given Freudenberg's predilections, it was not surprising that he saw his own future attached to the coming man: 'it had always been assumed that in the normal course of events he would come to the leadership and that I would continue as press secretary'. (*Interview, 1977.*) In February 1966, at a time when the ALP federal executive was threatening to expel Whitlam from the party because he chose to differ publicly with its views on state aid to private schools, Freudenberg resigned his position with Calwell in protest and went back to a newspaper job. A year later, when Whitlam was elected leader, he asked Freudenberg to come back. Freudenberg was appointed Whitlam's press secretary on the day Whitlam assumed the leadership, 8 February 1967, and remained at 'the leader's'[5] side until Whitlam's resignation after a second crushing electoral defeat in 1977 (following the anti-Labor landslide of 1975).

Freudenberg did maintain a role in press relations, and as an adviser. He was perhaps more significant in the latter role before 1972 than after:[6]

He was the talker-through with Whitlam of the continuing political stream . . . In working with Gough it was important not only to share his basic political outlook, but also to have a feeling for those things that were important to him, like history, opera . . . Graham had that . . . [he could] get that empathetic warmth that makes the relationship work . . . it has to have dimensions over and above the political . . .

(*Race Mathews, interview, 3 January 1982.*)

But his primary role was to collaborate with Whitlam in giving voice to 'the vision'. His was the hand behind the landmark speeches of the Whitlam era, and he gives a telling anecdote concerning one of the most important of these, the 1972 ALP policy speech:

It was not so much a public meeting as an act of communion and a celebration of hope and love. Touching the author lightly on the shoulder, a curious ritual that had developed between us before major speeches on which we had collaborated, an act not of superstition but of remembrance of things past, Whitlam said, 'It's been a long road, comrade, but we're there.'[7]

There could hardly be more direct testimony to Freudenberg's part as a 'secret sharer' in Whitlam's ascent.

Whitlam was, of course, central to the collaboration:

[Whitlam] . . . depended upon a very close, on-going relationship with the people who were writing speeches for him — the sort of relationship he had with me . . . Because you're living with the bloke from day to day, you know what he wants to say. If a speech comes up, you don't really have to sit down with him for an hour and say, 'What are we going to talk about here?' — you know what he's going to talk about, and you do it . . . you write it.

. . . The early speeches and pamphlets were, of course, entirely Whitlam's. But then you look at the later ones. In terms of who put the words down, it might be entirely Freudenberg. But look at the consistency between them. The last one just depends so utterly on the first one. Whoever put down the words, there can be no question who is the true — what's the Shakespeare thing? — the 'only true begetter': Whitlam.

You look at any speech I wrote for Calwell, and compare it with any speech I wrote for Whitlam . . . there's no comparison in the quality of the ideas, the calibre of the argument . . . Clearly the only difference is Whitlam, but that difference is crucial.   (*Interview, 1977.*)

None of this, however, undercuts Freudenberg's share in the undertaking. One feels it is not entirely accidental that Freudenberg lights on the Shakespearean metaphor: if Whitlam's were the seminal ideas, it was Freudenberg's words that brought them to fruition (only a couple, after all, can 'beget' anything). Elsewhere, Freudenberg spoke of the merging of their contributions:

there's a mutual thing in this, give and take . . . I adopted his style, he adopted mine. It would be very difficult to say where one began and the other ended. He always accused me of being too dithyrambic — I had to look it up in the dictionary of course. It meant . . . I go a bit heavy on the rhetoric. He admits his own style is too desiccated, too dry, too spare and sparse. The combination wasn't bad, I think.

(*Interview, 1977.*)

Others were in no doubt concerning Freudenberg's contribution:

He was one of the best political speech writers in the world, probably as good as Sorensen with Kennedy. And because of his quality and indispensibility, he could demand concessions from Whitlam (in terms of adopting an independent work style, keeping unusual hours and so on).[8]

Indeed Freudenberg himself suggests that, despite working through others, he has become one of the principal articulators of the ALP cause: '. . . it is a tremendous satisfaction to feel, to know that one is in fact one of the principal articulators of a particular cause'. (*Interview, 1982.*)

After the events of 1975, which left Freudenberg so shattered he left the country — ('I had to go overseas, to get the country out of my system as much as anything else.' *Interview, 1977*) — Freudenberg returned to Australia to write his history of the Whitlam years[9] whilst he was on leave from Whitlam's staff. He then returned to Whitlam's office until 1977, after which he went to work for NSW ALP leader, Neville Wran. In 1983, he was, like Barron, 'borrowed' from Wran's staff by Hawke for his election campaign. After Hawke's election, Freudenberg took up a position negotiated between Wran and Hawke, where he worked as consultant and speech writer for both of them.

In Freudenberg and Whitlam we have the story of men with complementary needs, affinities, and aspirations. No modern leader, given the complex demands of office, can do everything himself — it is the minder's role (in the words of one adviser) 'to do the things the leader would do for himself if only he had time'.[10] But Whitlam was perhaps more than usually dependent upon functionaries. His was a style that in a sense was predicated on gaps, on leaving openings for loyal allies whom he assumed would come to his service and supply what he lacked. Freudenberg was one of these. He had the skills to help Whitlam articulate his vision. He also had interests and attributes which enabled him to establish an empathetic and affectionate relationship with his principal: the sort of reliable support any leader needs, as George pointed out (see chapter 6). Whitlam, in turn, provided something for Freudenberg. Freudenberg's own early aspirations to stand at the hub of events in his own right had been thwarted when he found himself lacking the capacities for public life (capacities Whitlam had in abundance). But he could through collaboration with Whitlam participate in making history. He could not only be involved in events, but also later establish a claim as keeper of the historical record.[11] More, he could become 'principal articulator of the cause'.

Analysts of significant achievement have frequently remarked on the occurrence of partnerships, pairing, or twinship in facilitating that achievement.[12] In many cases, collaboration seems to be a condition of productivity and creativity (which is to say, generativity). Whitlam and Freudenberg present such a case (though of course Whitlam had other partners at the time, and Freudenberg was later to work effectively for Wran and Hawke). In psychological terms, Freudenberg was, as it were, incorporated by Whitlam as part of a larger self, affirming the grandeur which Freudenberg himself attributed to Whitlam.[13] Thus, Whitlam's boundless self-confidence was confirmed: as long as followers like Freudenberg fed into his project, contributing 'what he would do himself if only he had the time', he never had to confront limitations to the self and its powers.[14] In turn, Freudenberg found an alter ego who mirrored the ideal qualities he had once looked for in himself but had had to abandon; his aspirations would not now have to be sacrificed but could be achieved through more indirect means. Their productive relationship was based on a simple enough form of symbiosis, but such pairing may, as Little argues, be integral to groups around leaders like Whitlam, and crucial to their success.[15] Certainly the Whitlam/Freudenberg case provides us with an instructive instance of the dovetailing of skills and needs between an adviser and a politician, and of the way both their contributions are essential to (and meld in) the results achieved.

7

The Development of the Minder's Career

To an increasing extent, modern society makes it necessary to use experts to provide the basic information essential to political decisions, as well as, in many cases, to execute these decisions. The specialized knowledge of the experts is applied, for instance, whenever civil servants provide background material for their political masters. On the other hand, it is becoming increasingly clear that politicians must also have a considerable amount of independent knowledge if they are not merely to become the tools of their own civil servants.[1]

The story of the rise of personal advisers is, at the simplest level, an elaboration of the response to two factors: modern society's demand for the services of the exponents of specialized 'knowledge', and the disjunction between the expectations of ambitious socially interventionist governments (which may be impelled by electorate demands for state action in broadening areas) and the responses of mass bureaucracies. The model of complementary exchange between institutions supposed to be concerned with policy and institutions intended to provide advice comes under strain, and the minders are called to play a part in (even, created by) the pattern of institutional change.

There are two vantage points that can be taken in interpreting the developments that have been discussed here. The first recognizes the relatively timeless element of 'court politics' in political life. The second concentrates on the particularity of institutional evolution in bourgeois parliamentarist societies.

The ubiquitous pattern of patronage and cronyism that is a sub-theme of political leadership has already been mentioned. Many pragmatic considerations can be taken to account for it, but at base there seems to be a needs relationship based on a typological distinction between the leaders and their personal advisers. Each needs the other to fulfil their ambitions. Mainstream politicians, it might be argued, specialize in adversary relations — they interpret the world in confrontational terms (or are socialized by political life to do so).[2] It may be that they are drawn into it by a special urge to combine knowledge with idealism[3] or to stand at the hub of events,[4] but once arrived there is little opportunity for them to stand aside and think in terms of principle or philosophy rather than conflict. There are others, however, also moved by a strong urge to be at the centre of events, but who find some impediment in 'combat politics', and so seek an alternate route to the inner circle by service to the leader. These can never stand first in their own right, but on the other hand they are freed to stand aside from the daily conflict, to think in abstract terms, to consider the long term, to reinject ideals.[5] Thus exists the psychological (and role) differentiation between the politicians and their minders, and the affinity between them.

These distinctions between mainstream politicians and their advisers can be elaborated. It has come to seem to me that three of the central characteristics of those undertaking *any* political work are a preoccupation with aggression and conflict, a propensity for constantly reworking the attachment/autonomy dilemma which confronts us all, and an exaggerated desire to be 'in the know'.

To amplify some of the observations in chapter 5: where politicians specialize in confrontation, advisers choose a role which avoids the public display of aggression. The backroom role avoids open conflict, and establishes a distance between decisions (formally taken by another) and their consequences (which must be accepted as the responsibility of the politician). Arguably, therefore, the choice of a backroom role indicates some difficulty in coping with aggression, and a hesitance to live with the consequences of actions. Both predilections could be rooted in the predicament of the 'adult civilized' child, who remains aloof from peers but inevitably finds some barriers in relation to the adults towards whom he is oriented. Such a situation is conducive of frustration and rage, but how can this be expressed without further endangering the child's marginal status? Thus may be born intellectualizing defences against rage[6] and an enduring difficulty with the playing out of aggression. In so far as these tendencies relate to assertiveness, they have ramifications for the achievement of autonomy.

The dilemma we all face is that we are interdependent social beings, socialized into pushing for autonomy. Dependence on social others cannot be overcome, without sustained work on the distinction between 'self' and 'other' the notion of 'self' could not be achieved, indeed would be meaningless. Politics brings the dilemma into sharp resolution, as ambitious individuals give up the autonomy of acting alone in favour of collective action in pursuit of their ambitions. But the central problem of attachment or separateness apparently continues to have resonance for political work. For the backbenchers I surveyed in an earlier monograph, for instance, the vehicle for progress was the party (attachment), but these people had formerly led lives of independent achievement (education, career advancement, upward mobility) and in some senses showed a strong drive for separateness through politics: they demanded, for instance, to be recognized as leaders (outstanding figures) in their communities, and it was evident that many expected to progress in the parliamentary sphere simply through the recognition by others of their personal qualities.[7] In contrast, advisers have been seen to be not necessarily party socialized, not necessarily personifications of the party consensus, and so they seem to preserve intellectual autonomy without such strident display. Yet they are constrained by dependence on a minister, forced to join their ambitions to a greater enterprise, and they are heavily reliant upon the whim and patronage of their minister. They find themselves replaying the early life scenario of dependence versus autonomy as they pursue their ambitions in an 'official family'.

The sense of knowing what is going on, being 'at the centre', was for many of the backbenchers I spoke to at least as important as the power to shape those events, as I have argued elsewhere.[8] The politician wants 'the whole pulsing life of the nation . . . brought to a focus under his eyes and within his touch'.[9] Advisers share this ambition. While their raison d'être lies in their dealings in information and knowledge, they too frequently testify to the push to be 'at the centre', for instance: 'I wanted to work for Whitlam because that was where the action was. He was clearly the prime mover in the party, and in the government'.

To an extent, advisers and backbenchers are playing minor variations on the central matters of autonomy and knowledge. But a pivotal contrast emerges in their dealings with aggression, and this casts them in differing — though complementary — roles. Yet these speculations must be qualified by the realization that backbenchers and advisers necessarily develop different attributes for success. The backbencher must display the attributes of the 'party man' and develop the habits of orthodoxy, while the adviser is more dependent upon displaying expertise, or at least clarifying and putting the other's 'thoughts into words'. The adviser's work is that of intellectualization, much more than is that of the politician.

This book has shown the pattern as it has emerged in modern western societies: it is a story predicated on the sociology of knowledge and the central place of the intelligentsia in contemporary institutions. When knowledge became a matter not of what was 'given' but of what could be discovered — that is, with the fragmentation of traditional society — the intellectual and the expert emerged. At the same time, as power became not a matter of divine ordinance but of contest and debate, the demand for ideas and intellectual legitimation drew the intellectual into the political orbit. There has long been discussion about whether command of knowledge and articulation thus makes intellectuals a 'new class' who will dominate modern politics.[10] This book has examined briefly the practical impediments that will prevent that situation. The intellectual who enters politics proper will be caught up in the battle for power, and the critical qualities of intellect will be diluted in the battle for survival.[11] The intellectual who enters the bureaucracy will be constrained to play the role of neutral expert, relinquishing the initiative to the politician, and operating in terms of precedent and institutional norms rather than of critical discourse.[12] To become an adviser offers some scope for 'boring from within',[13] but the intellectual thus engaged never stands at the centre in his own right. The critical tension between intellect and power is a constant of modern civilization.

Intellectuals are a modern phenomenon. Their predecessors stood in no doubt of their functional dependency on ecclesiastical or courtly patronage. The bearers of ideas in modern society, impressed with the importance of their knowledge, selling their skills on an 'open' market, seem free of such shackles. Yet just as counsellors stood in a functional relationship with kings, the story of the minders should indicate that intellectuals are constrained to stand in a functional relationship to the powerful in modern society. That society places so much value on their skills persuades the intelligentsia that they are headed for the premier place, and hence they are willing recruits to bureaucracy and politics. But the 'new class' never holds the reins.

Gramsci, in particular, reminds us that, 'every social group . . . creates together with itself, organically, one or more strata of intellectuals which give it homogeneity and an awareness of its own function not only in the economic but also in the social and political fields'.[14] Taking Gramsci's argument as analogy, it might be suggested that while both politicians and bureaucrats constitute part of the intelligentsia, along with the advisers (and, for that matter, business managers, journalists, academics, and so on), the intellectual function of the power élite falls to the advisers. The tasks of analysis and articulation are political, as the intelligentsia recognizes, but as has been noted the bureaucrat foregoes these to become a supposedly neutral expert in 'apolitical' information and administration, while the politician can pay little attention to them because of the survival demands of combat politics. At first, the institutional disjunction thus caused creates tension and strain at the institutional interface — and disillusion in a sector of the intelligentsia about politics and bureaucracy. But at the next stage the political stratum, in order to maintain its dominance, must demand help, and thus demands the services of personal advisers, incidentally creating avenues for precisely that sector of the intelligentsia obsessed with the importance of politics but disillusioned about the available avenues of electoral representation or public service.

Thus there are historically formed specialized categories for the intellectual function. They are formed in connection with all social groups, but especially in connection with the more important, and they undergo more extensive and complex elaboration in connection with the dominant social group.[15]

Yet this is a subsidiary role, a service role: speaking for the powerful is not the same as being in power.

The historical contingencies that shaped the group from which advisers are drawn can be further specified. Its members are of course products of the nuclear family, and of an ideology that emphasizes childhood development. Much suggests that they are dominantly products of the middle-class, of that section which values educational achievement. However, in generational terms they are also products of the post-war boom which entailed, among other things, wide scale embourgeoisement in terms of values (if not in realistic measures of economic relationships), and which had its practical effects in the wholesale expansion of tertiary training.

It is significant that the group's members are primarily of a cohort which completed undergraduate degrees in the 1960s and early 1970s (in the mid 1970s the Whitlam staffers were in their twenties and thirties, the Hawke staffers are now mainly in their thirties and forties). They are, in other words, of a period when political issues came to the fore, the campuses were 'radicalized', and political allegiance (both left and right) became an issue of profound concern — but when conventional institutional niches were anathema.

Intellectual acolytes, encouraged by proud (newly bourgeois?) parents to expect a place in the sun, freighted by family expectations (often they were the first generation to attend university), yet trained to look with reservations on conventional avenues of high achievement (politics, bureaucracy — business especially): where were they to realize their cherished ideals? Fortuitously, the 1970s — with the election of a Labor government distrustful of the public service, and on the conservative side the call for a rethinking of philosophy and policy attendant on its relegation to opposition — brought to flower the demand for personal advisers in Australia, and this provided their avenue. For the politically engaged intellectual in such circumstances 'government service represents a frontal attack on the interests who have hitherto made the significant decisions'.[16] In Australia, the primary experience of this has been in the post-war period, but Coser, in discussing 'Fabians' and 'New Dealers', provides earlier models of politically engaged intellectuals 'boring from within'.[17]

If an avenue to the inner circle is thus opened for the politically engaged intellectual, the cost of admission is always to stand in the shadows, to be the minder rather than the mover. The institutionalization of adviser roles is a symptom of the atomization of modern society and the division of labour. The special contribution of the advisers takes place in the private offices of the political executive, and not in the public forum. The conditions of their work demand that credit should go to their political masters: the advisers are the 'secret sharers' in modern politics. Therefore, it will always be difficult precisely to identify their contribution. One wonders, further, if they remain committed to preserving the secrets of the inner circle, because while revelation of the negotiations of decision-makers would erode it, this would also destroy the potential of access to the privileged status of the insider, privy to special information. Whatever the reason, the minders have done little to enrich our public life by breaking down the secrecy of decision-making which so shackles open government, particularly in Australia. It may be that the secrecy of policy decision-making is simply a corollary of bourgeois society '. . . in which every form of exchange and communication is based on a sort of anonymous turnover'.[18]

One powerful incentive towards keeping their counsel, however, is the way in which a period of service with the political executive may interlock with other careers where it will prove an advantage to have demonstrated 'sound' instincts. And so we must turn, finally, to consider what happens to advisers after their stint of political service.

While the elaborated structure of private offices has not yet existed long enough for anyone to have led a full career as a staffer, there does now exist the possibility of extended service in a role which until recently was regarded as a commitment for two or three years at most. There are staffers now working for the Hawke government who first worked for the Whitlam government in 1972, (though usually not without some break). There were some who worked for the L-NCP coalition opposition in the mid-1970s, and then for the Fraser government until 1983. There were some who worked for Labor in opposition 1975–83, and are now staffers in government. The long term potential of staffer roles is only now becoming evident.

The interchange between staff roles and politics proper cannot be ignored, even though it is a route followed by few. Race Mathews, whose career has already been touched on, was a teacher, then adviser of Gough Whitlam, then federal Labor parliamentarian, then adviser to Victorian State Labor leaders Frank Wilkes and John Cain, then State Labor MP and minister in the Cain government. South Australian Premier John Bannon, having been an industrial advocate for the AWU, worked on the staff of Minister for Labour Clyde Cameron in 1973, then returned to the South Australian public service, before entering State

parliament there in 1977. Peter Shack worked on the staff of a
federal member of parliament on leaving university (where he had
studied politics), entered federal parliament as a Liberal MP in
1977, lost his seat in the swing to Labor in 1983 when he went
to work on the staff of opposition leader Andrew Peacock, then
returned to parliament in the elections of 1984. Peacock also
employed a former Liberal MP, Barry Simon, as his senior private
secretary during his tenure of the Ministry for Industrial Relations
under Fraser. John Langmore, one time academic and adviser to
the government of Papua New Guinea in the mid-1970s, returned
to Australia to work for the leader of the federal parliamentary
Labor Party in 1975, and served as a Labor staffer for eight years
before taking a federal Labor seat in the 1984 elections. Peter
Wilenski and John Menadue both stood for party preselection
while working for Whitlam. These examples could be multiplied.
Nonetheless, the broader survey shows that it is a career route
that the majority of the minders do not consider.

Interchange with the public service has been a route which
carries heavier traffic. Despite the inevitable institutional friction
between the bureaucracy and the minders, governments *can*
choose to appoint their own to the public service, and the
bureaucracy in any case recognizes the advantages of personnel
with experience of the inner circle. Indeed, though it has been
seen that more public servants now enter the private offices by
choice than by secondment as in the past, few saw this period of
'political' service as an impediment to their future career. On the
contrary:

As a career public servant it doesn't do to get out of the mainstream for
too long — if you are seen to be politicized, it will adversely affect
promotion. But being here for eighteen months or so is fine. You get
a range of experiences and a variety of contacts from the meetings you
attend with the minister that you wouldn't get in a department until you
reached the most senior levels. You get an insight into what happens to
policy at the political end. You get a much more real sense of what
community perceptions are. All of these things are to your advantage
when you return to the department, and they recognize it.

(Labor staffer, 1983.)

This experience is regarded very favourably by the public service. It is
seen as sharpening your administrative and policy skills.

(Labor staffer, 1983.)

Besides this to and fro movement at middle levels of the bureaucracy, there have been high level lateral appointments of former advisers to the public service.[19] The trend started under Whitlam with the appointments of John Menadue as secretary of PM and C, Jim Spigelman as secretary of the department of the Media, and Peter Wilenski as secretary of the department of Labour and Immigration. It continued with instances like the appointment of Fraser's adviser Petro Georgiou to the directorship of the Institute for Multicultural Affairs. (Georgiou later returned to an adviser role on the staff of the Liberal leader succeeding Fraser, Andrew Peacock.) Menadue has gone on to a distinguished career as head of several departments under governments of both complexions. Wilenski pioneered the means of career advance through moving back and forth between adviser roles, bureaucracy and academia. Several federal government staffers have moved on to positions in State government public service: John Mant, for instance, became head of South Australia's department of Urban and Regional Affairs after serving as Whitlam's principal private secretary; later Richard Stevens, who had served on the staffs of several federal Country Party ministers, became head of the South Australian Fisheries department under a Liberal government. There have also been notable instances at State government level of private office staffers becoming departmental heads, as illustrated by David Hill's elevation from premier Wran's personal staff to the directorship of the NSW State Rail Authority. Other examples are the Queensland National-Liberal government's appointment of the premier's press secretary, Allen Callaghan, to a deputy secretaryship and later a full departmental secretaryship, or the South Australian Labor government's appointment of the premier's secretary, John White, to head the premier's department when that was first created.

Equally well travelled is the road from political advising to consultancy in business–government relations, and lobbying generally. Staff of the conservative government in particular have found positions with leading Australian companies.[20] Knowledge of how government works on the inside and of who to contact on particular matters in the public service is an asset highly valued by commercial interests whose advantage must these days be pursued through negotiation with government. Such knowledge is also a commodity valued by other governments, as revealed by the defenestration of former ALP *apparatchik* and lobbyist, David Combe, over his relations with a Russian agent.[21] This event brought to public attention the extent to which business–government, and intergovernmental, dealings have been permeated by lobbyists. Peter Sekuless's study of lobbyists in Australia underlines the extent to which many capitalize on knowledge gained first as ministerial staffers:

The lobbyists themselves are mostly people formerly employed on prime ministerial or ministerial staffs, ex-public servants, or political journalists. The common thread is knowledge and the ability to find out how and when decisions are made. The . . . head of Eric White's in Canberra was Frank Hamilton, who had been a press secretary to Country Party leader, John McEwen; International Public Relations Canberra Chief is George Kerr, a former press gallery correspondent; Eric Walsh who runs his own firm was in the press gallery before becoming press secretary to Gough Whitlam when he was prime minister; (Canberra Liaison) partner Jon Gaul was press secretary to William McMahon when he was prime minister and Billy Snedden when he was opposition leader, and my own experience was in journalism and the public service.[22]

Indeed, Sekuless's directory of Canberra lobbyists suggests that about half have had experience as ministerial staffers, and most of the rest have been public servants and journalists.[23]

The interchange between academia and government service has been another feature of the growth of adviser roles. Some intellectuals have taken knowledge developed as advisers within the system of government back into the broader intellectual life of the academic community. Wilenski and Kemp are examples of this. Their cases indicate that government service has been no barrier to rapid academic promotion. Many of the academic economists recruited by the governments of Whitlam, Fraser, and Hawke maintained some university commitments while commuting to Canberra — virtually all returned to professorial appointments or their equivalents on leaving ministerial private offices (for example Fred Gruen, John Rose, John Hewson, Cliff Walsh, Barry Hughes). Some academics have simply returned to positions within the university departments from which they took leave to serve a minister (Denis White, for instance, returned to the Monash University politics department after holding senior positions in Fraser's office). Among these academics, some have stimulated public debate on the significance of the adviser's role,[24] but none has yet published a sustained account or analysis of government service, or of decision-making in the inner circle — presumably for reasons akin to those adduced earlier.

This review indicates that while there is no security for the ministerial staffer, and no institutionally prescribed career path, the options facing him/her at the end of service are far from limited. Nor should the adviser's stint of political service be seen as a deviation in otherwise settled career patterns. The ministerial staff constitute a pool fed by a number of tributaries, but opening out into the mainstream. Service there is a means of transition for the intelligentsia from positions of little account to positions of influence and sometimes of power. The translation from relative nonentity to influential bureaucrat, highly placed business consultant, well-paid lobbyist, or senior academic, is common. In fact, it is commonly recognized by ministerial staffers that '. . . it's a high-risk job, but it brings the chance for high mobility with it'. (*Labor staffer, 1983.*)

This may be seen as part of a broader pattern in that the modern intelligentsia is characterized by occupational mobility,[25] but there is much to indicate that a trajectory through the ministerial staff may be the fast lane to success.[26] The knowledge developed within the system and the contacts with those in power, and also the networks built up through the reciprocal relations between politicans and minders contribute to this. Thus, the migration of federal ministerial staff to State public service and political positions — most evident after the fall of the Whitlam government — appeared to depend on contacts within such networks. Or, from a different tack, some lobbying firms have featured partnerships between individuals who have worked in government, but on opposite sides of the political fence,[27] suggesting that the corporate identity of the minders (and mutual recognition of what their experience gives them to sell) may come to transcend party divisions.

In discussing the rise of the ministers' minders, I have examined the evolution of institutions at the centre of political life. Personal advisers are a third force alongside the politicians and bureaucrats. They are part of the collective process of decision-making, and to understand that process all of its participants must be understood. The ministerial staff structure is now an institutional fact of Australian politics. But political executives everywhere will continue to need such assistance: it is a consequence of the complex demands on political leadership of modern society. If jobs on a minister's staff remain a short-term prospect for most, the enduring networks developed through that experience, the saleable skills and knowledge attained, and the articulation of the minder's role with other careers beyond mainstream politics, should prompt us to regard the ministers' minders in broader terms. Their emergence is a manifestation of the functional role of the intelligentsia in modern politics. They are here to stay.

Notes

1 Introduction

1 See for instance the divergent uses in Alan Ramsey, 'Hawke minders — like chalk and cheese', *The National Times*, 13–19 July 1984, pp. 5–6, where it is applied both to the consummate handler, Peter Barron, and to party adviser, Bob Hogg.

2 See H. L. Wilenski, 'The professionalization of everyone?', *American Journal of Sociology*, vol. 70, 1964, p. 158; and cf. D. P. Moynihan, 'The professionalization of reform', *The Public Interest*, no. 1, 1965, pp. 6–16.

3 See R. W. Connell, 'Intellectuals and intellectual work', in his *Which Way Is Up? Essays on Class, Sex and Culture*, Allen and Unwin, Sydney, 1983, pp. 244–7.

4 That is to say, this book does not pretend to cover everything associated with the questions it raises — there is certainly more to be done on the psychology of the minder, just as there should be a demand for more revealing, detailed and responsible accounts by 'insiders' in the policy process, as I suggest in the final paragraph of this Introduction.

2 Advisers and Advisory Structures in the Modern Age

1 Francis Bacon, 'Of Counsel', *Selected Writings*, Random House, The Modern Library, New York, 1955, p. 55.

2 See C. B. Macpherson, *Democratic Theory: essays in retrieval*, Clarendon Press, Oxford, 1973.

3 See Henry Parris, 'The Origins of the Permanent Civil Service 1780–1830', *Public Administration*, London, vol. 46, 1968, pp. 143–66.

4 Max Weber, *The Protestant Ethic and the Spirit of Capitalism*, Charles Scribner's Sons, New York, 1958; see also H. H. Gerth and C. W. Mills, (eds), *From Max Weber, Essays in Sociology*, Routledge and Kegan Paul, London, 1948.

5 Arthur Mitzman's biography of Max Weber takes as its central theme the sense of hopeless entrapment suffered by the sons of the bourgeoisie as they faced the organizational structures erected by their fathers, which dominated the modern age and seemed to deny the possibility of individual choice or rebellion. See Arthur

Mitzman, *The Iron Cage: An Historical Interpretation of Max Weber*, Grossett and Dunlap, New York, 1969.

6 Michels's theory grew out of his work on the bureaucratic and oligarchical tendencies of European socialist parties; see Robert Michels, *Political Parties*, The Free Press, Glencoe, 1949 (first published 1911).

7 See Ezra N. Suleiman, *Politics, Power and Bureaucracy in France: The Administrative Elite*, Princeton University Press, Princeton, N.J., 1974, chapter VIII, 'The Ministerial Cabinet', pp. 181–200.

8 Dorothy Pickles, *The Government and Politics of France: Volume 1, Institutions and Parties*, Methuen, London, 1972, pp. 79–80.

9 An unsystematic literature on this predated the 1960s, but the argument became formalized with Louis W. Koenig, *The Invisible Presidency*, Holt, Rinehart and Winston, New York, 1960; and Richard E. Neustadt, *Presidential Power: The Politics of Leadership*, John Wiley and Sons, New York, 1960. Polemical heat was added by Patrick Anderson, *The Presidents' Men*, Doubleday, New York, 1968; George E. Reedy, *The Twilight of the Presidency*, New American Library Inc., New York, 1970; and Carl Bernstein and Bob Woodward, *All the President's Men*, Secker and Warburg, London, 1974. For other major sources on 'the invisible presidency' see Fred I. Greenstein, *et al.*, *Evolution of the Modern Presidency: A Bibliographical Survey*, American Enterprise Institute, Washington, 1977, chapter 16.

10 See Lester G. Seligman, 'Presidential Leadership: The Inner Circle and Institutionalization', *The Journal of Politics*, vol. 18, 1956, pp. 410–26; p. 412.

11 See for instance, Michael Medved, *The Shadow Presidents: The Secret History of the Chief Executives and Their Top Aides*, Times Books, New York, 1979.

12 Alexander L. George and Juliette L. George, *Woodrow Wilson and Colonel House: A Personality Study*, Dover, New York, 1956.

13 Compare Thomas E. Cronin, *The State of the Presidency*, Little, Brown, Boston, 1975, p. 121.

14 Stephen Hess, *Organizing the Presidency*, Brookings, Washington, 1976, p. 8.

15 Bill Moyers in *The Washington Monthly*, February 1969.

16 See particularly Reedy, op. cit.

17 Alex Brummer, 'The disaster team at Reagan's right hand', *The Guardian Weekly*, vol. 132, no. 20, week ending 19 May 1985, p. 9.

18 Richard P. Nathan, *The Administrative Presidency*, John Wiley, New York, 1983, makes this point very effectively with reference to the Nixon administration.

19 See Thomas E. Cronin, ' "Everybody Believes in Democracy Until He Gets to the White House" ': An Examination of White

House–Departmental Relationships' in Aaron Wildavsky (ed.), *Perspectives on the Presidency*, Little, Brown, Boston, 1975, pp. 362–93.

20 R. A. Watson and N. C. Thomas, *The Politics of the Presidency*, John Wiley, New York, 1983, p. 319. Watson and Thomas provide a concise and up-to-date account of presidential staffing from Roosevelt to Reagan, see pp. 313–19.

21 Anderson, op. cit., p. 1.

22 John Hart, 'No Passion for Brownlow: Models of Staffing the Presidency', *Politics*, vol. 17, no. 2, November 1982, p. 94.

23 See, for instance, Richard E. Neustadt, 'White House and Whitehall', *The Public Interest*, no. 2, 1966, pp. 55–69.

24 On this point, see George W. Jones, 'The Prime Minister's Advisers', *Political Studies*, 21, 1973, p. 365; and George W. Jones, 'The Prime Minister's Secretaries: Politicians or Administrators?' in J. A. G. Griffith, (ed.), *From Policy to Administration*, Allen and Unwin, London, 1976, p. 37.

25 See Neustadt, 'White House and Whitehall', op. cit., p. 68.

26 Peter Kellner and Lord Crowther-Hunt, *The Civil Servants: An Inquiry into Britain's Ruling Class,* Macdonald, London, 1980, pp. 23–99.

27 Richard Crossman, *Diaries of a Cabinet Minister Volume 1*, Jonathan Cape, London, 1975, pp. 30–1.

28 Barbara Castle, 'Mandarin Power', *The Sunday Times*, 10 June 1973.

29 As does Anthony Sampson. See his *The Changing Anatomy of Britain*, Hodder and Stoughton, London, 1982, chapter 10.

30 Sampson, op. cit., pp. 421–2.

31 See for instance, Douglas Allen, 'Ministers and their Mandarins', *Government and Opposition: A Journal of Comparative Politics*, vol. 12, no. 2, 1977, pp. 135–49. Allen was Head of the Home Civil Service at the time this article was written.

32 Quoted in Sampson, op. cit., p. 169.

33 George W. Jones, 'The Prime Minister's Secretaries. . .', in Griffith (ed.), op. cit.

34 On 'the garden suburb', see Jones, 'The Prime Minister's Advisers', op. cit., p. 370; 'The Prime Minister's Secretaries. . .', in Griffith (ed.), op. cit., pp. 26–7; and 'The Prime Minister's Men', *New Society*, vol. 43, no. 798, 1978, p. 122. Jones's source is J. Davies, *The Prime Minister's Secretariat 1916–20*, R. H. Johns, Newport, 1951.

35 G. D. A. Macdougall, 'The Prime Minister's Statistical Section', in D. N. Chester, (ed.), *Lessons of the British War Economy*, Cambridge University Press, Cambridge, 1951, p. 68.

36 Jones, 'The Prime Minister's Men', loc. cit.

37 James Fox, 'The Brains Behind the Throne', *The Sunday Times*, 25 March 1973, reprinted in Valentine Herman and James Alt (eds), *Cabinet Studies: A Reader*, Macmillan, London, 1975, pp. 277–92.
38 Peter Kellner and Lord Crowther-Hunt, op. cit., pp. 221–2.
39 Sampson, op. cit., p. 226; Tony Benn, *Arguments for Democracy*, Jonathan Cape, London, 1981, p. 60.
40 See Rudolf Klein and Janet Lewis, 'Advice and Dissent in British Government: The Case of the Special Advisers', *Policy and Politics*, 6, 1977, pp. 1–25; Joan E. Mitchell, 'Special Advisers: A Personal View', *Public Administration*, London, vol. 56, 1978, pp. 87–98.
41 My description of the prime minister's policy unit is derived from George W. Jones, 'Harold Wilson's Policy-Makers', *The Spectator*, 6 July 1974, pp. 12–13.
42 This argument paraphrases Colin Campbell, *Governments Under Stress: Political executives and key bureaucrats in Washington, London, and Ottawa*, University of Toronto Press, Toronto, 1983, pp. 74–5.
43 The following comments derived from a reading of Colin Campbell, op. cit., pp. 77–82; Thomas D'Aquino, 'The Prime Minister's Office: Catalyst or Cabal', *Canadian Public Administration*, vol. 17, no. 1, Spring 1974; Richard Gwyn, *The Northern Magus: Pierre Trudeau and the Canadians*, Markham, Paperjacks, Ontario, 1981 (on the 'supergroup' especially); Marc Lalonde, 'The Changing Role of the Prime Minister's Office', *Canadian Public Administration*, vol. 14, no. 4, Winter 1971; Denis Smith, 'President and Parliament: The Transformation of Parliamentary Government in Canada', in Thomas Hockin, (ed.), *Apex of Power: The Prime Minister and Political Leadership in Canada*, Prentice-Hall, Scarborough, 1971; Denis Smith, 'Comments on the Prime Minister's Office: Catalyst or Cabal', *Canadian Public Administration*, vol. 17, no. 1, Spring 1974; Joseph Wearing, 'President or Prime Minister', in Thomas Hockin, (ed.), op. cit.
44 Compare, for instance, the summary description of the French *cabinet ministériel* in D. Pickles, loc. cit., with the account of the PMO in Patrick Weller, *First Among Equals: Prime Ministers in Westminster Systems*, Allen and Unwin, Sydney, 1985, pp. 142–4.
45 Karl Mannheim, *Ideology and Utopia*, Harcourt, Brace and World, New York, 1946, p. 105.
46 Henry Fairlie, 'The Politician's Art', *Harpers*, vol. 225, (1531), December 1977, p. 36.
47 Graham T. Allison, *Essence of Decision: Explaining the Cuban Missile Crisis*, Little, Brown, Boston, 1971.
48 George C. Herring, *America's Longest War: The United States and Vietnam 1950–1975*, John Wiley, New York, 1979.
49 Compare Joel D. Aberbach, Robert D. Putnam, and Bert A.

Rockman, *Bureaucrats and Politicians in Western Democracies*, Harvard University Press, Cambridge, Mass., 1981, p. 21.

Illustrative Biographies

1 This paraphrases the argument of historian Roland Mousnier, as cited in Elizabeth Wirth Marvick, 'Favorites in Early Modern Europe: A Recurring Psychopolitical Role', a paper delivered at the conference of the International Society of Political Psychology, Mannheim, West Germany, 23–27 June 1981 — printed version 23 September 1981, pp. 8–9. I draw heavily on Marvick pp. 8–11, p. 17 in this discussion of Wolsey, although biographical detail comes from other sources.
2 Neville Williams, *Henry VIII and his court*, Weidenfeld and Nicolson, London, 1971, p. 57.
3 Williams, op. cit., p. 58.
4 Much has been written about Colonel House. My chief source is Alexander L. George and Juliette L. George, *Woodrow Wilson and Colonel House: A Personality Study*, Dover, New York, 1964, supplemented by Michael Medved, *The Shadow Presidents*, Times Books, New York, 1979, chapter 5. (The subheading of this chapter is 'Dear, dear friend' which calls to mind Henry VIII's description of Wolsey.)
5 George and George, op. cit., p. 82.
6 See George and George, op. cit., pp. 240–316.
7 Cited in Marvick, op. cit., p. 10.
8 This is a key theme in the George and George biography.
9 My chief sources for this sketch of Bundy are Patrick Anderson, *The Presidents' Men*, Doubleday, New York, 1968; and David Halberstam, *The Best and the Brightest*, Random House, New York, 1972.
10 Anderson, op. cit., p. 260.
11 For a more detailed biographical note on Donoughue, see George W. Jones, 'Harold Wilson's Policy-Makers', *The Spectator*, 6 July 1974, p. 12.

3 The Search for Structures in Australia

1 Fred Johns, *Who's Who in Australia, 1927–28*, The Hassell Press, Adelaide, 1927, p. 230.
2 Keith Penny, 'The Origins of the Prime Minister's Department, 1901–1911', *Public Administration (Sydney)*, vol. XV, 1956, pp. 253–4. See also the heated parliamentary debate about Shepherd of 18 December 1911, *C.P.D.*, vol. LXIII, 1911, pp. 4622–26.
3 S. Murray-Smith, 'Deane, Percival Edgar (1890–1946)', *Australian*

Dictionary of Biography, vol. 8, Melbourne University Press, Melbourne, 1981, p. 261. See also, Fred Johns, op. cit., p. 73.

4 Murray-Smith, op. cit., p. 261.

5 ibid.

6 Some of Deane's remarks, however, should endure, such as his observation that the best view of Canberra is 'from the back of a departing train'. Quoted in S. Murray-Smith (ed.), *The Dictionary of Australian Quotations*, Heinemann, Richmond, Victoria, 1984, p. 63.

7 See Sir Lloyd Dumas, 'With Billy Hughes', *The Story of a Full Life*, Sun Books, Melbourne, 1969, chapter 4 pp. 20–9.

8 Robert Milliken, 'Cook, Bertie Stuart Baxter (1877–1968)', *Australian Dictionary of Biography*, vol. 8, Melbourne University Press, Melbourne, 1981, p. 94.

9 See Norman E. Lee, *John Curtin, Saviour of Australia*, Longman Cheshire, Melbourne, 1983, p. 34.

10 A. F. Davies, *Australian Democracy: An Introduction to the Political System*, Longmans, Melbourne, 1966, p. 12.

11 See A. Petridis, 'Australia: economists in a federal system' in A. W. Coats, (ed.), *Economists in Government: An International Comparative Study*, Duke University Press, Durham, N.C., 1981. pp. 65–6; C. B. Shedvin, *Australia and the Great Depression*, Sydney University Press, Sydney, 1970, chapter 10.

12 On 'the bureaucratic explosion', see Fred Alexander, *Australia Since Federation*, Nelson, Melbourne, 1976, pp. 151–2; Sol Encel, *Equality and Authority: A Study of Class, Status and Power in Australia*, Cheshire, Melbourne, 1970, pp. 67–9.

13 For further detail on Alfred Conlon and references to source material, see the biographical sketch and related notes in the section following this chapter.

14 For details of one such 'brains trust', see Coombs' account of the team assembled to devise and administer wartime rationing; H. C. Coombs, *Trial Balance*, Macmillan, Melbourne, 1981, pp. 17–19.

15 Coombs, op. cit., p. 6.

16 L. F. Crisp, *Ben Chifley: A political biography*, Angus and Robertson, Sydney, 1963, pp. 256–7. A more detailed account appears in 'Commonwealth Policy Co-ordination', *Public Administration (Sydney)*, vol. XIV, 1955, pp. 193–213.

17 For more detailed accounts of the IPA, see D. A. Kemp, 'The Institute of Public Affairs, 1942–47', B.A. Honours thesis, University of Melbourne, 1963; J. R. Hay, 'The Institute of Public Affairs and Social Policy', paper delivered at the seminar on Post-War Reconstruction, ANU, September 1981, mimeo; John Lonie, 'From Liberal to Liberal: the Emergence of the Liberal Party and Australian Capitalism 1900–45', in Graeme Duncan, (ed.), *Critical*

Essays in Australian Politics, Edward Arnold, Melbourne, 1978, pp. 72–5; Marian Simms, *A Liberal Nation: The Liberal Party and Australian Politics*, Hale and Iremonger, Sydney, 1982, pp. 14–21.

18 See, for instance, what happened to the Economic Policy Division of the Department of Post-War Reconstruction in Coombs, op. cit., pp. 29–30; and for a fuller account, L. F. Crisp, 'Central Co-ordination of Commonwealth Policy-Making: Roles and Dilemmas of the Prime Minister's Department', *Public Administration (Sydney)*, vol. XXVI, 1967, pp. 28–57.

19 Donald Horne, *The Lucky Country: Australia in the Sixties*, Penguin, Ringwood, 1964, p. 201.

20 Coombs, op. cit., pp. 267–8. It might be added that there developed a corps of permanent public servants who made a speciality of working as ministerial staffers, and more or less made their careers in a succession of private office roles.

21 See Alan Reid, *The Gorton Experiment*, Shakespeare Head Press, Sydney, 1971, pp. 381–2.

22 Coombs, op. cit., p. 285.

23 Daniel Bell, *The End of Ideology: On the Exhaustion of Political Ideas in the Fifties*, The Free Press, New York, 1960.

24 H. C. Coombs, 'The Commission Report', in Cameron Hazlehurst and J. R. Nethercote, (eds), *Reforming Australian Government: The Coombs Report and Beyond*, ANU Press, Canberra, 1977, pp. 49–50.

25 Quoted in C. J. Lloyd and G. S. Reid, *Out of the Wilderness: the return of Labor*, Cassell, North Melbourne, 1974, p. 310.

26 At least, some public servants have suggested this in interviews with this author, and have gone on to express the sentiment which follows in the next sentence.

27 M. Walsh, 'Political Circus Hides the Real Power', *Australian Financial Review*, 30 September 1974.

28 For a representative sample, see: Andrew Farran, 'Reflections on Policy Making and the Public Service', *Public Administration (Sydney)*, vol. XXXIV, 1975, pp. 156–70; Geoffrey Hawker, 'The bureaucracy under the Whitlam Government — and vice versa', *Politics*, vol. X, 1975, pp. 15–23; Geoffrey Hawker, *Who's Master, Who's Servant? Reforming Bureaucracy*, Allen and Unwin, Sydney, 1981; Geoffrey Hawker, R. F. I. Smith and Patrick Weller, *Politics and Policy in Australia*, University of Queensland Press, St Lucia, 1979; Michael Sexton, *Illusions of Power: The fate of a reform government*, Allen and Unwin, Sydney, 1979, chapter 9; R. F. I. Smith and Patrick Weller, 'Learning to Govern: The Australian Labor Party and the Institutions of Government, 1972–1975', *Journal of Commonwealth and Comparative Politics*, vol. 15, 1977, pp. 39–54; R. N. Spann, *Government Administration in Australia*,

Allen and Unwin, Sydney, 1979; Peter Wilenski, 'Labor and the Bureaucracy' in Graeme Duncan, (ed.), *Critical Essays in Australian Politics*, Edward Arnold, Port Melbourne, 1978, pp. 28–46; Peter Wilenski 'Ministers, public servants and public policy', *The Australian Quarterly*, June 1979, pp. 31–45; Peter Wilenski, 'Reform and its Implementation: The Whitlam Years in Retrospect', in G. Evans and J. Reeves, (eds), *Labor Essays 1980*, Drummond, Richmond, 1980, pp. 40–63. See also Peter Wilenski and Di Yerbury, 'Reconstructing Bureaucracy: Towards a Vehicle for Social Change', in J. Reeves and K. Thomson, (eds), *Labor Essays 1983*, Drummond, Melbourne, 1983, pp. 154–80.

29 This paragraph and much of the discussion which follows inevitably draws heavily on the pioneering work of C. J. Lloyd and G. S. Reid, op. cit., pp. 265–72; G. T. Briot and C. J. Lloyd, 'Ministerial Staff Members', Royal Commission on Australian Government Administration, submission 466, 1976; M. Roberts, 'Ministerial Advisers: a background paper', Royal Commission on Australian Government Administration, Research Paper no. 6, 1976; R. F. I. Smith, 'Ministerial Advisers: The Experience of the Whitlam Government', *Australian Journal of Public Administration*, vol. XXXVI, 1977, pp. 133–58. See also Roy Forward, 'Ministerial Staff in the Australian Government, 1972–1974: A Survey', in R. Wettenhall and M. Painter, (comps), *The First Thousand Days of Labor*, vol. 2, Canberra College of Advanced Education, Canberra, 1975, pp. 137–57; and Royal Commission on Australian Government Administration, *Report*, Australian Government Publishing Service, Canberra, 1976, pp. 103–5.

30 See J. M. Anthony, 'The Politics of the Bureaucracy and the Role of Ministerial Staff', in Wettenhall and Painter (comps.), op. cit. On the other hand, Humphrey McQueen refers to 'personalised staff appointments' as an element of 'restaurant socialism' spawned with the emergence of a new Labor élite in South Australia in the 1960s — see his *Gone Tomorrow*, Angus and Robertson, Sydney, 1982, p. 210.

31 On the staffing of the Prime Minister's office, for instance, a position paper was prepared by Peter Wilenski at Whitlam's behest — see Lloyd and Reid, op. cit., pp. 149–50.

32 Wilenski, 'Ministers, public servants and public policy', op. cit., p. 36. See also the discussion of the *cabinet ministériel* above.

33 This list is an amalgamation of those that appear in Briot and Lloyd, op. cit., pp. 3–4, Lloyd and Reid, op. cit., pp. 265–6; Roberts, op. cit., pp. 2–3; Smith, op. cit., pp. 135–6.

34 For a detailed account of classifications, see Briot and Lloyd, op. cit., p. 6; Smith, op. cit., p. 143.

35 Smith op. cit., p. 144.
36 ibid.
37 Hawker, 'The bureaucracy under the Whitlam Government . . .', op. cit., p. 19.
38 Lloyd and Reid, op. cit., p. 267.
39 Hawker, 'The bureaucracy under the Whitlam Government . . .', op. cit., p. 19.
40 I have gained this impression from my own interviews with staff.
41 Lloyd and Reid, op. cit., p. 268.
42 *The Age*, 28 August 1973.
43 Roy Forward lists Junie Morosi, Elizabeth Reid, Clem Lloyd, Peter Wilenski, Jim Spigelman, Harry Stein, Phillip Cairns, Ward McNally and Jim Anthony as having received wide publicity in the media between 1972 and 1975; see Roy Forward, 'Ministerial Staff Under Whitlam and Fraser', *Australian Journal of Public Administration*, vol. XXXVI, 1977, p. 159.
44 John Edwards, 'Political Scientists in Politics', paper delivered to the Australian Political Studies Association Conference, August 1973, p. 3.
45 'The Prime Minister's Private Staff', paper prepared by Dr Peter Wilenski; see note 31 above.
46 Wilenski, 'Ministers, public servants and public policy', op. cit., pp. 37–8.
47 Indeed, this has been the consensus of the papers cited here; see note 29 above.
48 This study, conducted by Dr R. F. I. Smith, was published by the RCAGA in *Appendix Volume One*, AGPS, Canberra, 1976. It is an earlier version of the paper that has been cited extensively throughout this discussion.
49 This was a feature that Whitlam stressed in early public discussions of the system.
50 Smith, op. cit., p. 145.
51 Wilenski, 'Ministers, public servants and public policy', op. cit., p. 37.
52 Anthony's paper, 'The Politics of the Bureaucracy and the Role of Ministerial Staff' (see note 30 above) was delivered at the Australian National University on 10 June 1975.
53 Sexton, op. cit., p. 192.
54 Wilenski, 'Ministers, public servants and public policy', op. cit., p. 36.
55 Robert Haupt, 'Treasury opts out', *Australian Financial Review*, 27 August 1974.
56 Michelle Grattan, 'Stone letter hits "meretricious players of the advisory stage"', *The Age*, 25 November 1982.

57 For instance, one of the government's revenue-raising measures, a
    tax on unearned income, was called the 'Spigelman tax' because of
    its identification with Whitlam adviser, Jim Spigelman. The idea for
    an adviser on women's affairs, and some of the women's
    programmes that stemmed from that, originated with Peter
    Wilenski. It is known that when Whitlam cooled towards Labor's
    proposed inquiry into the public service, which had been a pre-
    election promise, pressure from members of his private office
    helped to swing him around and facilitated the establishment of the
    RCAGA. (On this, see Hawker, Smith and Weller, op. cit.,
    pp. 232–7.)
58 For some responses illustrative of the disquiet of senior public
    servants, see Roberts, op. cit., pp. 26–37.
59 Compare the notion of a 'member-centered enterprise' elaborated in
    R. H. Salisbury and K. A. Shepsle, 'Congressional Staff Turnover
    and the Ties-That-Bind', *The American Political Science Review*,
    vol. 75, 1981, pp. 381–96.
60 James Walter, *The Acculturation to Political Work: New Members of the
    Federal Backbench*, APSA/Parliamentary Fellow Monograph, no. 2,
    Bedford Park, SA, 1979.

Illustrative Biographies

 1 There are, as yet, no sustained biographical essays on Alfred
    Conlon, though he is sporadically thrown up in the popular press
    as Australia's pre-eminent *éminence grise* (see for example 'The
    Master Puppeteer', *Nation*, vol. 1, no. 1, 26 September 1958, p. 12,
    which establishes a line followed by subsequent press references
    throughout the 1960s and 1970s). The most comprehensive body of
    information appears in John Thompson, (comp.), *Alfred Conlon: A
    Memorial by some of his friends*, Benevolent Society of New South
    Wales, Sydney, 1963. I have also drawn on Richard Hall, *The Real
    John Kerr: his brilliant career*, Angus and Robertson, Sydney, 1978,
    chapters 3 and 4; and Brian Jinks, 'Alfred Conlon, The Directorate
    of Research and New Guinea', *Journal of Australian Studies*, 12, June
    1983, pp. 21–33. References are also to be found in J. R. Kerr,
    Matters for Judgment, Macmillan, Melbourne, 1978, chapters 7 and 8;
    and in H. C. Coombs, *Trial Balance*, Macmillan, Melbourne, 1981.
 2 This is Jinks' description of Conlon's degree, see 'Alfred Conlon,
    The Directorate of Research . . .', op. cit., p. 21.
 3 Hall, op. cit., p. 37.
 4 This is the assertion of historian Brian Fitzpatrick, see Thompson,
    (comp.), op. cit., p. 5.
 5 For a sharply antagonistic view, see Gavin Long, *The Final
    Campaigns*, Australian War Memorial, Canberra, 1963.

6 This listing is derived from Jinks, op. cit., p. 25.
7 The best examination of this is Jinks, op. cit.; and cf. 'The Master Puppeteer', op. cit., p. 13.
8 See Jinks, op. cit., p. 29.
9 See Jinks, op. cit., pp. 23–4, and Hall, op. cit., p. 47.
10 Jinks, op. cit., p. 22.
11 Coombs is quoted in Thompson, (comp.), op. cit. He has also noted, 'I found Conlon and his associates intellectually stimulating company and believe that, despite the antagonism they provoked . . . the unit made significant and valuable contributions,' *Trial Balance*, op. cit., p. 198.
12 There are many passing references to Coombs in books about Australian politics and society since the 1940s. There are early biographical materials: John Hetherington's essay in his *Uncommon Men*, Cheshire, Melbourne, 1965, pp. 50–8; and Robert Moore's ABC-TV interview, printed in *Profiles of Power*, Australian Broadcasting Commission, Sydney, 1970, pp. 37–47. I interviewed Coombs myself in July 1977, for my own earlier research on the Whitlam government. But the most useful source of information, and that on which I have drawn most for this sketch, is Coombs' quasi-autobiographical book, *Trial Balance*.
13 Quoted in Hetherington, op. cit.
14 See Coombs, op. cit., p. 6.
15 ibid.
16 L. F. Crisp, *Ben Chifley: A political biography*, Angus and Robertson, Sydney, 1963, p. 187.
17 See 'The Master Puppeteer', op. cit., p. 12.
18 For Coombs' account of the Department, see *Trial Balance*, op. cit., pp. 22–32. Cf. Crisp, op. cit., chapter 13.
19 See my book, James Walter, *The Leader: a political biography of Gough Whitlam*, University of Queensland Press, St Lucia, 1980, p. 59.
20 See H. C. Coombs, 'The Commission Report' and 'The Future Bureaucracy' in Cameron Hazlehurst and J. R. Nethercote, (eds), *Reforming Australian Government: The Coombs Report and Beyond*, ANU Press, Canberra, 1977, pp. 49–58.
21 Recurrent references to Wilenski can be found in the press during the early period of the Whitlam government in 1973. He attracted a further flurry of notice at the time of his appointments to head the Department of Labour and Immigration in 1975, and the Department of Education and Youth Affairs in 1983. However, the most usefully detailed profile was published after his appointment to the chairmanship of the Public Service Board on 25 October 1983, written by Alan Ramsey, 'The Egghead Turns Mandarin',

The National Times, 9 to 15 December 1983, pp. 10–14. The best account of his contribution to the transition to power in 1972 can be found in C. J. Lloyd and G. S. Reid, *Out of the Wilderness: the return of Labor*, Cassell, North Melbourne, 1974. I interviewed Wilenski for my own earlier research on the Whitlam government in July 1977, and again, more directly with relation to this project, in January 1982.

22 See Ramsey, op. cit., p. 11.

23 ibid.

24 See an extended account of this in Lloyd and Reid, op. cit., pp. 151–2.

25 Ramsey, op. cit., p. 14.

26 A register of this can be found in his entry in W. J. Draper, (ed.), *Who's Who in Australia*, Herald and Weekly Times, Melbourne, 1983, p. 907.

27 A colleague of Wilenski's at the ANU spoke of him there as: '. . . like a Bourbon in exile, you know, he was always waiting for the call to return'.

28 Ramsey, op. cit., p. 10 gives a splendid account of the patterns of opposition and support for Wilenski's appointment to the Public Service Board, including the influence of advisers behind the scenes in the Finance Minister and the Prime Minister's private offices.

29 See my book, *The Leader*, op. cit., pp. 68–77.

4 Following the Whitlam Government's Lead

1 See Paul Kelly, *The Unmaking of Gough*, Angus and Robertson, Sydney, 1976, chapter 10; Russell Schneider, *War Without Blood: Malcolm Fraser in Power*, Angus and Robertson, Sydney, 1980, chapter 3.

2 The total approved establishment of leaders and office holders of the (Labor) opposition in November 1972 was 26; in December 1974, the (L–NCP) opposition leaders enjoyed an approved establishment of 41. CPD, Representatives, 5 December 1974, p. 4851.

3 Michelle Grattan, 'The Liberal Party', in Howard R. Penniman, (ed.), *Australia at the Polls: the national elections of 1975*, American Enterprise Institute for Public Policy Research, Washington, 1977, chapter 4, pp. 114–19.

4 Grattan, op. cit., p. 117.

5 G. T. Briot and C. J. Lloyd, 'Ministerial Staff Members', Royal Commission on Australian Government Administration, submission 466, 1974, p. 12.

6 John Edwards, *Life wasn't meant to be easy: a political profile of Malcolm Fraser*, Hale and Iremonger, Sydney, 1977, pp. 79–80.

7 David Kemp, 'A leader and a philosophy', in Henry Mayer, (ed.),

Labor to Power, Angus and Robertson, Sydney, 1973, pp. 48–59. Edwards gives us a commentary on the article, and its uses to Fraser, see Edwards, op. cit., pp. 87–93.

8 Schneider, op. cit., p. 39.

9 Fedor Mediansky and James Nockels, 'Malcolm Fraser's bureaucracy', *Australian Quarterly*, vol. 53, no. 4, 1981, p. 394.

10 Schneider, op. cit., pp. 37–8.

11 See R. F. I. Smith, 'Ministerial Advisers: The Experience of the Whitlam Government', *Australian Journal of Public Administration*, vol. XXXVI, 1977, p. 144, and cf. Mediansky and Nockels, op. cit., p. 405.

12 Peter Wilenski, 'Labor and the Bureaucracy', in Graeme Duncan, (ed.), *Critical Essays in Australian Politics*, Edward Arnold, Port Melbourne, 1978, p. 40.

13 Peter Samuel, 'A Ministry of Mouthpieces', *The Bulletin*, 10 July 1976, p. 11; Roy Forward, 'Ministerial Staff Under Whitlam and Fraser', *Australian Journal of Public Administration*, vol. XXXVI, 1977, p. 159.

14 Forward, op. cit., pp. 159–60.

15 Mediansky and Nockels, op. cit., p. 405.

16 Schneider, op. cit., chapter 5; Mediansky and Nockels, op. cit., pp. 395–400.

17 Geoffrey Hawker, R. F. I. Smith and Patrick Weller, *Politics and Policy in Australia*, University of Queensland Press, St Lucia, 1979, pp. 120–2.

18 Laurie Oakes, 'Return of the Eggheads', *The News*, (Northern Territory), 11 April 1981.

19 'Fraser's staff tops the "egg-head" poll', *The Age*, 21 February 1981.

20 See note 18 above.

21 Paul Kelly, 'Private team moves into PM's realm', *Sydney Morning Herald*, 17 February 1981.

22 These tables are derived from CPD, House of Representatives, 5 December 1974, p. 4845, and CPD, Senate, 19 August 1981, pp. 99–100. Virtually identical tables appear in Mediansky and Nockels, op. cit., p. 406.

23 See Anne Summers, 'Fraser looks over his shoulder as he faces future', *Australian Financial Review*, 2 January 1981.

24 Russell Schneider, 'The power vacuum behind the throne', *The Australian*, 1 January 1983. Schneider emphasizes how important the office had become under Fraser, and asserts that its staff 'can have as much influence on the workings of government as the ministers and public servants . . .'

25 See Scott Milson, 'Dr Kemp's medicine: do less, or lose office in 1983', *Sydney Morning Herald*, 1 January 1981; Nigel Wilson,

'Academic for Canberra', *The Age*, 3 January 1981; Stewart Firth, 'Mr Fraser makes sure he is Right', *Sydney Morning Herald*, 23 January 1981; and note the articles cited in notes 18, 19, 21 and 23 above.

26 Note, for instance Fia Cumming, 'Academics invade corridors of power', *The Australian*, 21 July 1982.

27 Michelle Grattan, 'Stone letter hits "meretricious players of the advisory stage"', *The Age*, 25 November 1982.

28 Professor Cliff Walsh, interviewed on the political economy of economic advice, ABC Radio, 'P.M.', 21 June 1983.

29 CPD, House of Representatives, 9 December 1976, p. 3718.

30 See J. M. Hutchinson, 'Staffers to Shadow Ministers', *Canberra Survey*, vol. 35, no. 11, 26 November 1982, p. 2; and CPD, House of Representatives, 5 December 1974, p. 4851.

31 In 1976, for instance, 38 per cent of the opposition staff establishment was secretarial and clerical (CPD, House of Representatives, 9 December 1976, p. 3718).

32 *Australian Labor Party National Committee of Inquiry Discussion Papers*, APSA Monograph no. 23, Australasian Political Studies Association, Bedford Park, SA, 1979.

33 See David Marr, 'Labor team gets ready to take reins of power', *The National Times*, 6–12 March 1983; Patrick Weller, 'Transition: taking over power in 1983', *Australian Journal of Public Administration*, vol. XLII, no. 3, September 1983, pp. 303–19.

34 See C. J. Lloyd and G. S. Reid, *Out of the Wilderness: the return of Labor*, Cassell, North Melbourne, 1974.

35 Weller, op. cit.

36 Lloyd and Reid, op. cit., pp. 14–33.

37 Weller, op. cit., p. 306.

38 The Chandler and Macleod memorandum was heavily based on excerpts from the work of Dr R. F. I. Smith as a consultant for the RCAGA, see above.

39 Marr's article, op. cit., quotes extensively from Hawke's letter.

40 Bill Butler, interview with the author, Canberra, 25 August 1983.

41 Much of my information on how the panel operated is derived from an interview with Mr Bill Butler and correspondence with Dr Peter Wilenski. However, all of the ministerial staff I interviewed in August 1983 readily gave their views of the panel.

42 Dr Peter Wilenski, correspondence with the author, 18 October 1983.

43 Jane Button, 'Directive on employment of PS senior staff', *Canberra Times*, 9 April 1983; see also Jack Waterford, 'Ministerial-staff job discrimination alleged', *Canberra Times*, 27 April 1983.

44 The text of these advertisements read as follows:

MINISTERIAL STAFF VACANCIES

The Australian Government invites applications from suitably qualified men and women for engagement in Ministerial offices.

Approximately three positions are located in each Ministers' office within the range of classifications of Ministerial Officer and Assistant Private Secretary (depending on qualifications and experience). Certain Press Secretary positions are also available. Salaries will be in accord with standard Public Service rates. For staff above Assistant Private Secretary level an additional allowance is paid in lieu of overtime. All positions are open to suitably qualified persons irrespective of gender, race or place of birth.

According to level the duties involve:
- management of the Minister's office.
- policy advising, research and assistance with policy formulation.
- liaison with the Minister's Department, correspondents and constituents.
- communication with Members of Parliament, organisations, the public and the media.
- preparation of briefings, speeches and press releases.
- other duties as directed by the Minister.

The work of all positions requires a high level of skill, involves long hours and much travel. A working knowledge of Australian politics and government and background in a particular policy area would be an advantage. Applicants may wish to indicate the area of Government activity in which they wish to work. Expressions of interest and applications, including details of the applicant's qualifications and experience and the names of three referees, should be addressed to:

> Ministerial Staff Advisory Panel,
> The Prime Minister's Office,
> P.O. Box E 4840,
> Queen Victoria Terrace, ACT. 2600.
> (phone (062) 70 2211)

by 16 March, 1983.

45 Bill Butler, interview with the author.
46 See CPD, Senate, 13 September 1983, p. 610.
47 This was explained to me by an officer of the Parliamentary and Ministerial Services section, Parliament and General Division, department of the Special Minister of State. Bill Butler also spoke of the MSAP deliberations concerning salary scales (interview with the author).

48 For instance, at an early stage the prime minister's office
   consolidated a Federal/State listing of personal staffs to Labor
   governments and oppositions, circulating it to all senior advisers,
   and enjoining them to maintain contacts and reciprocal briefings.
49 Paul Kelly, *The Hawke Ascendancy*, Angus and Robertson, Sydney,
   1984, p. 213.
50 See *Members of Parliament (Staff) Act 1984* (No. 64 of 1984), part II,
   'Ministerial Consultants'.
51 The media analysis of government under both Fraser and Hawke
   has emphasized their personal dominance — Fraser as the
   'strongman', Hawke as the most popular prime minister since
   Federation. Yet the developments discussed here have not arisen
   purely as a result of such personalizing tendencies; they are of a
   piece with the flow of power to the prime minister that has
   characterized the evolution of Westminster systems: see, for
   example, Richard Crossman, *Inside View: Three Lectures on Prime
   Ministerial Government*, Jonathan Cape, London, 1972, especially
   pp. 62–8.

Illustrative Biographies

 1 Data for this profile are drawn primarily from public sources, as
   indicated below. I worked in the University of Melbourne politics
   department during some of Kemp's period there. Kemp was
   interviewed for this project in January 1982, but the emphasis was
   on the prime ministerial private office and not on personal
   biography.
 2 At least, according to John Edwards — see his *Life wasn't meant to
   be easy: a political profile of Malcolm Fraser*, Hale and Iremonger,
   Sydney, 1977, p. 27.
 3 D. A. Kemp, 'The Institute of Public Affairs, 1942–47', BAHons.
   thesis, University of Melbourne, 1963.
 4 David Kemp, 'A leader and a philosophy', *Checkpoint*, no. 13,
   January 1973, pp. 3–13.
 5 Cf. Herbert Goldhamer, 'The Mirrors of Kings: Manuals of
   Statecraft', *The Adviser*, pp. 37–41.
 6 Paul Kelly, *The Unmaking of Gough*, Angus and Robertson, Sydney,
   1976, chapter 10; Russell Schneider, *War Without Blood: Malcolm
   Fraser in Power*, Angus and Robertson, Melbourne, 1980, chapter 3.
 7 Edwards, op. cit., p. 93, and see pp. 87–93.
 8 ABC-TV, 'Four Corners', 19 March 1978.
 9 D. A. Kemp, *Society and Electoral Behaviour in Australia*, University
   of Queensland Press, St Lucia, 1978.
10 David Kemp, 'Political Parties and Australian Culture', *Quadrant*,
   December 1977, pp. 3–13. See also D. A. Kemp, 'Social change

and the future of political parties: the Australian Case', in L. Maisel and P. M. Sacks (eds), *The Future of Political Parties*, Sage Electoral Studies Yearbook vol. 1, Sage, Beverly Hills, 1975, pp. 124–64.

11 Jim Carlton, MHR, former NSW Party president testified to this — ABC-TV, 'Four Corners', 19 March 1978. And see 'The secret ingredient in Fraser's success', *The National Times*, 16–21 January 1978, pp. 20–1.

12 Kemp, *Society and Electoral Behaviour . . .*, op. cit., pp. 348–9.

13 Kemp, 'Political Parties and Australian Culture', op. cit., p. 9.

14 Kemp, 'Political Parties and Australian Culture', op. cit., p. 5.

15 Cf. James Jupp, *Party Politics: Australia 1966–81*, Allen and Unwin, Sydney, 1982, p. 13.

16 ABC television's nationally broadcast current affairs programme, 'Four Corners', for instance, devoted large parts of two successive broadcasts to the Kemp thesis, on 19 and 25 March 1978.

17 See for example, R. W. Connell and Murray Goot, 'The End of Class, Re-run', *Meanjin*, vol. 38, no. 1, 1979, pp. 3–25.

18 ABC-TV, 'Four Corners', 19 March 1978. Cf. 'The secret ingredient in Fraser's success', *The National Times*, 16–21 January 1978, pp. 20–1.

19 Scott Milson, 'Dr Kemp's medicine: do less, or lose office in 1983', *Sydney Morning Herald*, 1 January 1981.

20 See for example, David Kemp, 'The national economic summit: authority, persuasion and exchange', *The Economic Record*, vol. 59, no. 166, September 1983.

21 His career received its first public notice during the ALP Federal Executive's intervention into the affairs of the Victorian State branch in 1970, was regularly assessed by the media during his tenure of the Victorian State secretaryship of the ALP, 1976–83, and was given its most intensive consideration by the press at the time of his appointment to Hawke's private office in March 1983. This profile, therefore, is derived from public sources as indicated below. Hogg was interviewed for this project in August 1983 — again with the emphasis on work in the prime minister's private office rather than on personal biography.

22 See James Walter, *The Leader, a political biography of Gough Whitlam*, University of Queensland Press, St Lucia, 1980, pp. 27–30, 251–2.

23 John Hurst, 'Bob Hogg — keeping things sweet for the boss', *The National Times*, 3–9 June 1983, p. 10.

24 Paul Molloy, 'Hawke offers Hogg a key job', *The Australian*, 8 March 1983. See also Paul Molloy, 'Hogg accepts PM's trouble-shooter post', *The Australian*, 9 March 1983; and Alan Ramsey, 'Who's who in Hawke's office', *The National Times*, 3–9 June 1983, pp. 7–12.

25 Peter Barron is the only one of the Australian advisers profiled here
   whom I have not interviewed in the course of my research. He was
   never 'available' when I was in Canberra. He is, however, frequently
   mentioned in the press, and I have relied on press coverage, and
   commentary from other advisers for this sketch. The best
   biographical detail I am aware of is to be found in two articles by
   Alan Ramsey, 'Hawke Minders — like chalk and cheese', *The
   National Times*, 13–19 July 1984, pp. 5–6, and 'The Backroom Boy',
   The National Times, 21–7 September 1984, pp. 3–5. I have relied
   heavily on these.
26 See for instance, the references to Barron in Anna-Maria Dell'Oso,
   'Wran: how a punch — and brother Joe — sent him to the top',
   Sydney Morning Herald, 19 June 1982, pp. 33–4.
27 Alan Ramsey, 'What faction wars mean to the ALP', *The National
   Times*, 27 April–3 May 1984, p. 5.
28 Ramsey, 'The Backroom Boy', op. cit., p. 4.
29 Paul Kelly, *The Hawke Ascendancy*, Angus and Robertson, Sydney,
   1984, pp. 399–402; Alan Ramsey, 'Who's Who in Hawke's Office',
   The National Times, 3–9 June 1983, p. 11.
30 Alan Ramsey, 'How Hawke Manages the Media', *The National
   Times*, 6–12 July 1984, p. 5.
31 See for instance, the stress on Barron's cynicism about *both* media
   and politics in Michelle Grattan, 'The media's battle for access', *The
   Age*, 10 September 1984, p. 13.
32 Ramsey, 'The Backroom Boy', op. cit., p. 5.
33 'Barron privately is dismissive of Hogg's influence . . . Hogg in
   turn is known to regard Barron and Richardson as "clod-hoppers"
   whose basic political instincts are often in conflict with Labor's best
   interests,' Ramsey, 'Hawke minders — like chalk and cheese', op.
   cit., p. 5.
34 Alan Ramsey, 'The Man from the Power Machine', *National Times*,
   21–7 October 1983, pp. 8–12; Geoff Kitney, 'How Hawke rules —
   O.K.?' *The National Times*, 11–17 May 1984, pp. 16–19.
35 Kitney, op. cit., p. 18.
36 Ramsey, 'The Backroom Boy', op. cit., p. 5.

5 Who are the Minders?

1 This description was coined by Adlai Stevenson.
2 For a persuasive and imaginative account of the dynamics of
  transition from simple to progressively more complex bureaucratic
  units, see Elliot Jaques, *A General Theory of Bureaucracy*,
  Heinemann, London, 1976, especially part 6, 'Models of
  Bureaucratic Organization'.

3 For the work of backbenchers, see for example H. V. Emy, 'The
  Role Perceptions of Federal M.P.s', in his *The Politics of Australian
  Democracy*, Macmillan, Melbourne, 1974 and James Walter, *The
  Acculturation to Political Work: New Members of the Federal Backbench*,
  APSA/Parliamentary Fellow Monograph no 2, Bedford Park, SA,
  1979; for the work of ministers, see Patrick Weller and Michelle
  Grattan, *Can Ministers Cope? Australian Federal Ministers at Work*,
  Hutchinson, Richmond, Victoria, 1981; for an attempt at sustained
  analysis of a prime minister at work, see James Walter, *The Leader:
  a political biography of Gough Whitlam*, University of Queensland
  Press, St Lucia, 1980 and on the bureaucracy, see R. N. Spann,
  Government Administration in Australia, Allen and Unwin, Sydney,
  1979.
4 The depiction of White House staffers here is based on P. S.
  Florestano, 'The Characteristics of White House Staff Appointees
  from Truman to Nixon', *Presidential Studies Quarterly*, 7 (4), Fall
  1977, pp. 184–91; and L. G. Seligman, 'Who Advises and Assists
  the President?', paper presented to the American Political Science
  Association, Chicago, Illinois, 30 August 1974.
5 Seligman, op. cit., p. 27.
6 For a representative sample, see 'An Army of Experts Storms
  Capitol Hill', *Time*, 23 January 1978, pp. 10–11; Dom Bonafede,
  'Reagan's "Brains Trust" — A Candidate is Known by the
  company He Keeps', *National Journal*, 12 (17), 26 April 1980,
  pp. 672–6; George J. Church, 'The President's Men', *Time*, 14
  December 1981, pp. 28–34; Bill Keller, 'Ronald Reagan's Inner
  Circle Combines "California Mafia" with Nixon and Ford Alumni',
  Congressional Quarterly Weekly Report, 38, 4 October 1980,
  pp. 2913–22; Larry Light, 'White House Domestic Policy Staff
  Plays an Important Role in Formulating Legislation', *Congressional
  Quarterly Weekly Report*, 37, 6 October 1979, pp. 2199–204; Donald
  Smith, 'Carter's Staff: Young, Informal, Fast Moving', *Congressional
  Quarterly Weekly Report*, 34, 25 September 1976, pp. 2600–2;
  Elizabeth Wynhausen, 'The President's Loyal Lieutenants', *The
  National Times*, 10–16 January 1982, p. 4.
7 On these general characteristics, see for example James Fox, 'The
  Brains Behind the Throne', in Valentine Herman and James Alt,
  (eds), *Cabinet Studies: A Reader*, Macmillan, London, 1975,
  pp. 277–95, especially pp. 281–2; G. W. Jones, 'Harold Wilson's
  Policy Makers', *The Spectator*, 6 July 1974, pp. 12–13; Joan E.
  Mitchell, 'Special Advisers: A Personal View', *Public Administration*,
  56, Spring 1978, pp. 87–98; and on the distinction between Labour
  and Conservative advisers, see Rudolf Klein and Janet Lewis,
  'Advice and Dissent in the British Government: The Case of

Special Advisers', *Policy and Politics*, 6, 1977, pp. 1–25, especially p. 17.

8 A sober account of the Canadian PMO is to be found in Colin Campbell, *Governments Under Stress: Political executives and key bureaucrats in Washington, London, and Ottawa*, University of Toronto Press, Toronto, 1983, pp. 77–82.

9 The best account of 'the Supergroup' is to be found in Richard Gwyn, *The Northern Magus: Pierre Trudeau and the Canadians*, Paperjacks Ltd, Markham, Ontario, 1981.

10 Gwyn, op. cit., p. 92.

11 And one might add similar evidence from very disparate countries, see for example 'Who Are Ohira's "Brains"?', *The Oriental Economist*, 47 (823), May 1979, pp. 9–12.

12 Roy Forward, 'Ministerial Staff Under Whitlam and Fraser', *Australian Journal of Public Administration*, XXXVI (2), June 1977, pp. 159–66. This discussion follows Forward's work in a comparative manner, and hence all references to Whitlam and Fraser staffers below derive from Forward's surveys except where I clearly indicate otherwise.

13 On the grounds that my interest was primarily in those who played, or could conceivably play, an advisory role, clerical and stenographic staff were excluded. Press officers, who had been part of ministerial private offices under previous administrations, were grouped in a separate unit, the 'Ministerial Media Group', under the Hawke government. At the time of my interviews, it appeared that they did not play an integral part in most ministerial offices and so they were excluded from this survey, although Forward had included them in his. I have indicated that by late 1984 the situation had changed, the media group had deteriorated, and the press secretary role within ministerial offices had been extended once more. In August 1983, when questionnaires were sent out, there were 85 persons in the categories of assistant private secretary and above (further positions existed, but were then unfilled). By March 1984, when results were consolidated, there had been 48 responses (56.5 per cent). Forward's first survey (of Whitlam staffers) was based on a 44 per cent response rate from the canvassed group, although he obtained a higher response rate by personal interviewing with the Fraser group.

14 See CPD, Senate, 13 September 1983, pp. 610–13; CPD, Senate, 19 August 1981, pp. 99–103. Note however, that the newly initiated 'Ministerial Media Group' (nine persons) is not included in the numbers recorded here for the Hawke ministry's staff establishment.

15 CPD, Senate, 13 September 1983, pp. 610–13.

16 CPD, Senate, 19 August 1981, pp. 99–103.
17 CPD, Senate, 13 September 1983, pp. 610–13.
18 See note 13 above.
19 The figures relate not to the current parliament, which had not
   been revised in the Parliamentary Handbook at the time of writing,
   but to parliament in 1982; see *Parliamentary Handbook of the
   Commonwealth of Australia: Twenty First Edition*, 1982. There is little
   to suggest that the pattern will have changed significantly, as it also
   held for earlier parliaments; see my work *The Acculturation to
   Political Work: New Members of the Federal Backbench*, op. cit., p. 6.
20 *Parliamentary Handbook of the Commonwealth of Australia: Twenty
   First Edition*, 1982.
21 Forward, op. cit., p. 164.
22 This should be qualified by noting, however, that if those staffers
   designated 'political types' (see below) are considered separately, the
   proportion which had once considered or would in future consider
   political candidacy rises to 53 per cent.
23 Forward, op. cit., p. 164.
24 Joel D. Aberbach *et al*, *Bureaucrats and Politicians in Western
   Democracies*, Harvard University Press, Cambridge, Mass., 1981,
   pp. 80–1.
25 Aberbach *et al*, op. cit., p. 69.
26 Though note Harold Lasswell's distinction between the
   'independent' and the 'cause-serving' intellectual, H. D. Lasswell,
   'Political constitution and character', *Psychoanalysis and the
   Psychoanalytic Review*, 46 (4), 1959, pp. 3–18.
27 See, for example, Erik Erikson, *Young Man Luther*, Faber and
   Faber, London, 1958; Isaac Kramnick, *The Rage of Edmund Burke:
   Portrait of an Ambivalent Conservative*, Basic Books, New York,
   1977; Arthur Mitzman, *The Iron Cage: An Historical Interpretation of
   Max Weber*, Grosset and Dunlap, New York, 1969; Jerrold Seigel,
   Marx's Fate: The Shape of a Life, Princeton University Press,
   Princeton, NJ, 1978.
28 A. F. Davies, *Skills, Outlooks and Passions: a psychoanalytic
   contribution to the study of politics*, Cambridge University Press,
   Cambridge, 1980, pp. 100–20.
29 Davies, op. cit., pp. 100–1.
30 *The National Times*, 9–15 December 1983.
31 Ann Rowe, 'A psychological study of eminent psychologists and
   anthropologists, and a comparison with biological and physical
   scientists', *Psychological Monographs*, 1953, pp. 1–55.
32 H. D. Lasswell, *Power and Personality*, Norton, New York, 1948,
   pp. 92–4.
33 James Walter, *The Acculturation to Political Work . . .*, op. cit.

34 Davies, op. cit., p. 101.

35 Edward Shils, 'Ideology' in David L. Sills, (ed.), *International Encyclopaedia of the Social Sciences*, Macmillan-Free Press, New York, vol. 7, pp. 66–75.

6 The Work of the Minders

1 Deborah Snow, 'Senior jobs await decision by Hayden', *Australian Financial Review*, 15 August 1984, p. 7. And for further evidence of the significance ascribed to the minders, see Geoff Kitney, 'Hawke Government concern at exodus of key staff', *The National Times*, 14–20 September 1984.

2 Klein and Lewis, 'Advice and Dissent in the British Government: The Case of the Special Advisers' *Policy and Politics*, 6, 1977; Mitchell, 'Special Advisers: A Personal View', *Public Administration*, 56, Spring 1978.

3 Seligman, 'Who Advises and Assists the President?', paper presented to the American Political Science Association, Chicago, Illinois, 30 August 1974.

4 Briot and Lloyd, 'Ministerial Staff Members', Royal Commission on Australian Government Administration, submission 466, 1974; Forward, 'Ministerial Staff Under Whitlam and Fraser' *Australian Journal of Public Administration*, vol. XXXVI, 1977; Roberts, 'Ministerial Advisers: a background paper' Royal Commission on Australian Government Administration, Research Paper no. 6, 1974–76; Smith, 'Ministerial Advisers: the Experience of the Whitlam Government' *Australian Journal of Public Administration*, vol. XXXVI, 1977. Chandler and Macleod as consultants to the ALP parliamentary opposition's transition planning team circulated a memorandum to all Shadow Ministers prior to the 1983 election which was a distillation of R. F. I. Smith's paper: see chapter 3.

5 Alexander George, *Presidential Decision-Making in Foreign Policy: The Effective Use of Information and Advice*, Westview Press, Boulder, Colorado, 1980, pp. 81–108.

6 It was not assumed that designated roles would be exhaustive, and respondents were invited to define alternative roles under the category 'other': none of them did so.

7 It is interesting that despite the establishment of a separate media group, and hence the exclusion of those designated press officers from this survey (see chapter 4, note 13), ministerial staff still spend roughly the same amount of time on this activity as had their predecessors.

8 Most of the comparative references in this chapter, as in the last, are to Forward, 'Ministerial Staff Under Whitlam and Fraser', op. cit. However, Forward does not report findings in *these* areas for

Fraser staffers. The figures for the Whitlam group referred to in the next two paragraphs are taken from his earlier paper: see Roy Forward, 'Ministerial Staff in the Australian Government 1972–74: A Survey', in Roger Wettenhall and Martin Painter, (eds), *The First Thousand Days of Labor, Vol. 2*, Canberra College of Advanced Education, Canberra, 1975, pp. 137–57.

9 Forward, 'Ministerial Staff Under Whitlam and Fraser,' op. cit., p. 164.

10 The Hawke staffers had been in position only six months and a few positions were still unfilled at the time this survey was initiated.

11 Forward, 'Ministerial Staff Under Whitlam and Fraser', op. cit., p. 165.

12 Forward does not report any Whitlam staffers responding in this category.

13 Interviews with Whitlam advisers were first obtained in the course of my research for a biography of Whitlam (see James Walter, *The Leader*, University of Queensland Press, St Lucia, 1980). An early discussion of ministerial staff appears in that book (pp. 68–77). My interest in the advisers grew after publication, and with the growth in that interest I went back to reinterview some of those respondents, this time concentrating on their *own* work rather than on Whitlam. At the same time I began to interview personal staffers to the then Liberal prime minister, Malcolm Fraser. When I set to work in earnest on this project in 1983, I spent a month in Canberra, interviewing a cross-section of the staff of the Hawke ministry, as noted in chapter 5.

14 After publication of this book I intend to lodge interviewing notes, tape recordings, and transcripts relating to this project and to earlier books on Whitlam and on new backbenchers, in the National Library. Those with a scholarly interest in further detail may pursue their enquiries there.

15 See Walter, *The Leader* . . ., op. cit., pp. 29–34.

16 Television interview by David Frost, August 1972.

17 See Neal Blewett, 'Labor 1968–72: planning for victory' in Henry Mayer, (ed.), *Labor to Power*, Angus and Robertson, Sydney, 1973, pp. 6–16; Michelle Grattan, 'The Liberal Party' in Howard R. Penniman, (ed.), *Australia at the polls: the national elections of 1975*, ANU Press, Canberra, 1977, pp. 103–42 (especially pp. 112–30); Patrick Weller, 'Transition: Taking Over Power in 1983', *Australian Journal of Public Administration*, vol. XLII, no. 3, September 1983, pp. 303–19.

18 ABC-TV's 'Nationwide' on 22 February 1983 gave a good account of the role of campaign advisers during the 1983 federal election campaign. Particular mention of the roles of Barron and Hogg

during the 1984 campaign was made on 'Nationwide' on 29 November 1984.

19 See Patrick Weller and Michelle Grattan, *Can Ministers Cope?* Hutchinson, Richmond, Victoria, 1981.

20 Michael Medved, *The Shadow Presidents: The Secret History of the Chief Executives and Their Top Aides*, Times Books, New York, 1979, p. 4.

21 On Kemp's and Harries' influence on Fraser's philosophy and policy, see for example, John Edwards, *Life Wasn't Meant to Be Easy*, Hale and Iremonger, Sydney, 1977, chapter 14; Paul Kelly, 'The Man Who Writes Our Foreign Policy', *The National Times*, 23–8 January 1978, pp. 14–17.

22 And on the importance of journalists in general (and not just press secretaries in particular) see Michelle Grattan, 'Dateline Canberra, a game of intrigue', *The Age*, 28 January 1978; David Barnett, 'The Howson Diaries: The View from Inside', *The Age Monthly Review*, vol. 4, no. 5, September 1984.

23 See Kelly, 'The Man Who Writes our Foreign Policy', op. cit.; Geoffrey Barker, 'Hobbes and the mind of Owen Harries', *The Age*, 13 December 1980.

24 Geoffrey Hawker, R. F. I. Smith and Patrick Weller, 'The Politics of Advice and the Making of the 1974 Budget', in their *Politics and Policy in Australia*, University of Queensland Press, St Lucia, 1979, pp. 251–73.

25 Robert Haupt, 'Treasury Opts Out', *Australian Financial Review*, 27 August 1974.

26 Michelle Grattan, 'The PM's Oracles: Two key economists', *The Age*, 22 June 1979.

27 Mark Westfield, 'The men who sank John Stone', *Australian Business*, 25 November 1982, pp. 31–4, especially p. 31.

28 Westfield, op. cit., p. 33.

29 Michelle Grattan, 'Stone letter hits "meretricious players of the advisory stage"', *The Age*, 25 November 1982.

30 ABC-Radio, 'P.M.', 21 June 1983; 'Former adviser tells of Treasury antagonism', *The Age*, 22 June 1983.

31 See for example, John Short, 'Stone still a force in the background', *Sydney Morning Herald*, 11 May 1984.

32 See all of the metropolitan daily newspapers on 16 August 1984, for reports of and commentary on Stone's resignation.

33 The first such critical attack on ALP government economic policy, containing passing swipes at the previous coalition government, occurred in Stone's 1984 Shann Memorial Lecture delivered in Perth on 27 August 1984. For extensive commentary, see *The Age* and the *Sydney Morning Herald*, 28 August 1984.

34 Dennis Thompson illuminates the extent of this problem by investigating the ethical issue of how to allocate responsibility in public life: see Dennis Thompson, 'Moral Responsibility of Public Officials: The Problem of Many Hands', *American Political Science Review*, 74, 1980, pp. 905–16; and 'Ascribing Responsibility to Advisers in Government', *Ethics*, 93, 1983, pp. 546–60.

35 I base this idea on the elaboration of the 'member-centered' enterprise in Robert H. Salisbury and Kenneth A. Shepsle, 'Congressional Staff Turnover and the Ties-That-Bind', *American Political Science Review*, 75, 1981, pp. 381–96, especially p. 382.

36 Irving Janis, *Victims of Groupthink*, Houghton Mifflin, Boston, 1972.

37 cf. Alexander George, op. cit., p. 93.

38 Joel D. Aberbach *et al.*, *Bureaucrats and Politicians in Western Democracies*, Harvard University Press, Cambridge, Mass., 1981, p. 240–1.

39 Aberbach *et al.*, op cit., p. 240.

40 This assertion is still supported by the surveys reported above, though some qualifying tendencies should be noted. In Australia, as Weller and Fraser argue, politicians are getting younger. (Patrick Weller and Sue Fraser, 'The Younging of Australian Politics', paper delivered at Australasian Political Studies Association Conference, University of Melbourne, 27–29 August 1984.) At the same time, advisers are getting older — a corollary of the institutionalization of ministerial staff. Whitlam staffers were in their twenties and thirties, Hawke staffers are more likely to be in their thirties and forties (in part because some are the same people: see Alan Ramsey, 'Hawke Government recalls some old familiar faces', *The National Times*, 1–7 March 1985). As a result, some staffers who worked for the Whitlam ministry, and now for the Hawke ministry, find themselves the same age as (and at least as politically experienced as) their new ministers.

41 This should bring us within the ambit of Little's work on political ensembles — brought together by a shared project. However, the characteristic way in which advisers relate to politicians cuts across the distinctions Little posits between ensembles. As I suggest below, advisers always seek a 'pairing' relationship, no matter what the style of the leader. The ensembles Little refers to consist of leaders and followers at large — perhaps distinctions break down as we approach the more narcissistic world of the inner circle. We might, at this level, have to revert to the particularity of Bion, or of Bales (see notes 42 and 46 below). See Graham Little, *Political Ensembles*, Oxford University Press, Melbourne, 1985.

42 The term is derived from Wilfred Bion, *Experiences in Groups*, Tavistock, London, 1961.

43 David Halberstam, *The Best and the Brightest*, Random House, New York, 1972.

44 George Herring, *America's Longest War: The United States and Vietnam, 1950–1975*, John Wiley, New York, 1979.

45 ibid.

46 I have mentioned above the important work of Bion, Janis and Little (see especially chapter 4 of Little's *Political Ensembles*, op. cit.). See also R. F. Bales, 'Task roles and social roles in problem solving groups', in E. E. Maccoby et al. (eds), *Readings in Social Psychology*, 3rd edn, Holt, Rinehart and Winston, New York, 1970; Alexander George, *Presidential Decision-making in Foreign Policy*, op. cit., especially chapter 4; Robert T. Golembiewski and Gerald J. Miller, 'Small Groups in Political Science', in Samuel Long (ed.), *The Handbook of Political Behaviour, Volume 2*, Plenum Press, New York, 1981, pp. 1–71.

Illustrative Biographies

1 The classic case of such intersecting biographies of politician and adviser has been referred to earlier: George and George, *Woodrow Wilson and Colonel House: A Personality Study*, Dover, New York, 1964.

2 See my book, *The Leader: a political biography of Gough Whitlam*, University of Queensland Press, St Lucia, 1980.

3 The significance of the reliance on successive allies as noted above is best understood in the light of Wilfred Bion's investigations of pairing relationship in small groups: see his *Experiences in Groups*, Tavistock, London, 1961. And see note 15 below.

4 David Malouf superbly represents Brisbane as it must have seemed to a bright, literate adolescent at just the time when Freudenberg was growing up there, in his *Johnno*, Penguin, Ringwood, Victoria, 1976.

5 Freudenberg instituted the practice of calling Whitlam 'Leader', which most of the rest of his staff adopted since they felt they could not call him Gough (and would not address him in such a detached mode as Mr Whitlam). See my book *The Leader*, op. cit., p. 72.

6 Freudenberg's own account of the Whitlam years, however, makes recurrent reference to episodes of consultation between Whitlam and himself even after 1972. See Graham Freudenberg, *A Certain Grandeur: Gough Whitlam in Politics*, Macmillan, Melbourne, 1977.

7 Freudenberg, op. cit., p. 229.

8 Race Mathews, seminar in Politics Department, University of Melbourne, 29 June 1976.

9 Freudenberg, *A Certain Grandeur*, op. cit. It was said, too, that he

was of considerable assistance to Whitlam when Whitlam produced his own account of the 1975 crisis, Gough Whitlam, *The Truth of the Matter*, Penguin, Ringwood, Victoria, 1979, which would accentuate the importance of their collaboration from Whitlam's side.

10 Race Mathews, University of Melbourne, 29 June 1976.

11 That is, he not only participated in history, but constructed a history. His book, *A Certain Grandeur*, despite being very much 'the authorized version', was a fine achievement, and had some claim to being the definitive account of the Whitlam period.

12 Bernard Meyer, for instance, makes some interesting notations on this in his chapter 'The Contribution of Psychoanalysis to Biography', in R. Holt and E. Peterfreund, (eds), *Psychoanalysis and Contemporary Science*, Macmillan, New York, 1972, pp. 373–91, especially pp. 380–3. A more complex account is to be found in Heinz Kohut, 'Creativeness, Charisma, Group Psychology: Reflections on the Self-Analysis of Freud', chapter 48 in P. Ornstein, (ed.), *The Search for the Self, Selected Writings of Heinz Kohut: 1950–1978*, vol. 2, International Universities Press, New York, 1978.

13 Thus, the title of Freudenberg's book.

14 And cf.: 'men who demand and need a great deal of attention from others are manifesting a kind of childlike helplessness which evokes an appropriate response . . . As with a small child, omnipotence and helplessness went hand in hand.' Anthony Storr, 'The Inner Man', in P. Stansky, (ed.), *Churchill: A Profile*, Macmillan, London, 1973, pp. 222–61, especially p. 244.

15 See Graham Little, *Political Ensembles: A psychosocial approach to politics and leadership*, Oxford University Press, Melbourne, 1985. His account of Whitlam as an Inspiring leader, and the importance of the pairing group in his effectivity, informs my remarks here.

7 The Development of the Minder's Career

1 Gunnar Heckscher, 'The Role of the Intellectual in Politics — A Swedish View', in H. Malcolm MacDonald, (ed.), *The Intellectual in Politics*, Humanities Research Center, University of Texas, Austin, 1966, p. 20.

2 See my work, *The Acculturation to Political Work: New Members of the Federal Backbench*, APSA/Parliamentary Fellow Monograph, no. 2, Bedford Park, SA, 1979.

3 ibid, pp. 42–3.

4 Cf. Sigmund Freud, 'Psychopathic Characters on the Stage', *Standard Edition*, vol. 7, Hogarth Press, London, 1960, pp. 305–10, especially p. 305.

216   *The Ministers' Minders*

5 These remarks are informed by Alistair Mant's useful distinction
   between those who see the world in terms of direct interaction,
   often of conflict, (whom he calls binary thinkers), and those who
   can withdraw from direct interaction and conflict to stand in a third
   corner and analyze in abstract terms (whom he calls ternary
   thinkers). The former are the fighters, the corporate raiders, and
   most of the politicians. These people of action have to be restrained
   by, or complemented by, ternary thinkers in the interests of good
   government. Advisers, it might be argued, *choose* to stand in the
   third corner (and see below). See Alistair Mant, *Leaders We Deserve*,
   Martin Robertson, Oxford, 1983.
6 And cf. Davies, *Skills, Outlooks and Passions: a psychoanalytic
   contribution to the study of politics*, Cambridge University Press,
   Cambridge, 1980, pp. 100–101.
7 Walter, *The Acculturation to Political Work . . .*, op. cit., p. 17, p. 43.
8 Walter, *The Acculturation to Political Work . . .*, op. cit., pp. 40–1.
9 H. Fairlie, 'The Politician's Art', *Harpers*, December 1977, p. 42.
10 See Robert J. Brym, *Intellectuals and Politics*, Allen and Unwin,
   London, 1980; Alvin W. Gouldner, *The Future of Intellectuals and the
   Rise of the New Class*, The Seabury Press, New York, 1979; George
   Konrad and Ivan Szelenyi, *The Intellectuals on the Road to Class Power*,
   Harvester, Brighton, 1979; Michael Walzer, 'The New Masters', *The
   New York Review of Books*, 20 March 1980, pp. 37–9. For an amusing,
   and reactionary, Australian view, see Alex Buzo, *Meet the New Class*,
   Angus and Robertson, Sydney, 1981; and cf. R. W. Connell,
   'Intellectuals and Intellectual Work' in his *Which Way Is Up? Essays on
   Class, Sex and Culture*, Allen and Unwin, Sydney, 1983, pp. 231–54;
   Sol Encel, 'Labor's New Class takes Command', *Australian Society*,
   vol. 3, no. 5, 1 May 1984, pp. 6–9.
11 Cf. G. E. Hansen, 'Intellect and Power: Some Notes on the
   Intellectual as a Political Type', *The Journal of Politics*, vol. 31,
   no. 2, 1969, pp. 311–28, especially p. 328.
12 See Lewis Coser, *Men of Ideas*, The Free Press, New York, 1969,
   p. 186, and pp. 315–24.
13 See Coser, op. cit., pp. 171–88.
14 Antonio Gramsci, *Selections from the Prison Notebooks*, Quintin Hoare
   and Geoffrey Nowell-Smith, (ed. and trans.), Lawrence and
   Wishart, London, 1971, p. 5.
15 Gramsci, op. cit., p. 10.
16 Robert K. Merton, 'The Role of the Intellectual in Public
   Bureaucracy' in his *Social Theory and Social Structure*, The Free
   Press, New York, 1968, p. 267.
17 Coser, op. cit., pp. 171–88.
18 Tibor Huzar, 'Changes in the Concept of Intellectuals', in A. Gella,

(ed.), *The Intelligentsia and the Intellectuals: Theory, Method and Case Study*, Sage Publications, Beverly Hills, 1976, p. 87.

19 A detailed review can be found in John Warhurst, 'The partisan factor in lateral appointments to public services', *The Australian Quarterly*, vol. 55, no. 2, Winter 1983, pp. 184–201.

20 See particularly Julie Flynn, 'Road to the top on the ministerial bandwagon', *The National Times*, 3–9 October 1982, pp. 14–15. And for a striking case study, see Richard Coleman, 'Alan Jones and the art of winning', *The Courier-Mail*, 15 June 1985.

21 The Hope Royal Commission Report into the relationship between one time ALP federal secretary and lobbyist David Combe and Russian agent Valeriy Ivanov was tabled in the House of Representatives on 6 December 1983. For extensive commentary, see all metropolitan daily newspapers for 7 December 1983. For an impassioned review of the injustice of the affair, see David Marr, *The Ivanov Trail*, Nelson, Melbourne, 1984.

22 Peter Sekuless, *The Lobbyists: Using Them in Canberra*, Allen and Unwin, Sydney, 1984, p. 9.

23 See Sekuless, op. cit., appendix 5, pp. 134–43.

24 Wilenski occasionally adverts to the role of ministerial staff in his published work, see for example his 'Ministers, public servants and public policy', *The Australian Quarterly*, June 1979. pp. 31–45, especially p. 36. David Kemp has made at least one public statement on the importance of private office staff (*Monash Reporter*, November 1983, p. 10), as has Cliff Walsh (*The Age*, 22 June 1983).

25 See for example Daniel Bell, *The Coming of Post-Industrial Society*, Basic Books, New York, 1973; and note Encel's commentary in 'Labor's New Class Takes Command', op. cit.

26 Precisely the thesis hammered by Flynn's 'Road to the top . . .' article (see note 20).

27 Sekuless notes this in the case of his own firm (see *The Lobbyists*, op. cit., p. vi), but it was also interesting to note that Combe (see note 21) had been negotiating to join forces with lobbyists who had formerly worked for Liberal ministers shortly before the point when his affairs came into the public spotlight.

Bibliography

ABERBACH, J. D., PUTNAM, R. D. and ROCKMAN, B. A. *Bureaucrats and Politicians in Western Democracies*, Harvard University Press, Cambridge, Mass., 1981.

ABERBACH, J. D. and ROCKMAN, B. A. 'The Overlapping Worlds of American Federal Executives and Congressmen', *British Journal of Political Science*, vol. 7, 1977, pp. 23–47.

ALEXANDER, F. *Australia Since Federation*, Nelson, Melbourne, 1976.

ALLEN, D. 'Ministers and their Mandarins', *Government and Opposition: a Journal of Comparative Politics*, vol. 12, no. 2, Spring 1977, pp. 135–49.

ALLISON, G. T. *Essence of Decision: Explaining the Cuban Missile Crisis*, Little, Brown & Co., Boston, 1971.

ANDERSON, P. *The Presidents' Men*, Doubleday & Company, Garden City, New York, 1968.

ANTHONY, J. M. 'The Politics of the Bureaucracy and the Role of Ministerial Staff', in Wettenhall, R. and Painter, M. (comps.), *The First Thousand Days of Labor*, vol. 2, Canberra College of Advanced Education, Canberra, 1975.

Australian Labor Party National Committee of Inquiry Discussion Papers, ASPA Monograph No. 23, Australasian Political Studies Association, Bedford Park, S.A., 1979.

BACON, F. *Selected Writings*, Random House, The Modern Library, New York, 1965.

BAKER, R. and PETERS, C. 'The Prince and His Courtiers: at the White House, the Kremlin, and the Reichschancellery', *Washington Monthly*, February 1973, pp. 30–9.

BALES, R. F. 'Task roles and social roles in problem solving groups', in Maccoby, E. E. et al. (eds), *Readings in Social Psychology*, Holt, Rinehart & Winston, New York, 1970.

BARKER, G. 'Hobbes and the Mind of Owen Harries', *The Age*, 13 December 1980.

BARNETT, D. 'The Howson Diaries: The View from Inside', *The Age Monthly Review*, vol. 4, no. 5, September 1984.

BELL, D. *The End of Ideology: On the Exhaustion of Political Ideas in the Fifties*, The Free Press, New York, 1960.

—— *The Coming of Post-Industrial Society*, Basic Books, New York, 1973.

BENN, T. *Arguments for Democracy*, Cape, London, 1981.

BENVENISTE, G. *The Politics of Expertise*, The Glendessary Press, Berkeley, 1972.

BERMAN, L. 'Johnson and the White House Staff', in Divine, R. A. (ed.), *Exploring the Johnson Years*, University of Texas Press, Austin, 1981, pp. 187–213.

BERNSTEIN, C. and WOODWARD, B. *All the President's Men*, Secker & Warburg, London, 1974.

BLEWETT, N. 'Labor 1968–72: planning for victory', in Mayer, H. (ed.), *Labor to Power*, Angus & Robertson, Sydney, 1973, pp. 6–16.

BONAFEDE, D. 'White House Report: Scholars tackle problem of presidential advisory system', *National Journal*, vol. 7, no. 22, 1975, pp. 1607–10.

—— 'White House Staffing: The Nixon Ford Era', in Cronin, T. E. and Tugwell, R. G. (eds), *The Presidency Reappraised*, Praeger, New York, 1977, pp. 151–73.

—— 'How the White House Helps Carter Make Up His Mind', *National Journal*, vol. 10, no. 10, 1978, pp. 584–8.

—— 'Reagan's "Brains Tɩust" — A Candidate is Known by the Company He Keeps', *National Journal*, vol. 12, no. 17, 1980, pp. 672–6.

BRIOT, G. T. and LLOYD, C. J. 'Ministerial Staff Members', Submission no. 466, *Royal Commission on Australian Government Administration*, AGPS, Canberra, 1976 (16 pp. including Appendix).

BROOKS, H. 'The Scientific Adviser', in Cronin, T. E. and Greenberg, S. D. (eds), *The Presidential Advisory System*, Harper & Row, New York, 1969, pp. 40–57.

BRUMMER, A. 'The disaster team at Reagan's right hand', *The Guardian Weekly*, vol. 132, no. 20, 1985, week ending May 19.

BRYM, R. J. *Intellectuals and Politics*, Allen & Unwin, London, 1980.

BRYSON, L. 'Notes on a Theory of Advice', *Political Science Quarterly*, vol. LXVI, no. 3, 1951, pp. 321–39.

BUTTON, J. 'Directive on employment of PS senior staff', *Canberra Times*, 9 April 1983.

BUZO, A. *Meet the New Class*, Angus & Robertson, Sydney, 1981.

CAMPBELL, C. *Governments Under Stress: Political Executives and Key Bureaucrats in Washington, London and Ottawa*, University of Toronto Press, Toronto, 1983.

CARBONE, D. J. 'The Executive Office of the Presidency as a Management Tool', *Perspectives on Defense Management*, Feb. 1967, pp. 27–38.

CAREY, W. D. 'Presidential Staffing in the Sixties and Seventies', *Public Administration Review*, vol. 24, no. 3, 1969, pp. 450–8.

CARLTON, J. 'The secret ingredient in Fraser's success', *The National Times*, 16–21 January 1978.

CASTLE, B. 'Mandarin Power: Ministerial Life Since 1964', *Sunday Times*, 6 June, 1973.

—— *The Castle Diaries 1974–76*, Weidenfeld & Nicolson, London, 1980.

CHURCH, G. J. 'The President's Men', *Time*, 4 December, 1981.

CONNELL, R. W. *Which Way is Up? Essays On Class, Sex and Culture*, Allen & Unwin, Sydney, 1983.

CONNELL, R. W. and GOOT, M. 'The End of Class, Re-run', *Meanjin*, vol. 38, no. 1, 1979, pp. 3–25.

COOMBS, H. C. 'The Commission Report', in Hazlehurst, C. and Nethercote, J. R. (eds), *Reforming Australian Government: The Coombs Report and Beyond*, ANU Press, Canberra, 1977, pp. 49–52.

—— 'The Future Bureaucracy', in Hazlehurst, C. and Nethercote, J. R. (eds), *Reforming Australian Government: The Coombs Report and Beyond*, ANU Press, Canberra, 1977, pp. 53–7.

—— *Trial Balance*, Macmillan, Melbourne, 1981.

COSER, L. *Men of Ideas*, The Free Press, New York, 1965.

CRISP, L. F. *Ben Chifley: A Political Biography*, Angus & Robertson, Sydney, 1963.

—— 'Commonwealth Policy Co-ordination', *Public Administration (Sydney)*, vol. XIV, 1965, pp. 193–213.

—— 'Central Co-ordination of Commonwealth Policy-Making: Roles and Dilemmas of the Prime Minister's Department', *Public Administration (Sydney)*, vol. XXVI, no. 1, March 1967, pp. 28–57.

CRONIN, T. E. 'Political Science and Executive Advisory Systems', in Cronin, T. E. and Greenberg, S. D. (eds), *The Presidential Advisory System*, Harper & Row, New York, 1969, pp. 321–35.

—— ' "Everybody Believes in Democracy Until He Gets to the White House": An Examination of White House-Department Relations', in Wildavsky, A. (ed.), *Perspectives on the Presidency*, Little, Brown & Co., Boston, 1975, pp. 362–93.

CRONIN, T. E. and GREENBERG, S. D. (eds), *The Presidential Advisory System*, Harper & Row, New York, 1969.

—— *The State of the Presidency*, Little, Brown & Co., Boston, 1975.

CROSSMAN, R. *Inside View: Three Lectures on Prime Ministerial Government*, Jonathan Cape, London, 1972.

—— *Diaries of a Cabinet Minister Vol. 1*, Jonathan Cape, London, 1975.

CUMMING, F. 'Academics invade Corridors of Power', *The Australian*, 21 July 1982.

CUNLIFFE, M. 'The Intellectuals: The United States', *Encounter*, vol. 4, no. 5, 1955, pp. 23–33.

DAALDER, H. 'Cabinet Reform Since 1914: Major Trends', in Herman, V. and Alt, J. (eds), *Cabinet Studies: A Reader*, Macmillan, London, 1975, pp. 243–76.

D'AQUINO, T. 'The Prime Minister's Office: Catalyst or Cabal?', *Canadian Public Administration*, vol. 17, no. 1, Spring 1974, pp. 55–80.

DAVIES, A. F. *Australian Democracy: An Introduction to the Political System*, Longmans, Melbourne, 1966.

—— *Skills, Outlooks and Passions: a psychoanalytic contribution to the study of politics*, Cambridge University Press, Cambridge, 1980.

DAVIES, J. *The Prime Minister's Secretariat 1916–20*, R. H. Johns, Newport, 1951.

DELL'OSO, A-M. 'Wran: how a punch — and brother Joe — sent him to the top', *Sydney Morning Herald*, 19 June 1982.

DESTLER, I. M. *Presidents, Bureaucrats and Foreign Policy: The Politics of Organisational Reform*, Princeton University Press, Princeton, N.J., 1972.

—— 'Comment: Multiple Advocacy: Some "Limits and Costs"'', *American Political Science Review*, vol. 66, no. 3, September 1972, pp. 786–90.

—— 'National Security Advice to U.S. Presidents: Some Lessons from Thirty Years', *World Politics*, vol. 29, no. 2, 1977, pp. 143–76.

DEXTER, L. A. 'Court Politics: Presidential Staff Relations as a Special Case of a General Phenomenon', *Administration and Society*, vol. 9, no. 3, 1977, pp. 267–83.

DRUCKER, P. F. 'How to Make the Presidency Manageable', *Fortune*, vol. XC, no. 5, November 1974, pp. 146ff.

DUMAS, L. *The Story of a Full Life*, Sun Books, Melbourne, 1969.

EDWARDS, J. Political Scientists in Politics. Paper delivered to the Australian Political Studies Association Conference, August 1973 — mimeo.

—— *Life wasn't meant to be easy: a political profile of Malcolm Fraser*, Hale & Iremonger, Sydney, 1977.

EMY, H. V. *The Politics of Australian Democracy*, Macmillan, Melbourne, 1974.

ENCEL, S. *Equality and Authority: A Study of Class, Status and Power in Australia*, Cheshire, Australia, 1970.

ENCEL, S. 'Labor's New Class Takes Command', *Australian Society*, vol. 3, no. 5, 1 May 1984, pp. 6–9.

ENCEL, S., WILENSKI, P. AND SCHAFFER, B. (eds), *Decisions: Case Studies in Australian Public Policy*, Longman Cheshire, Melbourne, 1981.

ERIKSON, E. *Young Man Luther*, Faber & Faber, London, 1958.

FAIRLIE, H. 'The Politician's Art', *Harpers*, vol. 225 (1531), December 1977, pp. 33–46 and 123–4.

FARRAN, A. 'Reflections on Policy Making and the Public Service', *Public Administration (Sydney)*, vol. XXXIV, no. 2, 1975, pp. 156–70.

FINN, C. E. 'Advising the President', *Commentary*, vol. 61, no. 2, 1976, pp. 87–9.

FLORESTANO, P. S. 'The Characteristics of White House Staff Appointees from Truman to Nixon', *Presidential Studies Quarterly*, vol. VII, no. 4, 1977, pp. 184–91.

FLYNN, J. 'Road to the top on the ministerial bandwagon', *The National Times*, 3–9 October 1982.

FORWARD, R. 'Ministerial Staff of the Australian Government 1972–74: A Survey', in Wettenhall, R. and Painter, M. (comps), *The First Thousand Days of Labor*, Canberra College of Advanced Education, Canberra,

1975, pp. 137–57.

—— 'Ministerial Staff Under Whitlam and Fraser', *Australian Journal of Public Administration*, vol. XXXVI, no. 2, 1977, pp. 159–66.

FOX, J. 'The Brains Behind the Throne', in Herman, V. and Alt, J. (eds), *Cabinet Studies: A Reader*, Macmillan, London, 1975, pp. 277–92.

FREUD, S. 'Psychopathic Characters on the Stage', *Standard Edition, Vol. 7*, Hogarth Press, London, 1960, pp. 305–10.

FREUDENBERG, G. *A Certain Grandeur: Gough Whitlam in Politics*, Macmillan, Melbourne, 1977.

FRITH, S. 'Mr Fraser Makes Sure He is Right', *Sydney Morning Herald*, 23 January, 1981.

GEORGE, A. L. 'The Case for Multiple Advocacy in Making Foreign Policy', *American Political Science Review*, vol. 66, no. 3, September 1972, pp. 751–85.

—— 'Rejoinder to "Comment" by I. M. Destler', *American Political Science Review*, vol. 66, no. 3, September 1972, pp. 791–5.

—— *Presidential Decisionmaking in Foreign Policy: The Effective Use of Information and Advice*, Westview Press, Boulder, Colo., 1980.

GEORGE, A. L. and GEORGE, J. L. *Woodrow Wilson and Colonel House: A Personality Study*, Dover, New York, 1956.

GERTH, H. H. and MILLS, C. W. (eds), *From Max Weber, Essays in Sociology*, Routledge and Kegan Paul, London, 1948.

GOLDHAMER, H. *The Adviser*, Elsevier, New York, 1978.

GOLEMBIEWSKI, R. T. and MILLER, G. J. 'Small Groups in Political Science', in Samuel Long (ed.), *The Handbook of Political Behaviour*, vol. 2, Plenum Press, New York, 1981, pp. 1–71.

GOULDNER, A. W. *The Future of Intellectuals and the Rise of the New Class*, The Seabury Press, New York, 1979.

GRAMSCI, A. 'The Intellectuals', *Selections from the Prison Notebooks* (ed. and trans. Quintin Hoare and Geoffrey Nowell Smith), Lawrence & Wishart, London, 1971.

GRATTAN, M. 'The Liberal Party', in Howard R. Penniman (ed.), *Australia at the Polls: the national elections of 1975*, American Enterprise Institute, Washington, 1977, pp. 103–42.

—— 'Dateline Canberra, a game of intrigue', *The Age*, 28 January 1978.

—— 'The PM's Oracles: Two key economists', *The Age*, 22 June 1979.

—— 'Stone letter hits "meretricious players of the advisory stage"', *The Age*, 25 November 1982.

—— 'The media's battle for access', *The Age*, 10 September 1984.

GREENSTEIN, F. I. Presidents, Advisers and Decisionmaking: Vietnam 1954 and 1965 — A Perspective for Comparison. Paper prepared for delivery at the Presidency Research Group Panels, 1982 Annual Meeting of the American Political Science Association, Denver, Colorado — mimeo.

GREENSTEIN, F. I. et al. *Evolution of the Modern Presidency: A Bibliographical*

Survey, American Enterprise Institute, Washington, 1977.

GWYN, R. *The Northern Magus: Pierre Trudeau and the Canadians*, Paperjacks, Markham, Ontario, 1981.

HAINES, J. *The Politics of Power*, Jonathan Cape, London, 1977.

HALBERSTAM, D. *The Best and the Brightest*, Random House, New York, 1972.

HALL, R. *The Real John Kerr: his brilliant career*, Angus and Robertson, Sydney, 1978.

HALLMAN, H. W., EWALD, W., SORENSEN, T., GAITHER, J., and HARPER, E. 'Advising the President: A Panel', *The Bureaucrat*, vol. 3, no. 1, 1974, pp. 21–42.

HANSEN, G. E. 'Intellect and Power: Some Notes on the Intellectual as a Political Type', *The Journal of Politics*, vol. 31, no. 2, 1969, pp. 311–28.

HARARI, E. 'Japanese Politics of Advice in Comparative Perspective: A Framework for Analysis and a Case Study', *Public Policy*, vol. 22, no. 4, 1974, pp. 537–77.

HARRIS, R. J. 'The Inner Circle: Old Friends May Play a Very Important Role in Reagan Presidency', *Wall Street Journal*, vol. 196, no. 114, 1980, pp. 1 and 29.

HART, J. 'No Passion for Brownlow: Models of Staffing the Presidency', *Politics* vol. 17, no. 2, 1982, pp. 89–95.

—— 'Staffing the Presidency: Kennedy and the Office of Congressional Relations', *Presidential Studies Quarterly*, vol. XIII, no. 1, Winter 1983, pp. 101–10.

HAUPT, R. 'Treasury Opts Out', *Australian Financial Review*, 27 August 1974.

HAWKER, G. 'The bureaucracy and the Whitlam government — and vice versa', *Politics*, vol. X, no. 1, May 1975, pp. 15–23 (esp. pp. 18–20).

—— *Who's Master, Who's Servant? Reforming Bureaucracy*, Allen & Unwin, Sydney, 1981.

HAWKER, G., SMITH, R. F. I. and WELLER, P. *Politics and Policy in Australia*, University of Queensland Press, St. Lucia, 1979.

HAY, J. R. The Institute of Public Affairs and Social Policy. Paper delivered at the Seminar on Post-war Reconstruction, Australian National University, September, 1981.

HECKSCHER, G. 'The Role of the Intellectual in Politics — A Swedish View', in MacDonald, H. M. (ed.), *The Intellectual in Politics*, Humanities Research Center, The University of Texas, Austin, 1966, pp. 15–23.

HELLER, W. W. 'Economic Policy Advisers', in Cronin, T. E. and Greenberg, S. D. (eds), *The Presidential Advisory System*, Harper & Row, New York, 1969, pp. 29–39.

HELMER, J. 'The Sociology of Higher-Level Advisory Functions', *Melbourne Journal of Politics*, no. 7, 1975, pp. 35–46.

HELMER, J. and MAISEL, L. 'Analytical Problems in the Study of Presidential

Advice: The Domestic Council Staff in Flux', *Presidential Studies Quarterly*, vol. VIII, no. 1, 1978, pp. 45–67.

HERMANN, C. F. and HERMANN, M. G. The Impact of Decision Units on Foreign Policy Behaviour. Paper prepared for the Fourth Annual Meeting of the International Society of Political Psychology, University of Mannheim, Federal Republic of Germany, 24–27 June 1981 — mimeo.

HERRING, G. C. *America's Longest War: The United States and Vietnam 1950–1975*, John Wiley, New York, 1979.

HESS, S. *Organizing the Presidency*, Brookings, Washington, 1976.

HETHERINGTON, J. *Uncommon Men*, Cheshire, Melbourne, 1965.

HOLLANDER, P. *Political Pilgrims: Travels of Western Intellectuals to the Soviet Union, China, and Cuba, 1928–1978*, Oxford University Press, New York, 1981.

HORNE, D. *The Lucky Country: Australia in the Sixties*, Penguin, Ringwood, 1964.

HURST, J. 'Bob Hogg — keeping things sweet for the boss', *The National Times*, 3–9 June 1983.

HUTCHINSON, J. M. 'Staffers to Shadow Ministers', *Canberra Survey*, vol. 35, no. 11, 26 November, 1982.

HUZAR, T. 'Changes in the Concept of Intellectuals', in Gella, A. (ed.), *The Intelligentsia and the Intellectuals: Theory, Method and Case Study*, Sage Publications, Beverly Hills, 1976, pp. 77–109.

IMMERMAN, R. H. 'Eisenhower and Dulles: Who Made the Decisions?', *Political Psychology*, vol. 1, no. 2, Autumn 1979, pp. 3–20.

JANIS, I. L. *Victims of Groupthink*, Houghton Mifflin, Boston, 1972.

—— Preventing groupthink in policy-planning groups: theory and research perspectives. Paper delivered at the second annual meeting of the International Society of Political Psychology, Washington, 24 May 1979 — mimeo.

JAQUES, E. *A General Theory of Bureaucracy*, Heinemann, London, 1976.

JINKS, B. 'Alfred Conlon, The Directorate of Research and New Guinea', *Journal of Australian Studies*, no. 12, June 1983, pp. 21–33.

JOHNS, F. *Who's Who in Australia, 1927–28*, The Hassell Press, Adelaide, 1927.

JONES, G. W. 'The Prime Minister's Advisers', *Political Studies*, vol. XXI, no. 3, 1973, pp. 366–75.

—— 'Harold Wilson's policy-makers', *The Spectator*, 6 July, 1974, pp. 12–13.

—— 'The Prime Minister's Secretaries: Politicians or Administrators?', in Griffith, J. A. G. (ed.), *From Policy to Administration*, Allen & Unwin, London, 1976, pp. 13–38.

—— 'The Prime Minister's Men', *New Society*, vol. 43, no. 798, 19 January 1978, pp. 121–3.

JUPP, J. *Party Politics: Australia 1966–81*, Allen & Unwin, Sydney, 1982.

KELLER, W. 'Ronald Reagan's Inner Circle Combines "California Mafia" with Nixon and Ford Alumni', *Congressional Quarterly Weekly Report*, vol. 38, 1980, pp. 2913–22.

KELLNER, P. and CROWTHER-HUNT, N. *The Civil Servants: An Inquiry into Britain's Ruling Class*, Macdonald, London, 1980.

KELLY, P. *The Unmaking of Gough*, Angus and Robertson, Sydney, 1976.

—— 'The Man Who Writes Our Foreign Policy', *The National Times*, 23–28 January 1978.

—— 'Private Team Moves into PM's Realm', *Sydney Morning Herald*, 17 February 1981.

—— *The Hawke Ascendency*, Angus and Robertson, Sydney, 1984.

KEMP, D. The Institute of Public Affairs 1942–47, BA Honours thesis, University of Melbourne, 1963.

—— 'A leader and a philosophy', in Mayer, H. (ed.), *Labor to Power*, Angus and Robertson, Sydney, 1973, pp. 48–59.

—— 'Social change and the future of political parties: the Australian Case', in Maisel, L. and Sacks, P. M. (eds), *The Future of Political Parties*, Sage Electoral Studies Yearbook, vol. 1, Sage, Beverly Hills, 1975, pp. 124–64.

—— 'Political Parties and Australian Culture', *Quadrant*, December, 1977, pp. 3–13.

—— *Society and Electoral Behavior in Australia*, University of Queensland Press, St Lucia, 1978.

—— 'The National economic summit: authority, persuasion and exchange', *The Economic Record*, vol. 59, no. 166, September 1983, pp. 209–19.

'Kennedy's Inner Circle: Liberal, Young, Untried', *U.S. News & World Report*, vol. 87, 1979, p. 36.

KERR, J. *Matters for Judgement*, Macmillan, Melbourne, 1978.

KISSINGER, H. A. 'The Policymaker and the Intellectual', in Cronin, T. E. and Greenberg, S. D. (eds), *The Presidential Advisory System*, Harper & Row, New York, 1969, pp. 156–68.

KITNEY, G. 'How Hawke rules — O.K.?', *The National Times*, 11–17 May 1984.

KLEIN, R. and LEWIS, J. 'Advice and Dissent in British Government: The Case of the Special Advisers', *Policy and Politics*, vol. 6, 1977, pp. 1–25.

KOENIG, L. W. *The Invisible Presidency*, Holt, Rinehart & Winston, New York, 1960.

KOHUT, H. 'Creativeness, Charisma, Group Psychology: Reflections on the Self-Analysis of Freud', in Ornstein, P. (ed.), *The Search for the Self, Selected Writings of Heinz Kohut: 1950–1978*, vol. 2, International Universities Press, New York, 1978, Chapter 48.

KONRAD, G. and SZELENYI, I. *The Intellectuals on the Road to Class Power*, Harvester, Brighton, 1979.

KRAFT, J. 'Kennedy's Working Staff', *Harpers Magazine*, December 1962, pp. 29–36.

—— 'The Washington Lawyers', in Cronin, T. E. and Greenberg, S. D. (eds), *The Presidential Advisory System*, Harper & Row, New York, 1969, pp. 150–5.

KRAMNICK, I. *The Rage of Edmund Burke: Portrait of an Ambivalent Conservative*, Basic Books, New York, 1977.

LALONDE, M. 'The changing role of the Prime Minister's Office', *Canadian Public Administration*, vol. 14, no. 4, Winter 1971, pp. 509–37.

LASSWELL, H. D. *Power and Personality*, Norton, New York, 1948.

—— 'Political Constitution and Character', *Psychoanalysis and the Psychoanalytic Review*, vol. 46, no. 4, 1969, pp. 3–18.

LEE, N. E. *John Curtin, Saviour of Australia*, Longman Cheshire, Melbourne, 1983.

LIGHT, L. 'White House Domestic Policy Staff Plays an Important Role in Formulating Legislation', *Congressional Quarterly Weekly Report*, vol. 37, 1979, pp. 2199–204.

LITTLE, G. *Political Ensembles*, Oxford University Press, Melbourne, 1985.

LLOYD, C. J. and REID, G. S. *Out of Wilderness: the return of Labor*, Cassell, North Melbourne, 1974.

LLOYD, C. J. and TROY, P. N. *Innovation and Reaction: The life and death of the Federal Department of Urban and Regional Development*, Allen & Unwin, Sydney, 1981.

LONG, G. *The Final Campaigns*, Australian War Memorial, Canberra, 1963.

LONIE, J. 'From Liberal to Liberal: the emergence of the Liberal Party and Australian Capitalism 1940–45', in Duncan, G. (ed.), *Critical Essays in Australian Politics*, Edward Arnold, Melbourne, 1978, pp. 47–76.

MACDOUGALL, G. D. A. 'The Prime Minister's Statistical Section', in Chester, D. N. (ed.), *Lessons of the British War Economy*, Cambridge University Press, Cambridge, 1951, pp. 68ff.

MACPHERSON, C. B. *Democratic Theory: essays in retrieval*, Clarendon Press, Oxford, 1973.

MCQUEEN, H. *Gone Tomorrow*, Angus and Robertson, Sydney, 1982.

MANNHEIM, K. *Ideology and Utopia*, Harcourt, Brace & World, New York, 1946.

MANT, A. *Leaders We Deserve*, Martin Robertson, Oxford, 1983.

MARR, D. *The Ivanov Trail*, Nelson, Melbourne, 1984.

—— 'Labor Team Gets Ready to Take Reins of Power', *The National Times*, 6–12 March 1983.

MARVICK, E. W. Favorites in Early Modern Europe: A Recurring Psycho-political Role. Revised version of a paper presented at the annual meeting of the International Society of Political Psychology, Mannheim, West Germany, June 23–27, 1981 — mimeo.

MEDIANSKY, F. and NOCKELS, J. 'Malcolm Fraser's Bureaucracy', *Australian Quarterly*, vol. 53, no. 4, 1981, pp. 394–418.

MEDVED, M. *The Shadow Presidents: The Secret History of the Chief Executives and their Top Aides*, Times Books, New York, 1979.

MERTON, R. K. 'The Role of the Intellectual in Public Bureaucracy', in Merton, R. K. (ed.), *Social Theory and Social Structure*, The Free Press, New York, 1968.

MEYER, B. 'The Contribution of Psychoanalysis to Biography', in Holt, R. and Peterfreund, E. (eds), *Psychoanalysis and Contemporary Science*, Macmillan, New York, 1972, pp. 373–91.

MICHELS, R. *Political Parties*, The Free Press, Glencoe, 1949 (first published 1911).

MILLIKEN, R. 'Cook, Bertie Stuart Baxter (1877–1968)', in *Australian Dictionary of Biography*, vol. 8, Melbourne University Press, Melbourne, 1981, pp. 94–5.

MILSON, S. 'Dr Kemp's Medicine: do less, or lose office in 1983', *Sydney Morning Herald*, 1 January 1981.

MITCHELL, J. E. 'Special Advisers: A Personal View', *Public Administration*, vol. 56, Spring 1978, pp. 87–98.

MITZMAN, A. *The Iron Cage: An Historical Interpretation of Max Weber*, Grossett & Dunlap, New York, 1969.

MOLLOY, P. 'Hawke offers Hogg a key job', The *Australian*, 8 March 1983.

MOORE, R. *Profiles of Power*, Australian Broadcasting Commission, Sydney, 1970.

MOYNIHAN, D. P. 'The Professionalization of Reform', *The Public Interest*, no. 1, 1965, pp. 6–16.

MURRAY-SMITH, S. 'Deane, Percival Edgar (1890–1946)', in *Australian Dictionary of Biography*, vol. 8, Melbourne University Press, Melbourne, 1981, pp. 261–2.

NATHAN, R. P. *The Administrative Presidency*, John Wiley, New York, 1983.

NAVEH, D. 'The Political Role of Academic Advisers: The Case of the U.S. President's Council of Economic Advisers; 1946–1976', *Presidential Studies Quarterly*, vol. XI, no. 4, 1981, pp. 492–510.

NEUSTADT, R. E. *Presidential Power: The Politics of Leadership*, John Wiley & Sons, New York, 1960.

—— 'White House and Whitehall', *The Public Interest*, no. 2, 1966, pp. 55–69.

—— 'Approaches to Staffing the Presidency', in Cronin, T. E. and Greenberg, S. D. (eds), *The Presidential Advisory System*, Harper & Row, New York, 1969, pp. 11–24.

—— 'Staffing the Presidency: Premature Notes on the New Administration', *Political Science Quarterly*, vol. 93, no. 1, 1978, pp. 1–14.

OAKES, L. 'Return of the Eggheads', *The News* (Northern Territory), 11 April 1981.

OKUN, A. M. 'Three Pitfalls for Presidential Advisers', *Monthly Labor Review*, vol. 97, no. 3, 1974, pp. 43–4.

Oriental Economist, 'Who are Ohira's "Brains"?', vol. 47, no. 823, May 1979, pp. 9–12.

OSBORNE, J. 'Nixon's Command Staff', *The New Republic*, 15 February 1969, pp. 13–15.

—— 'Nixon's Home Guard: Discipline and Order but an "Open" Image', *The New Republic*, 22 February 1969, pp. 11–13.

PARLIAMENTARY LIBRARY. *Parliamentary Handbook of the Commonwealth of Australia: Twenty First Edition*, Australian Government Publishing Service, Canberra, 1982.

PARRIS, H. 'The Origins of the Permanent Civil Service 1780–1830', *Public Administration* (London), vol. 46, 1968, pp. 143–66.

PEARSON, D. and ALLEN, R. S. 'The Men Around the President: A Group Portrait', *Harper's Magazine*, vol. 168, February 1934, pp. 267–77.

PENNY, K. 'The Origins of the Prime Minister's Department, 1901–1911', *Public Administration (Sydney)*, vol. XV, 1956, pp. 249–55.

PETRIDIS, A. 'Australia: economists in a federal system', in Coats, A. W. (ed.), *Economists in Government: An International Comparative Study*, Duke University Press, Durham, N.C., 1981, pp. 65–97.

PETRIE, C. *The Powers Behind the Prime Ministers*, Macgibbon & Kee, London, 1958.

PICKLES, D. *The Government and Politics of France: Volume 1, Institutions and Parties*, Methuen, London, 1972.

RAMSEY, A. 'Who's Who in Hawke's Office', *The National Times*, 3–9 June 1983.

—— 'The Man from the Power Machine', *The National Times*, 21–27 October 1983.

——'The Egghead Turns Mandarin', *The National Times*, 9–15 December 1983.

——'What faction wars mean to the ALP', *The National Times*, 27 April–3 May 1984.

—— 'How Hawke Manages the Media', *The National Times*, 6–12 July 1984.

—— 'Hawke minders — like chalk and cheese', *The National Times*, 13–19 July 1984.

—— 'The Backroom Boy', *The National Times*, 21–27 September 1984.

—— 'Hawke Government recalls some old familiar faces', *The National Times*, 1–7 March 1985.

RAVEN, B. H. 'Nixon's Group', *Journal of Social Issues*, vol. 30, no. 4, 1974, pp. 297–320.

REEDY, G. E. *The Twilight of the Presidency*, New American Library Inc., New York, 1970.

REID, A. *The Gorton Experiment*, Shakespeare Head Press, Sydney, 1971.

ROBERTS, C. *LBJ's Inner Circle*, Delacorte Press, New York, 1965.

ROBERTS, M. 'Ministerial Advisers: A Background Paper', Research Paper no. 6, *Royal Commission on Australian Government Administration*, AGPS, Canberra, 1976.

ROCHE, J. P. and SACHS, S. 'The bureaucrat and the enthusiast: An exploration of the leadership of social movements', in McLaughlin, B. (ed.), *Studies in Social Movements: A social psychological perspective*, The Free Press, New York, 1969, pp. 207–22.

ROSE, R. 'The President: A Chief But Not an Executive', *Presidential Studies Quarterly*, vol. VII, no. 1, Winter 1977, pp. 5–20.

—— 'British Government: The Job at the Top', in Rose, R. and Suleiman, E. N. (eds), *Presidents and Prime Ministers*, American Enterprise Institute, Washington, 1980, pp. 1–49.

ROWE, A. 'A psychological study of eminent psychologists and anthropologists, and a comparison with biological and physical scientists', in *Psychological Monographs*, 1953, pp. 1–55.

RUSH, A. E. How Kings Take Counsel: Effective and Ineffective Use as Perceived by Top Executives. Paper delivered to International Society of Political Psychology Conference, Washington, 24 May 1979 — mimeo.

SALISBURY, R. H. and SHEPSLE, K. A. 'Congressional Staff Turnover and the Ties-That-Bind', *American Political Science Review*, vol. 75, 1981, pp. 381–96.

SAMPSON, A. *The Changing Anatomy of Britain*, Hodder & Stoughton, London, 1982.

SAMUEL, P. 'A Ministry of Mouthpieces', *Bulletin*, 10 July, 1976.

SCHEDVIN, C. B. *Australia and the Great Depression*, Sydney University Press, Sydney, 1970.

SCHNEIDER, R. *War Without Blood: Malcolm Fraser in Power*, Angus and Robertson, Sydney, 1980.

—— 'The Power Vacuum Behind the Throne', The *Australian*, 1 January 1983.

SEIGEL, J. *Marx's Fate: The Shape of a Life*, Princeton University Press, Princeton, N.J., 1978.

SEKULESS, P. *The Lobbyists: Using Them in Canberra*, Allen & Unwin, Sydney, 1984.

SELF, P. *Administrative Theories and Politics*, University of Toronto Press, Toronto, 1973.

SELIGMAN, L. G. 'Developments in the Presidency and the Conception of Political Leadership', *American Sociological Review*, vol. 20, no. 6, December 1955, pp. 706–12.

—— 'Presidential Leadership: The Inner Circle and Institutionalization', *The Journal of Politics*, vol. 18, 1956, pp. 410–26.

—— Who Advises and Assists the President. Paper presented to the American Political Science Association, Chicago, 30 August 1974 — mimeo.

SEMPLE, R. B. 'Nixon Staff Had Central Role in Missile Decision', *The New York Times*, 19 March, 1969, p. 22.

SEXTON, M. *Illusions of Power: The Fate of a Reform Government*, Allen & Unwin, Sydney, 1979.

SHILS, E. 'Ideology', in Sills, D. L. (ed.), *International Encyclopaedia of the Social Sciences*, vol. 7, Macmillan–Free Press, New York, pp. 66–75.

SHORT, J. 'Stone still a force in the background', *Sydney Morning Herald*, 11 May 1984.

SIDEY, H. 'The White House vs. The Cabinet: Hugh Sidey Interviews Bill Moyers', *Washington Monthly*, vol. 1, no. 1, February 1969, pp. 2–9, 78–80.

SIMMS, M. *A Liberal Nation: The Liberal Party and Australian Politics*, Hale and Iremonger, Sydney, 1982.

SMITH, D. 'President and Parliament: The Transformation of Parliamentary Government in Canada', in Hockin, T. (ed.), *Apex of Power: The Prime Minister and Political Leadership in Canada*, Prentice-Hall, Scarborough, 1971, pp. 308–250.

—— 'Comments on the Prime Minister's Office: Catalyst or Cabal', *Canadian Public Administration*, vol. 17, no. 1, Spring 1974, pp. 80–84.

—— 'Carter's Staff: Young, Informal, Fast Moving', *Congressional Quarterly Weekly Report*, vol. 34, 1976, pp. 2600–2.

SMITH, R. F. I. 'Ministerial Advisers: The Experience of the Whitlam Government', *Australian Journal of Public Administration*, vol. XXXVI, no. 2, June, 1977, pp. 133–58 — and see an earlier version, Appendix IJ, *Royal Commission on Australian Government Administration*.

SMITH, R. F. I. and WELLER, P. 'Learning to Govern: The Australian Labor Party and the Institutions of Government, 1972–75', *Journal of Commonwealth and Comparative Politics*, vol. 15, 1977, pp. 39–54.

SNOW, D. 'Senior jobs await decision by Hayden', *Australian Financial Review*, 15 August 1984.

SORENSON, T. C. *Decision Making in the White House: the olive branch or the arrows*, Columbia University Press, New York, 1963.

SPANN, R. N. *Government Administration in Australia*, Allen & Unwin, Sydney, 1979.

STUART, R. W. *The Thought Brigade: America's Influential Ghosts in Government*, Ivan Obolensky, Inc., New York, 1963.

SULEIMAN, E. N. *Politics, Power and Bureaucracy in France: The Administrative Elite*, Princeton University Press, Princeton, N.J., 1974.

SUMMERS, A. 'Fraser looks over his shoulder as he faces the future', *Australian Financial Review*, 2 January 1981.

THIRLWALL, A. P. (ed.) *Keynes as a Policy Adviser*, Macmillan, London, 1982.

THOMAS, N. C. 'Presidential Advice and Information: Policy and Program Formulation', in Thomas, N. C. and Brade, H. W. (eds), *The*

Institutionalized Presidency, Oceana Publications, Dobbs Ferry, New York, 1972, pp. 114–46.

THOMPSON, D. 'Moral Responsibility of Public Officials: The Problem of Many Hands', *American Political Science Review*, vol. 74, 1980, pp. 905–16.

—— 'Ascribing Responsibility to Advisers in Government', *Ethics*, vol. 93, 1983, pp. 546–60.

THOMPSON, J. (comp.) *Alfred Conlon. A memorial by some of his friends*, Benevolent Society of New South Wales, Sydney, 1963.

Time, 'An Army of Experts Storms Capitol Hill', January 23, 1978.

U.S. News & World Report, '12 Who Will Move to the Inner Circle', vol. 81, 1976, pp. 45–6.

—— 'White House Insiders', vol. 81, 1976, pp. 11–14.

VERBA, S. *Small Groups & Political Behaviour*, Princeton University Press, Princeton, N.J., 1961.

WALSH, M. 'Political Circus Hides the Real Power', *Australian Financial Review*, 30 September 1974.

WALTER, J. *The Acculturation to Political Work: New Members of the Federal Backbench*, APSA/Parliamentary Fellow Monograph, no. 2, Bedford Park, S.A., 1979.

—— *The Leader: A Political Biography of Gough Whitlam*, University of Queensland Press, St Lucia, 1980.

WALZER, M. 'The New Masters', *The New York Review of Books*, 20 March 1980, pp. 37–9.

WARHURST, J. 'The partisan factor in lateral appointments to public services', *Australian Quarterly*, vol. 55, no. 2, Winter, 1983, pp. 184–201.

WATERFORD, J. 'Ministerial-staff job discrimination alleged', *Canberra Times*, 27 April 1983.

WATSON, R. A. and THOMAS, N. C. *The Politics of the Presidency*, John Wiley, New York, 1983.

WEARING, J. 'President or Prime Minister?', in Hockin, T. (ed.), *Apex of Power: The Prime Minister and Political Leadership in Canada*, Prentice-Hall, Scarborough, 1971, pp. 326–43.

WEBER, M. *The Protestant Ethic and the Spirit of Capitalism*, Charles Scribner's Sons, New York, 1958.

WELLER, P. 'Transition: Taking Over Power in 1983', *Australian Journal of Public Administration*, vol. XLII, no. 3, September 1983, pp. 303–19.

WELLER, P. and GRATTAN, M. Can Ministers Cope? Possibilities for Change. Paper delivered at The Australian Political Studies Association Conference, Canberra, 27–29 August 1980 — mimeo.

—— and —— *Can Ministers Cope? Australian Federal Ministers at Work*, Hutchinson, Richmond, Victoria, 1981.

WELLER, P. and FRASER, S. The Younging of Australian Politics. Paper delivered at Australasian Political Studies Association Conference, University of Melbourne, 27–29 August 1984 — mimeo.

WELLER, P. *First Among Equals: Prime Ministers in Westminster Systems*, Allen & Unwin, Sydney, 1985.

WESTFIELD, M. 'The men who sank John Stone', *Australian Business*, 25 November 1982.

WHITLAM, G. *The Truth of the Matter*, Penguin, Ringwood, 1979.

WICKER, T. 'Johnson's Men: "Valuable Hunks of Humanity" ', *The New York Times Magazine*, 3 May 1964, p. 11. Reprinted in Polsby, N.W. (ed.), *The Modern Presidency*, Random House, New York, 1973, pp. 171–8.

WILDAVSKY, A. 'Salvation by Staff: Reform of the Presidential Office', in Wildavsky, A. (ed.), *The Presidency*, Little, Brown & Co., Boston, 1969, pp. 694–700.

WILDAVSKY, A. (ed.) *Perspectives on the Presidency*, Little, Brown & Co., Boston, 1975.

WILENSKI, H. L. 'The Professionalization of Everyone?', *American Journal of Sociology*, vol. 70, 1964, p. 158.

WILENSKI, P. 'Labor and the Bureaucracy', in Duncan, G. (ed.), *Critical Essays in Australian Politics*, Edward Arnold, Port Melbourne, 1978, pp. 28–46.

—— 'Ministers, public servants, and public policy', *The Australian Quarterly*, vol. 51, no. 2, 1979, pp. 31–45.

—— 'Reform and its implementation: The Whitlam Years in Retrospect', in G. Evans and J. Reeves (eds.), *Labor Essays 1980*, Drummond, Richmond, 1980, pp. 40–63.

WILENSKI, P. and YERBURY, D. 'Reconstructing Bureaucracy: Towards a Vehicle for Social Change', in Reeves L. and Thomson K. (eds), *Labor Essays 1983*, Drummond, Melbourne, 1983, pp. 154–79.

WILLIAMS, M. *Inside Number 10*, Weidenfeld and Nicolson, London 1972.

WILLIAMS, N. *Henry VIII and his Court*, Weidenfeld & Nicolson, London, 1971.

WILSON, N. 'Academic for Canberra', *The Age*, 3 January 1981.

WOLFINGER, R. E., SHAPIRO, M. and GREENSTEIN, F. I. *Dynamics of American Politics*, 2nd edn, Prentice-Hall, Englewood Cliffs, 1980.

WOLFSON, E. M. Presidents and Advisers: Filtering the Two-Way Flow of Information. Paper delivered at Annual Meeting of the American Political Science Association, Washington, 1–4 September 1977 — mimeo.

WYNHAUSEN, E. 'The President's Loyal Lieutenants', *The National Times*, 10–16 January 1982.

Index